TAKING
LE TISS

TAKING LE TISS

MY AUTOBIOGRAPHY

MATT LE TISSIER

HarperSport
An Imprint of HarperCollinsPublishers

To my wife,
my children and my parents

First published in paperback in 2010 by
HarperSport
an imprint of HarperCollins*Publishers*
77–85 Fulham Palace Road,
Hammersmith, London W6 8JB
www.harpercollins.co.uk

1 3 5 7 9 10 8 6 4 2

A catalogue record of this book is
available from the British Library

ISBN 978-0-00-731092-0

Printed and bound in Great Britain by
Clays Ltd, St Ives plc

All photographs provided courtesy of the author or the
Southern Daily Echo with the exception of:
Guernsey Press 1lml, 1bl; Brian J. Green 2tl;
Press Association 3tl, 4tr, 4mr; Solent News 6tl

Mixed Sources
Product group from well-managed
forests and other controlled sources
www.fsc.org Cert no. SW-COC-001806
© 1996 Forest Stewardship Council

FSC is a non-profit international organisation established to promote the
responsible management of the world's forests. Products carrying the FSC
label are independently certified to assure consumers that they come
from forests that are managed to meet the social, economic and
ecological needs of present and future generations.

Find out more about HarperCollins and the environment at
www.harpercollins.co.uk/green

Contents

Foreword
By Alan Shearer

I wasn't surprised when Matt asked me to write the foreword to his autobiography. After all, I did all his work for him when we were teammates so it is only fitting I should help him now. The big surprise is that he hasn't asked me to write the whole thing – with him adding the one brilliant punchline which people will remember and talk about for ever.

Matt might not have been noted for his work-rate, but he is one of the most naturally gifted players it has been my privilege to play with. He could do things with a ball which left you, literally, speechless. His skill and technique were sublime and the really annoying thing is that it all came so naturally to him. The rest of us would be working our backsides off, chasing, closing down, taking knocks and tackling, while he would amble around like he didn't have a care in the world. Then, suddenly, he'd explode into life and win the game with a piece of pure genius. And he got almost as much pleasure creating goals for others. If you made a run, you knew he had the ability to find you with an exquisite pass or cross.

I had to do all the running for him. Well, we all did. We were told to get the ball and give it to Matt because he had the ability to create something special. People thought he was lazy but what they don't appreciate is that he concentrated on doing his running in all the right areas. We, his teammates, knew that if we lost possession he was never going to chase back and help. You accepted that because when the ball was played forward and there was just a sniff of goal, he'd be on it in a flash.

Once you got to know him, you realized he cared passionately about winning and scoring – and about Southampton Football Club. That's why he stayed there his whole career when he could have had his pick of teams. He had several opportunities to leave but he didn't see why he should, and he was single-minded enough to dig his heels in when others were saying he should go. You have to applaud him because that sort of loyalty is very rare.

I can identify with that because that's just how I felt about Newcastle – it was always my dream to play for them. But I have a lot of affection for the Saints. They were my first club and I am very sad to see what has happened to them in recent years. I know it has hurt Matt, who gave so much to keep them in the Premier League against the odds for so many years. And he provided the fans with wonderful entertainment along the way.

He was capable of scoring from virtually anywhere. Some of his goals were absolutely breathtaking. Even when I was playing against him, there were times I almost found myself applauding his goals. But Matt was not just a great goal-scorer – he was a scorer of great goals. Some of them left you puzzling, 'How the heck did he do *that*?'

I'll never forget the one he put past his big mate Tim Flowers for Southampton, at Blackburn. He beat a couple of men as though they weren't there and then fired into the top left corner from 35 yards. There was no luck about it, he knew exactly where he wanted to put the ball. It was a really special goal, and the fact he beat Tim all ends up gave him even more satisfaction. Tim has never lived it down even though we won the game. It always seemed to be Newcastle or

Blackburn he scored against. He really seemed to enjoy scoring against my teams.

Being a similar age, we always had a bit of friendly rivalry going right from our days together in the Southampton youth team. And we are still good friends now – even though we are the exact opposite in terms of lifestyle and looks.

He has never been your stereotypical footballer, either on the field or off. The club's nutritionists must have wondered how he was still alive, let alone playing at the top level. His idea of a diet was picking the lettuce out of his burger. And he hasn't changed now that he has retired. Even as a TV pundit he looks like a sack of spuds – or as though he has eaten one. He's never bothered what people think of him. He openly admits, 'This is the way I am, take me or leave me.' And everyone respects that. They are quick to poke fun at his failings – but always in a good-natured way. He takes it well – with his body size and dress sense he hasn't got any choice – and he can certainly dish it back. In spades.

I have to say he is perfect for Sky's *Soccer Saturday* show because he is so laid back, but his wit is as sharp as his shooting. He can laugh at himself and has the perfect sense of humour for that show, coupled with the fact he knows the game inside out and isn't afraid to speak his mind.

This autobiography has been written very much in that vein – self-deprecating with a great sense of his own worth and a lot of jokes. And obviously it has been written by someone else because it is far too much like hard work for Tiss. But I bet he takes all the credit.

Introduction

If you are hoping for smut and scandal from this book then look away now. A lot of 'celebrities' rely on revelations about their personal lives in order to sell books, but I have always been a very private person so there's no sleaze here. It's Tiss and Dell not Kiss and Tell.

So if I guard my privacy so carefully, why write an autobiography? Mainly because my Sky colleagues Jeff Stelling and Phil Thompson have recently published books, and I thought if they could get in the bestseller list with such a pile of tosh, I might as well have a go. Thommo said he found it so therapeutic that the idea suddenly became very tempting.

Southampton supporters have been asking me to tell my story ever since I finished playing, but I wanted to wait until I had achieved something else. Now, with the popularity of Sky's *Soccer Saturday* and the controversial double relegation of the Saints, it seems the perfect time to talk about my career at The Dell and why I stayed with one supposedly unfashionable club for my whole career when I could have got far more money, and maybe medals, by moving.

There have been a lot of misconceptions about me over the years and a lot of wildly inaccurate stories in the press, so this is the perfect chance to put a few things straight. A lot of people think they know what went on – but they don't. Now I can say exactly what happened.

INTRODUCTION

I am acutely aware of my own failings, so I'm not going to gloss over the fact I didn't have the best diet and was never the greatest runner. I was once carried off in training after a fainting fit caused by eating too many sausage and egg McMuffins before we even started. Tim Flowers was asked to write a few lines for this book to describe me and he sent in: 'Matt Le Tissier signed for Southampton, ate a lot, scored some bloody good goals, should have left.' That pretty much sums it up so there's no point reading the book now – apart from the football, the fun and my forthright views about the likes of Alan Ball, Graeme Souness, Ian Branfoot, Rupert Lowe – and a certain Glenn Hoddle.

Unfortunately I never won the Footballer of the Year award; in fact the only vote I got each year came from the reporter on the *Southampton Echo*, so that hardly counted. But for a decade I did have my acceptance speech ready, just in case, and here it is …

'I really want to thank all the people who have been so important to me, starting with my mum and dad. I couldn't have wished for better parents. They were the most supportive people possible – but without interfering. They got the balance brilliantly right and I have them to thank for everything I have achieved in life. They had three kids by the time they were 20 but have remained married for 48 years, which is a fantastic achievement – although I think the reason they stayed together is because neither of them wanted custody of me. My grandparents have been superb and my brothers have been fantastic. All three of them could have been professional players but they have never shown any jealousy or resentment towards me, only pride and support.

My own children, Mitchell and Keeleigh, are growing up to be fantastic kids and have given me a lot of pleasure. I now have a new baby girl, Ava, with my wife Angela. We were together many years ago and there was a lot of love left over so she recently made the decision to come back to this country to see if we could make a go of it. It is wonderful to be married to her finally. We didn't think she could have children so she needed to have fertility treatment. There was only a 20 per cent chance of success but we were lucky it worked first time, and we are now blessed with Ava who is an absolute joy.

Family and friends are important to me and there are some people who really do need a special mention. Pete and Pat Ford, and their children Martin and Stuart, and the Phillips family all really helped me to settle when I first came to Southampton and homesickness might have been a problem. My "mum" in England, Celia Mills, has looked after me for the last 12 years and seen me through a lot. She is one of the loveliest people you could wish to meet.'

I also need to thank Jerome Anderson who was my agent during my playing days and never put me under any pressure to move, even though he would have made more money from a transfer. (If any young players ever want a good agent then go straight to him at the S.E.M. group.) And I must thank Richard Thompson who represented me during this book deal with HarperCollins, for whom Jonathan Taylor has been a big help. Thanks too to Jordan Sibley at Southampton Football Club for sourcing some of the photos, to the club photographer Paul Watts for taking them and to the *Southern Daily Echo* for supplying some of the older pictures. They say the camera never lies but do some of them seem to make me look overweight?

I also need to single out my golf buddies Laurie Parsonage, Ben Johnson and Paul Mico, one of the best DJs in Southampton. I'm absolutely obsessed with golf and I will always be grateful to pro

Richard Bland who allowed me to caddy for him on the European Tour, giving me the best time of my life outside football. He and his brother Heath are really good friends, along with taxi driver Mark Harris who has ferried Saints players around the city for years and knows all their secrets. If he ever wrote a book he'd make millions. In contrast, I must thank Mike Osman for costing me a fortune by persuading me to invest in a nightclub. Despite the huge loss, we have remained friends throughout, which must say something. I must also thank Big Dave and his wife Teresa who have been a big help in recent years.

Francis Benali and Claus Lundekvam are close mates but I have to thank all my former teammates, too numerous to mention individually, for doing my running and allowing me the licence to play the way I did. I couldn't have done it without them, and it was nice to know they were prepared to graft on my behalf.

I want to thank all my former managers but especially Alan Ball – and it is so sad he isn't here to read this. My time playing under him really defined me as a player and I must thank both him and Lawrie McMenemy for their joint efforts in finding the perfect position in the team for me. Thanks, too, to all the Saints staff I have worked with over the years, from the backroom team to the stadium personnel and, of course, I will always be grateful to all the Saints fans for their constant support and belief in me.

More recently I need to thank everyone at Sky for giving me the chance on *Soccer Saturday* and making me so welcome. They have ensured I can stay involved in football in a casual way, with no pressure or fear of getting the sack if results don't go well. And finally I must thank the man who has put all these words to paper, Graham Hiley, who was lucky enough to follow my entire career as the Saints correspondent with the *Southern Daily Echo*. Obviously when I was playing I needed people around me to do all the hard work, so I thought I'd carry on in the same vein and get Graham to do the writing while I just sat and talked. It is a tactic which has worked well for me over the years and you wouldn't want to change a winning formula – unless you are Ian Branfoot.

Preface

Even now people still ask me why I stayed with Southampton throughout my playing career when I probably could have earned a lot more money elsewhere. The fact is, I loved the club – and still do. That's why it breaks my heart to see where they are now. And that's why I almost gave up my job with Sky Sports to become the club chairman.

When I was playing we had four last-day escapes from relegation, some against almost overwhelming odds. And yet I always had a feeling that we would do it. Many fans say that it was all down to my goals but the fact is I couldn't have scored them without ten players alongside me. We had such a fantastic team spirit that we somehow survived every crisis – and I loved being part of it.

We punched above our weight for years while we were at the homely but inadequate Dell. With a capacity of just 15,200, the club desperately needed to move to a new stadium in order to continue competing at the highest level. I was so proud that my goals helped keep us in the Premier League long enough for St Mary's to be built – and when I retired at the end of the club's first season in their new home, I felt the future was secure.

But somehow the spirit of Southampton seemed to seep away and, through a catalogue of errors, this great club has slipped into the third tier of English football for the first time in 50 years. Worse than that, it almost went out of existence altogether. The financial problems which had dogged the Saints for more than a year suddenly came to a head in April 2009 when the holding company went into administration. It meant an automatic 10-point deduction and certain relegation, and there was a very real chance that, after 125 years, the club might fold.

I have always said I would do anything I can to help the Saints, so when I was asked to front a consortium to save the club, I readily agreed. It would have meant giving up my cushy number talking about games in the warmth of the Sky *Soccer Saturday* studio. It would have meant getting a proper job for the first time in my life, working in an office, starting at 9am ... and having to wear a tie! Perhaps it is for the best that our consortium couldn't quite put the finishing touches to the deal. Thankfully, another group did manage to step in and save the club – and I genuinely wish them well. Meanwhile I can get back to working four days a month – pretty much the same as when I was playing ...

HOD'S LAW

'YOU'LL NEVER PLAY FOR ENGLAND, YOU'LL NEVER PLAY
FOR ENGLAND!' THAT WASN'T THE FANS CHANTING,
IT WAS TERRY VENABLES AND GLENN HODDLE.

So how does a scrawny, incredibly talented kid from Guernsey get to
play for England? I'll tell you.

I grew up playing against three older, highly talented brothers –
that sharpened me up. And then I flew to the mainland and joined the
nearest top-flight club. Southampton. I played for the England Under-
20s and B side and then, finally, when I was 25, I got the call. Terry
Venables was the new England manager and I was in his first squad
for a home friendly against Denmark. I couldn't believe it. I came off
the bench to replace Paul Gascoigne. It was a fairly low-key game but
I felt 10ft tall when I went on. I didn't get much chance to shine but
we won 1–0 and I reckoned I was now on my way to becoming a
regular. That was in 1994.

It had been my dream to play for England for as long as I can
remember. I used to watch these superstars on a flickering black and
white television and imagine that it was me pulling on the white jersey
in the World Cup Finals. And yet, when the first call came, I didn't go.

I'd had a few training camps at schoolboy level but my first real international recognition came in 1987 when I was selected for the England Under-20 tour to Brazil. Saints were on a close-season trip to Singapore at the time and I was meant to fly direct from there to South America but I twisted an ankle. Chris Nicholl gave me a fitness test and effectively wrote me a note excusing me from games. It was nothing to do with the fact that I had a holiday booked in Tenerife.

I told Gordon Hobson, an older journeyman pro in the best sense of the word. He couldn't grasp that I had turned down the chance to play for the Under-20 squad. He thought I was mad. Even at that young age I was a cocky git and I knew I was young enough to get in again the following year. And I did. Graham Taylor picked me alongside the likes of Neil Ruddock, David Howells, Kevin Pressman and Carl Leaburn, a tall skinny lad from Charlton who was a bit like John Fashanu and a real handful.

We played three games in Brazil. I scored in the first two with Neil Ruddock setting me up for one, and then Carl Leaburn was picked to play in the final match. It would have been his first appearance for England but he made the mistake of going shopping when he had been told to rest – and he bumped into Graham Taylor who promptly dropped him. It didn't matter because it rained heavily and the match was called off. The humidity out there was unbelievable. I know I wasn't the fittest but I was struggling to breathe after 10 minutes.

I never actually played for the England Under-21 side, probably because I was picked for the England B-team instead. I made my debut for them against the Republic of Ireland on what appeared to be a potato field in Cork. It was an awful day. It hammered down with rain, again – to the disgust of the VIPs including Southampton manager Chris Nicholl because they all had to sit out in the open. And all the subs had to sit on a gym bench and got drenched. The only ones with any shelter were the press who were put in the Perspex team dug-outs. It could only happen in Ireland. I had a shocker, but then so did everyone else, and we lost 4–1.

Now, under my Southampton manager Alan Ball I was playing the best football of my career, scoring and creating goals for fun and there was a growing campaign to get me in Terry Venables' full England team. There was even a CD 'Bring Him On For England' by a Southampton band called the Valley Slags. When they mimed to it on the pitch at half-time during a home game against Leeds, the lead singer almost caused a riot by standing in front of the Leeds fans trying to get them to join in.

Terry didn't speak to me much but I enjoyed his coaching. The sessions were short and sharp with the emphasis on skill; on being comfortable on the ball. That's what counted. I came on as a sub against Greece and Norway before I got my first start in a home friendly against Romania in October 1994. I played the full 90 minutes but had only a couple of half chances in a 1–1 draw. It was tight and scrappy and I had to fit into the formation, and that was never my strength. At times I really did think that some of the more established players (and NO, I won't name names) saw me as a threat given their occasional reluctance to give me the ball.

And what did the media say? Having campaigned to get me in the team they now had a go at me. I was a sub against Nigeria and then the Pro Tissier movement started up again. Terry was under a fair bit of pressure to play me, with many feeling he hadn't given me a fair chance (it couldn't possibly be because I'd turned him down at Spurs when he tried to buy me, could it?). So far I had figured mainly as a bit-part player. Then I was picked for that extraordinary infamous match against the Republic of Ireland in Dublin. Some reckoned he was actually setting me up *to fail* by picking me for a match against a team then noted for its physical approach and long-ball game. The pitch certainly wasn't conducive to good football.

But I wasn't thinking about that at the time. I was just thrilled to get my second start and then it all went horribly wrong because the England fans went beserk and rioted. The flashpoint came when Ireland took the lead after 25 minutes, but the tension had been increasing for hours. We thought it was just routine crowd trouble, but then came the seats and missiles. People ask were you frightened and the answer is 'WHAT D'YOU THINK?' The game was cut short but

HE ORDERED ME TO SEE A DIETICIAN. AND A FAT LOT OF GOOD THAT DID.

Terry never picked me again. In fact, I was the only one dropped from his next squad but he did at least have the decency to phone and tell me, though he didn't give a reason. And I was too stunned to ask. Instead he put his faith in Paul Gascoigne and probably felt he couldn't play two 'luxury' players. To be fair Gazza was outstanding in Euro 96, but I don't think I got a chance to prove I could be equally influential.

When Terry was replaced by Glenn Hoddle, my schoolboy idol and another manager who had tried to buy me (when he was at Chelsea), I reckoned things were looking up. We were similar players and I hoped he'd give me a fair chance, especially when the media got going, but this time with a succession of scare stories that I might play for another country. Because I came from the Channel Islands I was eligible to play for any of the Home Countries. And because all my previous caps had been in friendlies, I could still opt to play for Ireland, Scotland or Wales. Well, in theory. But it was never on. My dream had always been to play for England, though that didn't stop the Wales manager Bobby Gould saying he'd love to pick me. There was even a story linking me with France, which was bonkers. In fact, when I was in my early twenties my dad did get phone calls from the French FA asking about my availability. Michel Platini was the manager and his assistant, Gerard Houllier, kept ringing dad badgering him to talk to me. But it was never going to happen. The only good thing was that it increased the pressure on Glenn to play me in a competitive match so that I couldn't play for another country, and that's exactly what he did in his first match in charge, bringing me off the bench for NINE whole minutes in a World Cup qualifier away to Moldova when England were already 3–0 up and the game was stone dead. And then he had a go at my brother Carl.

Glenn picked me for the vital World Cup qualifier against Italy at Wembley in February 1997 but it was overshadowed by a massive row because the team was leaked to the press. Glenn was furious and actually blamed my brother when another player had leaked the news because he had been dropped and he got the hump. Big time. Glenn hauled me in front of him that lunchtime and had a right go at me. That was the only one-to-one I ever had with him as England manager, and come to think of it I only had one when he was the manager at Southampton when he ordered me to see a dietician. And a fat lot of good that did, if you'll pardon the pun.

It wasn't a great night against Italy. We lost 1–0 although I did go close to scoring with a header, but the press were out for me. What they didn't know was that I was struggling with injuries. I needed a hernia operation and I'd also torn the tendon from my heel to my toe. It was horrible, and I was having to run on the outside of my foot but I had to keep playing because Saints were near the bottom of the table. I told Glenn I was OK to play for Southampton but I didn't think I could do myself justice playing for England. He asked if I would mind going to see his faith healer Eileen Drewery because she might be able to help. I wasn't rude but just said I'd prefer not to because that wasn't my sort of thing. And that was the last full England squad I was in. Any connection? Ask Glenn.

Glenn did pick me for an England B game against Russia at Loftus Road in April 1998, which was like a final trial match for the fringe players before the World Cup Finals in France 98. I was on a hot streak, pretty close to my best, and had scored seven goals in the last nine games of the season for Saints. A lot of people were pushing my claims, so Glenn put me in the B game. It was Last Chance Saloon. Peter Taylor took charge of the team and I was very impressed by his training and ideas. I knew I must be in with a shout of making the preliminary 30-man squad because Glenn was getting blood tests done for all the candidates, and I was one of only three (with Les Ferdinand and Darren Anderton) in the B team to be tested.

The game couldn't have gone any better. I know I've got a reputation for playing in fits and starts but this was one of my best ever 90 minutes. Everything went right. I scored a hat trick, hit the woodwork twice and ended up with the captain's armband for the last 10 minutes of a 4–1 win. I was besieged by the media afterwards. They were taking it for granted that I'd get selected. I tried to play it down, at least in public; I didn't want to appear arrogant or over-confident but inside I was BUBBLING. I walked away from the ground with my parents and Angela (now my wife) on a real high and I was pestering my mum to let me get a bag of chips but she told me I had to eat properly if I was going to the World Cup. And did Glenn pick me? No way. I only heard when my brother saw the news on Teletext and told me. It was like being punched in the stomach; I felt sick, bewildered and absolutely devastated. It was the most disappointing moment of my career.

There was a widely held theory that Glenn had been hoping I'd fail in the Russia match, which would let him off the hook with the fans and the media. Then he tried making out that Russia weren't very good – in which case why did he organize a match against *them*? – and while that's true I did get a hat trick. You can only beat what's in front of you. And if Russia were so weak, how come Darren Anderton and Les Ferdinand got in the squad? To make matters worse, Glenn rang a few people on the fringes of the squad to let them know they weren't in it, but he must have lost my number. I still have no idea why he made that decision. I shouldn't think he regrets it though – people that arrogant are never wrong. To make matters worse, he didn't take Paul Gascoigne either. I could just about have accepted it if he had thought that Gazza was better than me *but he didn't take a playmaker at all*, which I found very strange.

Or maybe we got on so badly because I didn't sign for him at Chelsea. In fact, I didn't even agree to speak to him. He must have rated me, though I think it was actually the director, the late Matthew Harding (who died in a helicopter crash), who wanted me. If I'd kicked up a stink and said I wanted to go then I think Saints would have sold me, but I said I was happy. I didn't want to leave. I loved the club and the city and felt at home there, and that was always very important. A lot of people told me I was mad because Chelsea was a bigger club and it would have been a chance to play for Hoddle.

My agent rang me and said Glenn still wanted to talk to me, even though I insisted I was staying put, but again I said 'No'. I knew that if I did speak to him – and he was my idol – he might change my mind. All that happened three years before he said 'No' to me, dropping me from the 30-man squad. When I was growing up my uncle always said you should never meet your heroes because they always let you down. Bloody hell, he was right!

After that I hastily booked a holiday to get away and watched the World Cup Finals on TV. I was never churlish enough to want England to fail just because I had been left out and I was gutted when England went out to Argentina. I was furious at the injustice when Sol Campbell had a perfectly good goal disallowed and was bitterly disappointed when we went out on penalties. I'd have given anything to be out there taking one.

Looking back, being snubbed was a crushing blow and I wonder if it had a bigger impact on my career than I then realized, because I never reached the same heights again. It was as though the ultimate goal had been snatched away from me and my greatest incentive had gone. It had always been my ambition to play for England and now I knew that was it.

MY UNCLE ALWAYS SAID YOU SHOULD NEVER MEET YOUR HEROES BECAUSE THEY ALWAYS LET YOU DOWN. BLOODY HELL, HE WAS RIGHT!

Glenn and I have since made up, although we will never be close friends. We were both staying in the same hotel on a golfing trip in Dubai in 2006 and I decided to clear the air. I walked in to breakfast one day and there he was, sitting on his own, so I went and sat with him. He looked surprised – and a bit wary. I think he wondered what was coming but I just said that life is too short for any bad feelings, and I wanted to sort things out. I admitted that I'd made mistakes while playing under him and I apologized, even though I actually felt he was far more in the wrong than me. I felt it was right to apologize and get the ball rolling. It was actually quite a hard thing to do and I got quite emotional because I really had idolized him. I told him that he'd been my hero. He was a fantastic footballer and someone I'll admire for his skills. Always.

It was equally tough because the rift and the not speaking to each other had gone on for so long, and here I was making the first move when I didn't really think I had anything to be sorry for. But we cleared the air, shook hands and moved on. I bear no grudges and wish him all the best with his academy in Spain. It's a terrific idea, taking on lads who have been released by clubs, working on their weaknesses and trying to get them back into professional football. Glenn will be good at that because he won't have to manage players with massive opinions and the lads will be desperate to get back into football. They'll take on board everything he says, no argument, so he'll probably get on well with them. But I still find it sad he isn't managing a top club and, if he does get the chance, I hope he'll have learned from his mistakes. If he could get a semblance of man-management he'd be a huge asset to any club.

SOUTHAMPTON
HERE I COME

THE ENTIRE TOTTENHAM TEAM WATCHED OUR MATCH.
I'D LIKE TO SAY I TURNED ON THE STYLE, BUT I MADE
A COMPLETE IDIOT OF MYSELF …

The stereotypical British pro footballer is said to be a gutsy, bust-a-gut, working-class northener. And me? I come from Guernsey, best known for its cows, in the Channel Islands, closer to France than England. And you can't get more south than that.

At school I was a good all-round sportsman, i.e. good at anything which involved a ball – tennis, squash, snooker, table tennis, hockey and particularly cricket. If I hadn't made it as a footballer I'd have tried to become a professional cricketer because I was a pretty decent wicketkeeper, mainly because that was the only position which did not involve much running. I remember scoring 164 not out in a 20-over game, which is still a Guernsey record. And I was amazed, while researching this book, to find that I broke several school athletics records including the 75m, 55m hurdles and the 6 x 10m shuttle runs (when you sprint to the first marker, touch the ground, sprint back to the start and then run to the second marker, touch the ground, and so on). It is mind-boggling because I was always the first one to drop out when we had to do them at Southampton.

To be fair, there was precious little else to do on Guernsey apart from going to the beach. So it was sport, Sport, SPORT. The island was obsessed with it, and I came from a very sporting family. I was born on October 14, 1968, the youngest of four boys, after Mark, Kevin and Carl. I turned up as an afterthought, or because my parents wanted a girl.

My mum and dad (Ruth and Marcus) got married at 16 and had had three children by the time they were 19 – and they are still happily together – despite the strain of looking after the four of us. They've been behind everything I have ever achieved, but the only principle I didn't follow involved hard work. They grafted like mad when we were young, often holding down two jobs each to ensure we didn't go without. We grew up on an estate and didn't have a lot. It was a bit rough and ready but not a bad place, and when you are a kid you don't really think about your surroundings, you just accept that's how life is. And Guernsey was a fantastic place to grow up, with wonderful beaches close by. It was so safe. It really was the kind of place where people didn't lock their front doors or their cars, and I must admit I'm quite pleased two of my kids are growing up there. The only thing people weren't relaxed about was sport, particularly when it came to competing against Jersey.

Both me and my brothers inherited our skill from our dad, who was good at softball, cricket and football and had trials with Arsenal. He was a lightning quick right-winger and I think the Gunners would have signed him but for a bad ankle injury. Mark was a solid defender and the only one of us ever to win Man of the Match in the annual Muratti game between Guernsey and Jersey. He was a decent player but not quite on a par with Kevin and Carl who could have both made it as pro footballers. In fact Kevin was a better finisher than me. He was an out and out centre-forward in the Alan Shearer mould and lethal in front of goal. He broke the Guernsey scoring record and averaged a goal a game over 20 years. Carl was a bit more like me and played deeper. He was skilful and creative and Guernsey's leading midfield scorer.

Both had the chance to make it as pros but suffered from homesickness. Kevin had trials with Middlesbrough, who were keen to take him but they were close to going bust at the time. He went to Oxford United and did so well that they offered him a professional contract but he turned it down. I was gobsmacked. Even at 13 I knew all I wanted to be was a professional footballer. Carl had trials with Southampton who offered him an apprenticeship but, again, he didn't want to leave Guernsey. That may seem bizarre but unless you have grown up there, you can't understand what a close-knit, insular place it is. But it did make me realize that being a professional footballer wasn't a pipedream. The fact that two of my brothers had been

THE FACT THAT TWO OF MY BROTHERS HAD BEEN OFFERED TERMS SHOWED IT COULD BE DONE. IN FACT IT MADE ME MORE DETERMINED THAN EVER.

offered terms showed it could be done. In fact it made me more determined than ever, and my parents started to take steps to ensure that I didn't suffer from homesickness if and when I got the chance to go. They encouraged me to go on school trips and residential soccer schools to get me used to being away from home. I have no idea where they got the money from but, somehow, they managed to scrimp and save in order to get me off the island. So when the time came for me to go, I was up for it.

For my thirteenth birthday I went away to a soccer skills week at Calshot Activity Centre near Southampton. I wouldn't say it was done on the cheap but my prize for being Player of the Week was two photographs, one of Kevin Keegan and one of Lawrie McMenemy – both unsigned. The sad thing is I still have them, and they are still *not* autographed. By now I was starting to realize I was pretty good at football and was playing regularly against much older opposition without looking out of place. That was partly because I had three talented older brothers and because I had the ability to cope with it.

The first sign of that came when I played in the final of the island's Under-11 school tournament. I was just eight (and physically there's a big difference between an eight-year old and a lad not quite 11) but I scored both goals to give my school, Mare de Carteret, a 2–0 win over Vale. It was my first ever medal and I remember thinking, 'I'm bloody good at this!' Even then I knew how to swear, although my vocabulary soon expanded as I learned to shout at referees.

By 1983 I was playing regularly for Guernsey's Under-15 side and I still remember the Muratti Cup Final against Jersey that year. We were the warm-up act before a friendly between the full Guernsey side and Tottenham Hotspur, the team I supported as a boy. I was a huge fan, mainly because I idolized Glenn Hoddle who was everything I ever wanted to be as a player. His skill, touch, vision and finishing were sublime. It was 1–1 when the Tottenham team arrived and they actually watched our match. We could see them all in the stand with the likes of Ray Clemence, Ossie Ardiles, Steve Archibald and Glenn watching us. I'd like to say I turned on the style but I made a complete idiot of myself.

With seven minutes remaining I was pushed in the box and we got a penalty – and I made a hash of it. I put the kick wide, a cardinal sin. A free shot from just 12 yards. It is the first penalty I remember missing and it had to be in front of the Spurs players. They weren't best pleased because it meant our match went to extra-time so they had to wait to play their game. We won in the end but I was still mortified at missing in front of so many big names.

My dad was a big Spurs fan so I supported them too, and I'll never forget when they reached the FA Cup Final in 1981. Every year my dad and a group of mates went to the final. I have no idea how he got tickets, but it always coincided with his birthday so it was his big annual treat to himself. He was more excited than ever when Spurs got to that final, and I nipped home from school at lunchtime to say goodbye but he told me not to bother going back for the afternoon, and handed me a ticket for the match. I was absolutely stunned. Instead of going back for lessons I was suddenly packing my bag and flying to the mainland to see Spurs v Manchester City at Wembley. Obviously, having me there cramped his style a bit because it meant he had to look after a 12-year-old boy instead of going out for a few drinks, so I'll always be grateful. We didn't get to see Spurs lift the Cup as it finished 1–1 and, in those days, there'd be a replay, but it was still an amazing experience and I was more determined than ever to make it as a pro.

I remember the thrill of walking up Wembley Way, jostling with thousands of other fans, seeing the Twin Towers (before they became an arch) and dreaming that one day Michael Gilkes would be cup-tied and that I'd get to take his place. I was absolutely buzzing as I handed in my ticket at the turnstiles and walked inside the stadium for the first time. Excitement? I nearly exploded. I can still recall walking out into that giant concrete bowl and seeing that famous pitch down there in front of me. I loved every second of the build-up, the flags, the scarves, even the smell of the place. It was then the most magical day of my life and I vowed I'd would be back as a player.

I was already on the right path. Manchester Utd didn't exactly come knocking, but when I was 14 Oxford offered me a trial, ironically in a game against Southampton. I stayed with Keith and Gill Rogers, friends of my dad and the people who had got Kevin his trial. Ray Graydon was the youth team coach at the time and he'd pick me up each day and take me to training. Oxford wanted me back and said it would be easier if I lived there so I left Guernsey to start school in Oxford, and I absolutely hated it. I didn't know anyone and wanted to leave after the first lesson. I think I managed two full days – so at least I gave it a good go.

Keith put me on a flight back to Guernsey and I think he was a bit annoyed, not least because the same thing had happened with Kevin. I just wasn't ready. I hope he didn't take it personally but it was too soon for me to leave home. Oxford were doing well then under Jim Smith, and had got to the League Cup Final, but I knew Southampton were interested. I had another chance. They'd spotted me playing for Guernsey Schools when we came over on tour and were keen for a closer look. They said they were happy for me to finish my schooling in Guernsey, and would wait to make a decision about an apprenticeship until I was 16. That was better. I still have the letter, addressed to 'Matthew Le Tissieur'. Maybe they were already thinking ahead to shirt printing, charging £1 a letter.

When I went to Southampton I stayed with Andy Cook and Leroy Whale who were also on schoolboy terms. Their families made me very welcome and I had no hesitation accepting the apprenticeship. My parents had received a letter from the manager Lawrie McMenemy but again my name was spelled wrongly, and the letter stressed the importance of finishing my exams. Bizarrely it said, 'I will quite understand if you do not want to tell Matthew of this offer until after he has completed his exams, but please let me know his decision *within a week.'*

Of course they told me, and I was always going to accept. My parents had ensured I was used to the surroundings at Southampton and that I was ready to move away. It also took all the pressure off my exams because I knew they didn't matter. I was never too fussed about schoolwork though I was pretty good at mental maths, which came in handy for working out goal difference, and I once won the Guernsey Eisteddfod Society Certificate of Merit for an essay about a dream in which I scored the winning goal in the World Cup Final. In short, I always just did enough because I always knew I'd be a footballer.

By that stage I knew I was head and shoulders above everyone I was playing against, often scoring five or six goals a game in the Under-16s and Under-18s leagues and also turning out at adult level for Vale Rec Reserves. And then I got a call for the England Under-17 training camp, which was a huge honour. It was also an opportunity to fiddle the expenses and make a few quid. We were able to claim train fare, food and taxi fares when of course I actually got a lift. Julian Dicks and Andy Hinchcliffe were also in the group, along with around 50 others I'd never heard of

MANCHESTER UTD. DIDN'T EXACTLY COME KNOCKING BUT WHEN I WAS 14 OXFORD OFFERED ME A TRIAL.

before or since. It's quite astonishing how many of that group never made it at *any* level, so there must have been something seriously wrong with either the scouting or the development. Who's to blame –

the talent scouts or the players with no desire? Me – I'd had a burning ambition from the age of eight. I never thought about anything but football. I knew I was good on Guernsey, but what about on the mainland? What was the competition like? Did I have any? It didn't take me long to realize that the answer was 'No'.

When news spread that I was moving away to join Southampton, I received a special presentation at the Guernsey FA annual awards evening. Former QPR goalkeeper Phil Parkes handed me a framed cartoon which had appeared on the back of the local paper. It said, 'Best wishes Matt for a long and successful career in England – from all the Channel Island goalies.'

Was I confident? It was weird. I was on a high because I'd just enjoyed a great season and I had faith in my own ability, but I was stepping into the unknown.

KNOCKED INTO SHAPE BY THE HAIRDRIER

WE WERE ALL LISTENING OUTSIDE THE DRESSING ROOM AS IT ALL KICKED OFF AND CHRIS NICHOLL THUMPED MARK DENNIS.

There was just one great big obstacle: I'd been suspended for the first two youth matches. All the bookings were for dissent and I had to appear before the Guernsey Island FA where we argued that a ban could harm my prospects at Southampton. Thankfully they voted by six votes to five to overturn the ban and give me a severe warning about my future conduct. So that obviously worked well!

I had always been quick to voice my opinion. I still remember one schools match which we struggled to win away. The ref was one of the teachers at their school and he did all he possibly could to get them a win. I was only 13 or 14 but I let him have it. As we came off the pitch the ref went up to our coach and said he needed to 'Keep an eye on that Le Tissier, and tell him to calm down and stop arguing.'

I overheard and said to my mate, 'He's talking out of his arse.' Too loudly. The next thing I'm being frogmarched to the coach's car and he's driving me straight home to tell my parents, but what he didn't know was that my mum had been at the game and she'd seen that the ref was a disgrace. A cheat. She stuck up for me but made it quite clear I had to be more careful in future.

And I remembered that at Southampton. What was it like there? Now Saints have a well-run lodge where all the trainees stay, but in those days you had digs, and it was pot luck what sort of family you ended up with. You were driven to someone's front door and told, here's your new home. I was very lucky and stayed with Pete and Pat Ford. Pete is a massive Saints fan who has one of the biggest collections of autographs I have ever seen, and he had two football-mad sons, Martin and Stuart, who were then 11 and nine. I went from being the youngest of four to the oldest of three, so instead of getting beaten up the whole time I was suddenly the one dishing it out!

I was getting £26 a week with a £4 win bonus and £2 for a draw, which was quite good as a percentage of the wage. We also got £16 every four weeks to buy a monthly bus pass. The clever ones soon realized that the date was on the back and that drivers never checked it, so we didn't bother renewing it and pocketed the £16. Most of my money went on fruit machines. They didn't exist on Guernsey and the bright lights were one hell of an attraction. I ended up losing big time in the amusement arcades. I'd just signed as a professional on £100 a week but I was already £1,500 overdrawn. It sounds like it was out of control but I knew I had a £5,000 loyalty bonus coming at the end of the season and that I could easily pay it off. As addictions go this was nothing, but I can see why some players get hooked. You get such a big buzz on match days that you desperately feel the need to recreate that during the week, and gambling is a quick-fix thrill. And don't forget footballers have plenty of time to kill. I played snooker. Straight after training I'd go to the Cueball Snooker Club where I became good friends with Warren King, the resident pro who got as high as Number 35 in the world. I thought I was pretty good until I played him. I'll never forget him rattling off a 145 break against me. He used to give me a head start of 60 and it'd go up by 10 each frame until I won. I had a couple of century breaks in practice but the most I ever managed in a match was 89. I'd stay there until it was time for the last bus home.

On the playing side there were nine of us apprentices, of which five of us made a decent living out of the game. Andy Cook went on to play for Pompey and Exeter, Steve Davis had a long career at Burnley before moving into coaching, Allen Tankard played for Port Vale for a long time and Franny Benali became a Southampton legend. He set up my first goal as an apprentice in a 4–2 win over Reading. I missed a penalty in that match but got an easy tap-in when Franny crossed from the left. Bizarrely, for a man who only ever scored one senior goal, he started out as a striker. At 15 he was a big strapping centre-forward but then he stopped growing and, as the others caught up, he moved further and further back, first to midfield and then full-back. If he had been two or three inches taller he'd have made a top-class centre-back. He was an excellent man-marker and very disciplined, except when the red mist descended. Like many of the game's hard men he's quiet off the field, one of the nicest guys you could meet – articulate, kind and gentle – but hard as nails on the pitch.

The youth team coach was Dave Merrington, who was a terrific bloke and a huge influence on me, but he was terrifying. He was a teak-tough, no-nonsense Geordie. There are very few things in life which faze me but Dave in full flow was awesome. The original hairdrier-blaster, long before Fergie. He was actually very religious, which you'd never guess from his language, but he was wonderful, warm and infectious. We had some great fun but were terrified of him. When Dave blew his top we knew he'd have us running, running and RUNNING, and I hated that. He didn't take any backchat or slacking but was absolutely brilliant, and even the likes of Alan Shearer still hail him as the biggest influence on their careers. He was brilliant for me, and never tried to stifle my talent. All the apprentices still keep in touch with him but, bloody hell, he was tough.

In those days they really made apprentices work for a living. It isn't like that today, where many have agents and boot deals and cars. Our system was better, even though I hated it. Besides training we had to pick up the dirty laundry, sweep the floors, clean the dressing rooms and showers, and Heaven help anyone who slacked.

One day a PFA rep called in to talk to the players, including the apprentices. We were all summoned so we couldn't finish cleaning the dressing room. While we were in the meeting, Dave walked past and saw some kit on the floor and went ballistic. He stormed into the players' lounge with a face like thunder and ordered us all downstairs immediately. He pointed to the dirty kit and asked why it was there. We said we'd been told to go to the meeting but he just barked that we should have finished the cleaning first. He gave us 10 minutes to complete the job, and to get changed and ready on the running track. He ordered us to do 40 laps while he sat in the corner of the stand and counted them. We jogged round as a group while he ticked them off until he got to 36. When we completed the next lap, he called 36 *again*. No one dared correct him, so next time he called 37 and then 37 *again*, and so on, until eventually he reached 40, making us do four EXTRA laps. He made his point all right. I'll never forget that, or the time one of the lads thought it would be funny to press the fuel cut-off button in the youth team mini-bus. No matter what he tried,

Dave couldn't start it. We all thought it was hilarious until he told us to run back. And in those days, before Saints bought their own training ground, we trained a good six miles from The Dell. We weren't best pleased but it was one time we actually got the better of Dave. We'd gone no more than 400 yards when a truck drove past. We got a lift and jumped on the back. He dropped us off near The Dell so we waited a while then sprinted the remaining half mile to make it look like we were knackered, and I was.

We had a good squad and won the South East Counties title both seasons I was an apprentice. In fact that was the last winner's medal I got. With the ability we had, and the likes of Alan Shearer and Rod Wallace in the year below, we should have won the FA Youth Cup. I remember we got drawn against West Ham who tanked us 5–0 at The Dell and Dave went mental, and ordered us all in for training at 6am the next day. Up to that point I thought there was only one six o'clock in the day so it came as a real shock. We all made it apart from Andy Cook, who turned up at 8.45 because he lived in Romsey and there were no early buses. He was taken round the track for some severe running which took the heat off the rest of us.

DAVE WENT MENTAL, AND ORDERED US ALL IN FOR TRAINING AT 6AM THE NEXT DAY. UP TO THAT POINT I THOUGHT THERE WAS ONLY ONE SIX O'CLOCK IN THE DAY.

For all his bluster you could have a laugh with Dave, at the right time, although it took me about a year to learn when to do it. I took a bit of a chance after a game at Spurs. I had an absolute shocker in the first half and Dave laid into me at half-time telling me I had

10 minutes to improve or I was off. After about five minutes I scored and I had a decent second half. Dave used to phone through the match details for the *Pink*, the local sports paper. He was writing his notes after the game and asked me what time I scored. I said, 'Five minutes after you told me I had 10 minutes or I was off.' The rest of the lads held their breath but I got away with it. It was certainly a better retort than Alan Shearer managed when he was having a 'mare in one game. It was a blustery day and he couldn't trap a bag of cement. The wind was howling and the rain was swirling and Dave was absolutely caning Alan from the touchline. Finally, in desperation, Alan turned round and yelled, 'I can't see because of the wind.' That was right up there on a par with his answer at the pre-match meal before his first-team debut. He was asked what he wanted in his omelette and he replied, 'Egg.'

Dave's approach wouldn't work now, partly because it's not politically correct and partly because many of the apprentices now have too much money, fast cars, inflated opinions of themselves, too much bargaining power and agents who'll approach another club the moment there's a problem. Some of them have even got agents and boot deals *before* they sign YTS forms. (I was 20 before I got my first car. I failed my first driving test because I nearly crashed. I was waiting at a roundabout and thought I saw enough of a gap to get through – and there wasn't. But I passed second time, bought myself a second-hand Ford Fiesta for £1,100 and thought I was pretty cool.) Clubs are scared of losing their talent so they give apprentices the kid-glove treatment, not the iron fist.

We all mucked in as cleaners and scrapers and that really made us appreciate the good times when we actually made it. We were basically part-time paid slaves. Each apprentice had to look after a pro, which basically meant cleaning his boots and making sure his training kit was ready on time. I looked after Joe Jordan and David Armstrong. At Christmas they were supposed to give a tip as a thank you. Trust me to get a Scotsman. I got the lowest tips, but that might be because Joe got the dirtiest boots. I was more interested in playing head tennis.

I vowed that when I got to be a pro I'd look after my apprentice well. The one who did best out of me was Matthew Oakley. I gave him a bonus of £5 for every goal I scored from 1993–95, some of my best years, which cost me a fortune. I remember Alan Shearer had his boots cleaned by a young lad called Kevin Phillips. For some reason we played him at right-back but decided he wasn't good enough, which was hardly surprising because he was a striker. Saints didn't offer him professional terms and he drifted into non-league football with Baldock Town before being snapped up by Watford and

ALAN SHEARER WAS ASKED WHAT HE WANTED IN HIS OMELETTE AND HE REPLIED, 'EGG.'

then Sunderland, where he became one of the most prolific goalscorers in Premier League history. Every club has players who slip through the net and go on to prove them wrong, but that was a pretty big mistake and, in fairness, a rare one for Southampton. But it's a good lesson for any youngster with self-belief and talent. You can still make it.

As apprentices we also had to work in various departments of the club to understand what everyone did, and how hard the staff worked. We also did one day a week at college, and the club placed great importance on that. With such a high percentage of youngsters failing to make the grade as players, they wanted to ensure that we all had qualifications to fall back on if necessary. I did a BTech in 'Sports and Leisure Something Or Other'. I've no idea what it was because I didn't finish the course. I signed as a pro in my second year as soon as I reached my eighteenth birthday.

My first professional contract was worth £100 a week, rising to £120 in the second year. My negotiations with the manager Chris Nicholl consisted of him telling me what I would get and me saying, 'Thanks very much.' He was quite scary, as Mark Dennis found out. There were a lot of big names in the first-team squad including the likes of Peter Shilton, Jimmy Case and Mark Wright, and it was tough for Chris to impose his authority in his first major job in management. He hit the roof when he learned that Mark Dennis's preparation for the home leg of the League Cup semi-final against Liverpool consisted of him playing snooker until 2am, so he decided to have it out with him in front of the rest of the lads.

We were all listening outside the dressing room when it kicked off. Chris was absolutely boiling and hit out and cut Mark's eye with a right-hander. He thought Mark was going to hit him, so he got his retaliation in first. Mark had pushed him to the limit and Chris snapped. He was a big man and I don't think many people would have fancied their chances in a fist fight with this big, bruising ex-centre-half. Mark Wright took Mark Dennis to hospital for stitches, and typically Denno just wanted to come straight back and finish it off once he'd been patched up. He stormed back into the changing room to find Chris having a shower, naked in all his glory. Thankfully Mark Wright stepped in and calmed it down, which was unusual for him. As soon as he was dressed, Chris went up to see a senior club official and told him he had just punched Mark Dennis. 'It's about time some-body did,' came the reply.

IT'S STUART PEARCE – 'OH ... MY ... GOD!'

IT WAS LIKE ONE OF THOSE KIDS' CARTOONS WHERE
A FEARSOME BULL IS SNORTING STEAM AND PAWING
THE GROUND BEFORE CHARGING.

I got my proper first team start – and I don't mean as a sub – when I was 17, playing in a Division One (now the Premier League) game against Spurs. That was a big one. The team I'd supported as a boy. The team with Glenn Hoddle, my idol. He was everything I wanted to be. I was fascinated by what he could do with a ball and by his range of passing with both feet. He was a great volleir and scored some fantastic goals from outside the box. Everything he did I tried to emulate. I can't put into words just how important he was to me.

Things had been building up nicely because I'd already made my debut at St James' Park – no, not Newcastle, Exeter – after I'd been included in the pre-season tour. I was still in my second year as an apprentice, and came on for the last 20 minutes of a 1–1 draw and was chuffed to read the write-up in the *Southampton Echo* which said I'd had a confident baptism and stole the show with some dazzling ball work. That gave me a real confidence boost because in those days I thought the press knew what they were talking about. I'd always read the papers if I had done OK but not if I'd had a stinker. I didn't need some reporter rubbing it in, and if someone is slagging you off that's not good for the confidence. I'd pick and choose when to read the papers, and I'd tell any young players to do the same.

My first senior appearance at The Dell came a few weeks later as a sub in a 4–1 win against Benfica in a testimonial match for Nick Holmes, although I didn't play very well. Then I was called in to the senior squad for a league game at Norwich on August 30, 1986. These days, with five or even seven subs, it's easier for a youngster to get on the bench, but back then there was only one sub allowed so it was a big ask to give the number 12 shirt to a kid. We were 3–2 down when I was sent on for the last 15 minutes with instructions to change the game, and I did. We lost 4–3.

First thing on the Monday morning I was summoned to Chris Nicholl's office and I remember thinking I had only been on for 15 minutes so I couldn't have had time to do that badly, but he wanted to let me know I'd be starting the following night. Giving me 24 hours' notice was a brilliant decision. Normally he didn't announce the team until the day of the match, but he knew it wouldn't be easy for my family to get over from Guernsey. And he knew how important they were to me, so he gave me the nod which was a lovely touch. In the end 24 friends and family came over, although I have no idea how I managed to get them all tickets.

It was fantastic just to be told I was starting, but even more special because it was against Spurs. The fact I had 24 hours' notice meant I had plenty of time to get nervous, but I spent most of the build-up wondering whether my parents were going to get there. There was only one seat left on the plane so Mum told Dad to take it and promised she would get there somehow. She ended up getting a boat and a lift so it really was a case of trains, planes and automobiles. The butterflies grew as the match drew nearer and I was a bit worried about the physical side as I was just a skinny lad and didn't know how to look after myself at that time – but that's what Jimmy Case was there for! I got a lot of support from all of the lads who were really helpful.

Bizarrely, I don't remember too much about the game, which zipped by in a blur. I know I started on the right wing and that we won 2–0 with goals by Colin Clarke and Danny Wallace, and I played the full 90 minutes, which was a bit of a surprise. My big moment was when Mark Blake hit a ball out from the back. It was going over my shoulder but I produced a bit of great control, brought the ball down and cut inside Mitchell Thomas and slipped a reverse pass to Danny Wallace, putting him one-on-one. He rounded the keeper but slotted it into the side-netting just as I was ready to celebrate my first assist. I also remember Chris Waddle – CHRIS WADDLE of all people – got booked for a foul on me. Five minutes from time I got cramp in both hamstrings but no one noticed and I didn't care because I was on such a high.

My debut gave me a massive boost because I now knew I could play at that level and not look out of place. And of course the £35 win bonus came in very handy. That doesn't sound much now, especially compared to the players' huge salaries, but I have never been motivated by money. The biggest basic wage I ever earned was £3,950 per week. That was from the four-year contract I signed in July 1997. The first year I received £3,450 per week, the second I got £3,700 per week and in the third £3,950 per week. And the fourth year? £3,450, but that's a chairman for you (thank you, Rupert Lowe).

People always ask if I wish I was playing now with all that money in the game and my answer is always the same ...

Of course I bloody well do.

Though I was never money-motivated, when I see very ordinary players getting 10 or even 20 times what I did, it does rankle. On the other hand I played in a fabulous era, the money was decent and you didn't get the intrusive media. And I don't think I'd have got away with eating the way I did, or playing with such freedom. I couldn't have put up with that, not even for £60,000 a week. I certainly think I was good enough for the modern game but the big question is, would I have been given the chance? If I was coming through the ranks as a young lad now clubs would probably take one look at my work-rate and get rid of me.

So what's wrong with the modern game? Where shall I start?

- It's taken much too seriously in every way, as a business, sports science, you name it.
- The players don't look as though they enjoy it, like we did.
- There is too much pressure. It's so serious.
- I'd love to see more home-grown players being brought through the system without all these big buys from abroad. Certain clubs develop their own talent but not enough.
- And the money is now quite staggering; clubs need to ask if they are getting value for the vast salaries they are paying out.

Rant over. I was very grateful for that win bonus against Spurs. We were given the day off after the game and I spent most of it reading match reports. The *Echo* described me as a 'mere slip of a lad' for the first and only time in my career. We trained on the Thursday and the Friday and I kept my place for the Saturday home game against

Nottingham Forest. I felt really confident as I lined up on the right wing and then I saw Forest's left-back Stuart Pearce and just thought, 'Oh ... My ... God!' It was like one of those kids' cartoons where a fearsome bull is snorting steam and pawing at the ground before charging.

Stuart was the scariest man I have ever played against, by a mile. All I can say is it is a good job Saints played in dark-coloured shorts. I was terrified. His thighs were wider than my torso. I think I got three kicks in that first half, and all from him. The first time he clattered me it was like 'Welcome to the First Division son.' To be honest I didn't even try and take him on. The look in his eyes was enough. It was a steep learning curve for me but I can't have done too badly because I got seven out of 10 in the paper even though we lost 3–1. Colin Clarke brought us level at 1–1 with 16 minutes to go, but they won with two goals from Gary Birtles and one from Neil Webb. It's just as well there was only one sub back then because otherwise I might well have been off.

I found myself back on the bench after that and I was probably lucky not to be dropped altogether. In fact Chris Nicholl made a special point of kicking lumps out of me in training. I think he was trying to toughen me up and to get me used to facing players like Stuart Pearce. Chris had a real mean look in his eyes and you could tell he meant every kick, but I really believe he thought he was doing the best for me. After that I spent quite a lot of time on the bench, which was

STUART WAS THE SCARIEST MAN I HAVE EVER PLAYED AGAINST, BY A MILE. ALL I CAN SAY IS IT IS A GOOD JOB SAINTS PLAYED IN DARK-COLOURED SHORTS.

very frustrating. I think he was trying to protect me and bring me through slowly, just like Sir Alex Ferguson did with Ryan Giggs.

I, of course, thought I was good enough to play every week and reckoned I'd tell Chris, really tell him, well, once I got a bit braver. He was scary, an old-fashioned tea-cup thrower. After a defeat he had a terrible habit of picking on one person, normally me because I was the youngster. Very few dared answer back but I remember one game at home to QPR when it was 1–1 with 15 minutes left and we lost 4–1. It was rare for us to be turned over at The Dell like that, and two of the goals came from outside the area. Tim Flowers was in goal and didn't get anywhere near them.

Chris stormed into the dressing room and slammed the door. No one dared make eye contact because we knew he'd be going for someone. Thankfully it was Tim. Chris yelled, 'Goalie, you've let in two goals from outside the box and got nowhere near them. Have your eyes ever been checked?' Tim couldn't help himself and replied, 'No, they have always been blue.' How he wasn't the second player to be punched by Chris I'll never know. Chris was so stunned he didn't know what to say.

Tim always had a reply but even he was dumbfounded after one game when he was injured while conceding the second goal. We were 2–1 down at half-time and Tim hobbled off the pitch. The physio Don Taylor was checking his ankle in the dressing room and Chris was laying into him as he lay there in agony. Don eventually managed to get a word in edgeways and said Tim would have to be subbed and would need to go to hospital for an x-ray.

Chris paused and then, in his distinctive northern accent, said, 'If it's broken, sorry. If not, W****R!'

I GET RON ATKINSON FIRED AND FERGIE HIRED

'CHRIS NICHOLL WAS QUITE RELUCTANT TO GIVE ME A CHANCE IN MY EARLY DAYS BUT WHENEVER THE GAME WAS NOT GOING WELL, THE SAINTS FANS WOULD CHANT: "WE WANT LE TISSIER". I WAS NEVER ONE FOR DOING MUCH WARMING UP BUT I KNEW IF I JOGGED UP THE TOUCHLINE THE CROWD WOULD START SINGING MY NAME – AND IT USED TO WIND UP THE MANAGER NO END – SO I DID IT EVEN MORE!'

One of the great things about coming through the ranks was having a minder to look after me on the field. Jimmy Case took it upon himself to look after the young players. If anyone tried to kick us, he would note their number and give them a whack; anyone, that is, except Stuart Pearce. After 40 minutes of that game against Forest, I jogged inside and said, 'Jim that's *three times* he's done me'. Jimmy just said, 'Not today son!'

It was brilliant having senior players like Jimmy Case, Mark Dennis and Joe Jordan as minders on the field and being able to work with them in training. Joe was so fit, one of the best trainers I worked with – not that I followed his example. It was quite daunting though to be training alongside such big names as Peter Shilton. I grew up watching him play for England and suddenly I was a cocky 17-year-old trying to chip him in training. It felt quite bizarre. He was the greatest keeper I'd ever seen and there I was trying to take the mickey out of him. I very rarely succeeded, but when I did, he hated it. Back then there was no such thing as a goalkeeping coach so Shilts used to take the sessions for the keepers, working with Phil Kite and my old mate Keith Granger.

> **I GREW UP WATCHING SHILTON PLAY FOR ENGLAND AND SUDDENLY I WAS A COCKY 17-YEAR-OLD TRYING TO CHIP HIM IN TRAINING.**

There were times when Shilts would turn up for training looking a bit rough. We would go out and warm up then I would turn round after 20 minutes to see him walking off the field and heading for home. He was a law unto himself and just trained when he felt like it. For the majority of the time he trained like a Trojan and would really put himself and the others through a tough session. I really used to look forward to the times when he was on top form because it would be really difficult to get a shot past him and you got a real high if you did it. He hated being beaten, even in training.

It took me two months to get off the mark but I'll never forget my first goals, and nor will Ron Atkinson. They came in a Littlewoods Cup tie against Manchester United at The Dell on November 4, 1986. We were 2–0 up when I came off the bench to score twice in a 4–1 win. The referee, Lester Shapter, allowed my first despite a massive shout for offside. There was a long kick from the keeper, Colin Clarke challenged in the air but the ball actually came off their defender. If Colin had made contact then I'd have been offside but I ran on and chipped the keeper.

I was so excited that I slid on both knees towards the fans at the Milton Road end of the ground – and then I saw the ref consulting the linesman. My heart sank because I thought I was going to look a complete arse if he disallowed it, but thankfully it stood. My second came from a Jimmy Case corner and I rose majestically (the only way to describe it!) to score with a downward header so my first two goals for Saints came, strangely, with my left foot and my head. Two days later Ron's time was up and he was sacked. I didn't feel guilty because it wasn't down to that one result but it was definitely the final straw. I did think it was a shame that he lost his job because he was a good manager but, as it turned out, that was Fergie's big chance. I hadn't done the rest of the league any favours.

Four days later I scored my first league goal but it counted for nothing as we got thumped 3–1 at Sheffield Wednesday. I was sent on when we were already 3–0 down so I was never likely to have much impact, but Jimmy Case chipped one through for me to run on to and lob over Martin Hodge. I was on a high. With three goals in four days I thought it was the start of something good but Chris didn't put me in the team for the next game, home to Arsenal. Maybe he was trying to keep my feet on the ground, but I have always believed in picking your best players and the ones in form. In fact it was a good one to miss because we lost 4–0, but I got a big boost from an article by Saints legend and record goalscorer Mike Channon who described me as the new Ian Rush. He called me deceptively quick and said my football brain would take me a long way and that Liverpool should try to sign me. So on the one hand my ego was soaring but on the other I spent a lot of that season on the bench, usually being sent on with the instruction to try and rescue the game. I very rarely got on when we were winning. But I do remember having fantastic support from the crowd. Whenever we were drawing the Milton Road end would start chanting 'We want Le Tissier'. Chris Nicholl was quite stubborn; the more the fans chanted my name, the more reluctant he became to put me on. I was never one for doing much warming up but I knew if I jogged up the touchline the crowd would start singing my name – and it used to wind up the manager no end – so I did it even more!

Chris thought I wasn't physically developed enough to play 90 minutes. Looking back, I see he was trying to protect me a bit BUT in my opinion, and I have told him this, I think he went too far. He should have given me more starts. I proved I could last a full match when I scored my first senior hat trick. It came in the snow against Leicester in the first week of March. I put us 1–0 up at half-time when Mark Wright knocked the ball down in the box and I crashed it into the roof of the net with my left foot. I remember Chris Nicholl had to virtually force Mark Wright back onto the pitch after the interval – he was refusing to go because it was so cold. I've never seen anything like it. His ears had turned blue and he was determined to stay in the warmth of the dressing room. Danny Wallace set me up for my second, a tap-in at the far post from his cross from the left. And then, with eight minutes left, came the *pièce de résistance*. I picked the ball up just inside the Leicester half and set off on a mazy run. The pitch was heavy and sodden and the snow was swirling around and I got a bit lucky when Russell Osman came in to tackle me and the ball fell back into my path. The better you are, the luckier you get. My first shot was blocked by the goalkeeper Ian Andrews but it came back to me and I rammed it in.

The best thing was that it came on a rare weekend when my dad came over to watch. It was the first time since my debut because it wasn't usually worth trekking over from Guernsey just to see me sit on the bench. I immediately got the lads to sign the ball and gave it to my dad to thank him and my mum for all their amazing help and support. And I lapped up the headlines, particularly 'The Wizard In The Blizzard' which was a damn sight better than 'Matt The Hat – And Dad Came Too'.

Even better, I reckoned I'd made my point with Chris Nicholl. I couldn't just last 90 minutes against tough, physical opposition in the freezing cold but score by the bucket. But no. Nothing changed, even though the fans were begging for me to play. I remember Chris said he didn't give a monkeys about all the pressure on him to play me. As he very delightfully said, 'With a face like mine, you don't get hurt by criticism.'

PUNCH UPS, HANGOVERS AND LADY BOYS

'IF WE ARE GOING TO GET A ROLLOCKING AT 8.30
IN THE MORNING THEN IT MAY AS WELL BE FOR
SOMETHING WORTHWHILE!'

Everyone wants to know – what happens on club trips abroad? I'll tell you: sex, drinks and fights.

At that time I wasn't old enough to drink, and didn't want to. And on just £100 a week I didn't have a lot of spare spending money so, while the rest of the lads went out drinking in Singapore in 1987, I stayed in the hotel. My vice was nipping out to KFC for a bargain bucket at one o'clock in the morning. But for the rest of the lads it was like they'd they had been let off the leash – and it was quite an eye-opener for an innocent young lad.

On our last night I was woken at 2am by my room mate who had better remain anonymous. He told me to get out of the room for half an hour. As a 17-year-old I had no idea why or where I was supposed to go. He told me to go and sit in reception and, as I went out, this *thing* walked in. I think it was a woman but you can't be sure out there. Certainly one of the lads got more than he bargained for when he took a 'woman' back to his room only to learn the truth when it was too late. Now if that had been me I'd never have told a soul. But he made the mistake of telling Jimmy Case in confidence, and as captain Jim felt it was his duty to ensure everyone knew.

I did go out one night but I stayed sober and just sat at the bar enjoying watching everyone else get more and more drunk. At one point Jimmy Case caught my eye and started waving to someone over my shoulder. I thought that he'd seen someone he knew but, as he walked past me, he said, 'That feller keeps waving at me. I'm going to have a word with him.' It was only when he walked into a huge mirror that he realized it was his reflection and that he'd been waving at himself.

Jimmy loved a drink and was fantastic value on a night out. I remember one trip to Puerta Banus near Marbella. Jimmy started before we even left Heathrow so by the time we landed he'd already had quite a bit. On the way to the hotel he made the coach driver stop at a supermarket and bought even more beer so, by the time we checked in, a lot of the lads were pissed. They just dumped their stuff in the rooms and hit the town. By midnight Jimmy wasn't making too much sense, in fact he could barely stand.

Dennis Rofe, the first-team coach, was meant to supervise us and make sure we didn't go too far. Now Dennis liked a drink and a good night out as much as anyone. When he was a player at Leicester he once threw a punch at someone who was threatening him only to find it was his reflection in a shop window. So he had a lot in common with Jimmy, but even he could see that Casey was hammered. After some considerable effort he finally managed to pour Jim into a taxi and took him back to the hotel. Somehow he managed to prop Jim over his shoulder and dragged him into his room and threw him on the bed to sleep it off. As a responsible member of the coaching staff, Dennis thought he had better go right back and check on the rest of us, so he got the taxi back and walked straight into Sinatra's Bar. And there was Jimmy, sitting at the end of the bar, raising a toast. The look on Dennis's face was priceless, and to this day I have no idea how Jimmy got back before him.

Jimmy was a formidable character when he had been drinking, as I found out when I ended up playing cards with him until 5am on another trip. We were staying at the Atalaya Park Hotel on the Costa del Sol and he owed me £80, which was a fortune to me back then. We had no cash on us so we were just writing the stakes on bits of paper. Jimmy was getting more and more drunk and wouldn't let me go to bed while he was losing. Eventually he staggered away to the toilet so I legged it out the door and back to my room. I was sharing with Francis Benali who, incidentally, never got up to anything on these foreign trips. So he was well chuffed to be woken by me shouting that Jimmy had kept me prisoner for five hours and now owed me £80. Suddenly there was a loud bang on the door and I hissed 'Don't answer it.'

Next thing there was a loud bang on every door as Jimmy went down the corridor, trying to find someone who wasn't asleep. I conked out but was woken by a rap on the patio doors. Jimmy had climbed over his balcony and was standing outside trying to get in. We just hid and eventually he calmed down and went off. Next morning, when we left the room, we were greeted by the sight of Ray and Rod Wallace's door hanging off its hinges. It wasn't the normal flimsy door but a big, thick wooden one and Jim had just demolished it. Apparently he wanted someone to lend him some batteries for his personal stereo. It proved mighty expensive because the cost of the door got added to his bill. And no, I never did get that £80 – and I'm still not brave enough to ask for it.

The only time Jim had a drink ahead of a match was the night before the final game of the 1986–87 season. I was injured so I was back home in Guernsey but I heard all about it from Glenn Cockerill who was rooming with him, and who also liked the occasional drink. We were away to Coventry and both teams were safe and, with no prize money in those days, there was nothing riding on the match. So the lads had a few quiet drinks the night before, but Jim kept going all night. His breath was still reeking of alcohol when the game kicked off and he'd hardly had any sleep.

After five minutes we won a corner and Jim went up to take it. Coventry cleared it, broke and won a corner of their own. It was Peter Shilton's job to set up the defence and tell everyone who to mark, and he noticed that Jim was missing. Everyone looked round and eventually spotted him still at the other end of the pitch, where we'd had our corner, sat on a wall talking to a spectator. He was quickly subbed after that.

After games, the lads would usually end up at Jeeves nightclub, but as I've said, at 17 and 18 I didn't really drink. However I do remember being talked into going out one night for a few rounds. I was living in digs and didn't want to wake everyone at 2am so Jim said I could stay at his place. We got back there at 2.30am and Jim started cooking bacon sandwiches while I sat in the lounge. I honestly just wanted to see his medal collection because he had won just about everything in the game, except an England cap, which is unforgivable when you think of his talent. On international weeks at Liverpool he'd be training all on his own. Everyone else would be with England and Scotland, etc. He was different class and I just wanted to see his championship medal because I had never seen one. I was stood looking at his trophy cabinet when his wife Lana came downstairs to see who'd woken her up.

She had a bit of a go at Jim and I thought I was going to be in the middle of a domestic when she started having a go at me. She said, 'What do you think you are doing?' I stammered, 'Jim said I could stay here …' She hit back, 'No, I mean what d'you think you are doing trying to keep up with Jim? You've got no chance.' She packed me off to bed and warned me never to try that again. I was woken by the sound and smell of Jim cooking a full fry-up including eggs from the geese he kept in his garden.

JIM KEPT GOING ALL NIGHT. HIS BREATH WAS STILL REEKING OF ALCOHOL WHEN THE GAME KICKED OFF AND HE'D HARDLY HAD ANY SLEEP.

For such a hard-tackling, hard-drinking player Jimmy was very domesticated. On away trips he'd look after the whole team on the coach, making cups of tea and plates of toast. He was really happy doing it. Here was this senior pro, a real big name in the game who was happy to be the waiter. He also looked after his training kit. Most of the lads just chucked it on the floor to be cleared up by the apprentices but Jim always folded his up neatly. He was brilliant like that but very different when he'd had a few.

It was quite an eye-opener for a naïve young lad who had grown up on Guernsey with something of a sheltered upbringing. I don't think the wives were particularly pleased about these trips but it did us good to relax in a different country, and that togetherness played a huge part in keeping Saints in the top flight. We weren't the most talented team but we had a real bond and spirit which got us through a lot of matches. You certainly couldn't have a conversation without one of the lads taking the mickey. If you said something stupid, you instantly panicked wondering if anyone else would pick up on it, and invariably they did. Equally, there was a time and a place for it – which took me time to learn. I was always ready with a cheeky quip but it wasn't always appreciated. These trips were brilliant for banter and team spirit. And of course we went right OTT.

I remember when we almost got chucked out of the prestigious five-star Dona Filipa hotel on the Algarve. Why we went to a luxurious hotel during the season I'll never know. It was full of really posh people dressed smartly for dinner while we were in shorts and T-shirts, larking around and getting drunk. There were several complaints about us so the hotel manager summoned Dennis Rofe who called a team meeting for 8.30am, which we thought was a bit unreasonable as we'd only just got in. We had no idea what was going on.

Dennis read the riot act and said the hotel manager was on the verge of throwing us out but he'd managed to talk him into giving us one last chance, and we had to be on our best behaviour or we were out. There was suddenly quite a sombre mood but I didn't pick up on it because I hadn't sobered up and piped up, 'I thought if you were calling a meeting at 8.30 in the morning, it must be for something serious.' Dennis had a face like thunder.

Generally Rofey was good value on tour, mucking in with the lads. As first-team coach he was a kind of bridge between the players and manager, someone for us to moan to or laugh with. He was popular with the fans too because he had Saints running through him, despite the fact that the club sacked him three times. The first time was when Chris Nicholl got sacked in 1991. The board assumed that the new manager would arrive with a ready-made coaching team, but that wasn't the case. Ian Branfoot came solo so there was absolutely no reason for Rofey to go. Dave Merrington brought him back as youth team coach in July 1995, but he was sacked again a year later when Graeme Souness came in as manager and brought in his own team of coaches, most of whom weren't a patch on Dennis, who returned for a third spell in April 1998. He was appointed as Academy coach but worked his way up through the Reserves to regain his position as first-team coach in March 2001. But he was sacked again in December 2005 following the appointment of George Burley who discarded most of the coaching staff. It was Rofe justice (OK, OK) because all the players and fans liked him, especially because he wore his trademark T-shirt on the touchline even when it was freezing in midwinter. He'd even had a stint at the club as a half-time pitch announcer, winding up the crowd to get behind the team, cracking jokes and even singing.

He fancied himself as a bit of a crooner and never hesitated to lead a sing song when he'd had a few. I remember a pre-season tour of Sweden and, after the final game, the host club laid on a dinner and drinks in a Wild West barn. There was a bucking bronco which all the lads tried, the beer flowed and Dennis got up on stage to sing a few Roy Orbison numbers before delivering a thank-you speech. Dennis thought it would be a nice touch to finish by thanking them in their native tongue but made the mistake of asking our midfielder, Anders Svensson, to tell him the Swedish for 'Thank you and good luck.' Dennis could never quite understand the lack of applause as he actually told them to kiss an intimate part of the female anatomy. Stunned silence all round.

Then there was the time we almost ended the career of one of England's greatest ever strikers before it had begun. It was 1989 on a close-season trip to Portugal and Micky Adams, Neil 'Razor'

Ruddock and Barry Horne had been partying quite hard, ending up with Micky and 'Razor' having a punch-up even though they were best mates. They were thick as thieves but the punches were flying and I remember thinking it wasn't a fair fight looking at the size of them. But Micky, who's maybe 5ft 6in, could take care of himself; not for nothing was he known as Fusey because of his short temper. Anyway, everything quickly calmed down and I went back to my room while they resumed drinking until they had emptied their own mini-bars, and that's when they went looking for someone else's. Alan Shearer's.

Alan wasn't a big drinker so they decided there would be plenty of booze left in his fridge. He was relaxing in the bath as they burst into his room. 'Razor' emptied a bottle of vodka over Alan while Barry picked up his mini-bar and ran off with it down the corridor – as you do! Of course Alan jumped out of the bath and gave chase, unfortunately there were a load of glasses on top of the mini-bar and, as Barry raced off, they all smashed on the floor. Alan had nothing on his feet and as he ran through the shards of broken glass he practically severed three of his toes. They were cut to

WHICH BRINGS ME TO ANDY COOK AND HIS BIZARRE SEX-SPECTATOR INJURY ON A MID-SEASON BREAK ...

the bone and almost hanging off. Everyone sobered up pretty quick when they saw that. It is no exaggeration to say his career was hanging as precariously as his toes.

The only one sober enough to drive was a young lad called Steve Davis who went on to have a decent career as a player and coach with Burnley. He drove Alan to this primitive hospital where he was left in an A&E in a bed with no curtains beside an assortment of car crash and broken leg victims. Thankfully a doctor managed to sew the toes back on and no lasting damage was done, but I often wonder if he realized who he was treating and what a favour he did England.

Which brings me to Andy Cook and his bizarre sex-spectator injury on a mid-season break. We were staying at a hotel and one of the single lads brought a girl back to his room but left the curtains open. A Big Mistake. Of course we all climbed over the balcony from the next room to have a good look and, when he finally spotted us, we all clambered back apart from Andy who decided to jump to the ground. Next day in training he complained that his heel was sore but, when he was named in Saturday's team, he decided not to mention it because he wasn't a regular and wanted to play as much as possible. After 30 minutes he was subbed in pain and an x-ray showed he'd broken his heel with the jump. But sometimes things got even worse. Time to tell you about David Speedie, and how he joined Southampton.

In the autumn of 1992 we'd made our usual shocking start to the season. During the summer the club had decided to sell Alan Shearer, who had made it clear he wanted to move to bigger and better things. That was fair enough but Saints allowed themselves to be bullied by Blackburn through the negotiations, even though they were in the driving seat. Alan had three years left on his contract so Southampton did not have to sell, and they certainly did not have to accept any old deal. I think the directors' eye lit up with pound signs at the prospect of a British record fee, and they rushed the deal through in case Alan got injured. They even pulled him out of a pre-season trip to Scotland for the same reason.

To be fair to Ian Branfoot (read all about it in Chapter 9), he wanted to take Blackburn striker Mike Newell as part of the deal, but Rovers didn't want to let him go. Instead of playing hardball and holding out for a quality replacement, Saints caved in and sold Alan for £3m with NO sell-on clause. Even I can work out that if they had insisted on getting 20 per cent of any future fee then when Al eventually moved to Newcastle for £15m, Saints would have pocketed another £3m.

Instead of getting Mike Newell we ended up taking David Speedie. It seemed to me as though Speedo didn't want to be here. He never got what Southampton was about, and it looked to me as though he resented being used as a makeweight in the deal. So Ian Branfoot spent part of the fee on Kerry Dixon in the hope of recreating the successful Dixon/Speedie partnership at Chelsea. Kerry had been an ace striker in his time but his best days were behind him. He had lost that yard of pace and sharpness and Speedie just didn't settle. It was hardly a match made in heaven, and it didn't help the situation or the fans' mood when Branfoot made the staggering prediction that Speedie and Dixon would outscore Alan Shearer that season. Kerry got just two goals and Speedo precisely zero while Al had scored 16 by December, when he picked up a bad knee injury ruling him out for the rest of the campaign. The following season he scored 31. (Kerry did try and I set him up for both his goals, including his two-hundredth league strike at Leeds. I was through and could have shot but I knew he was on 199 and, the way things were going, this would be his only chance to get to 200 so I teed him up for a simple tap-in, and spurned my best chance to score at Elland Road. Leeds were the only established Premier League club that I failed to score against.)

Anyway, it is fair to say that David Speedie didn't really settle in at Southampton. I don't think he liked me and we certainly didn't get off on the right foot. When he joined, he met up with us at the airport as we were heading off on a pre-season tour. As it happened the Manchester United players were at the same airport and I was chatting to Lee Sharpe because we shared the same agent. When we arrived at our hotel David Speedie accused me of being a big-time Charlie who wanted to talk only to the United players, and he promptly launched a bar stool at my head. Which was a good start. But he surpassed that several weeks into the season after we lost 2–1 at home to QPR. The fans were restless, the mood was grim. So the manager Ian Branfoot decided to take us to Jersey in the Channel Islands for a bonding trip. It suited me because it meant I was able to get home to Guernsey but it meant that I missed all the excitement.

After a meal the lads had a clear-the-air meeting in the bar where they went through all the things they felt were going wrong. As the alcohol flowed, the debate became increasingly heated to the point where David Speedie and Terry Hurlock came to blows. Very few people would ever dare tangle with Terry Hurlock but David Speedie didn't worry about that. There were a few punches thrown and a bit of blood. Eventually it all calmed down and Speedo went off to clean himself up. As he walked back in Terry went to throw a heavy glass ash tray at his head – only for Micky Adams to get in the way. For once in his life Fusey was trying to act as peacemaker and paid the price, ending up with a cut on his forehead. To make matters worse, the hotel manager called the police and Micky ended up spending the night in the cells even though he'd done nothing wrong. Speedo was arrested and hauled before the courts the following morning before being sent home in disgrace.

I flew in from Guernsey a couple of hours later and turned up all bright and jolly. It was like gate-crashing a funeral. The mood in the camp was the most sombre I had ever experienced. There was no banter so I asked what was wrong and the lads looked at me as though I was an alien. There were no mobiles or Sky News in those days so I hadn't heard. I was gutted to have missed it because I could have lobbed in a few of my sarcastic hand-grenades and inflamed the situation. (I met David Speedie on a golf trip to Mauritius last year. We ended up rooming together and he couldn't have been nicer. He had certainly mellowed and I was even able to remind him of the bar stool incident without getting clouted. He was great company, good as gold and seemed very happy with life, so maybe he really didn't want to be at Southampton.)

Games in the Channel Islands were always special to me, but for the rest of the lads they were a good chance for a few drinks and to stock up on the Duty Free before it was abolished. I remember a friendly against Guernsey in 1995 when half the team were still drunk at kick-off. I was a bit disappointed because a lot of people had turned out to see us, and my son Mitchell was our mascot. He ran out in a Southampton shirt with '7 Daddy' on the back. He is 17 and very embarrassed by it now but it was cute at the time. We had to rely on a header from me to win the game 2–1 but I took it a bit personally that some of the lads couldn't stay sober for a match which meant a lot to me.

Not all the foreign trips were to glamorous locations. We had a horrible trip to East Germany to play Carl Zeiss Jena before the wall came down. I can't believe we went there; the club must have received a fair wedge to make it worthwhile. It was a real experience crossing the border, with East German armed guards searching every inch of the team coach. We were stuck there for at least an hour and the agent warned us not to do anything to antagonize the trigger-happy police. Even I knew when it was wise to keep quiet and we all sat there on our best behaviour – apart from John Burridge.

He was as mad as a bucket of frogs. He even slept with a football as part of his pre-match preparation and, when he was relaxing watching television, used to get his wife to suddenly throw oranges at him to test his reflexes. It was like Inspector Clouseau asking Kato to jump out and attack him. Anyway, 'Budgie' wasn't noted for doing or saying the right thing and he kept on at one particular border guard asking him if there were landmines in no-man's-land, the couple of miles of neutral territory between the two heavily armed border barriers. The guard steadfastly refused to answer him, so Budgie kept on asking. Eventually the guard admitted that there were mines in those fields and Budgie cracked, 'Well, how do you dig up your potatoes then?' Not the subtlest remark!

HE WAS AS MAD AS A BUCKET OF FROGS. HE EVEN SLEPT WITH A FOOTBALL AS PART OF HIS PRE-MATCH PREPARATION.

As we entered East Germany it was as though someone had flicked the view from colour to black and white. The whole place was so bleak and the poverty unbelievable. We had a stroll outside the hotel to try and buy souvenirs but the shops were empty apart from a few bits of rotting fruit. The food in the hotel was no better. We ate in a dungeon and it was the worst food I have ever tasted, but I did get one of the best tour gifts I ever received. Usually the players were given glassware or tacky commemorative souvenirs but we all got really nice watches from Zeiss.

The match was played in a stadium surrounded by a running track so there was very little atmosphere, and that was shattered by the sonic boom of East German fighters swooping low overhead every few minutes. But it meant a lot to the people that we were there. There was so little to brighten their lives that one guy cycled for four hours just to be there. We had a few souvenir pin badges to give out and each one caused a massive scramble, as though we were handing out food parcels. One guy burst into tears of joy at being given a simple badge.

Another grim trip was to Northern Ireland at the height of the troubles. We played a game at Cliftonville, a bizarre ground tucked right in the middle of terraced houses. We actually went in through someone's front door and out the back, into the stadium. Iain Dowie was a big player for Northern Ireland at the time but he was obviously the wrong religion as far as the home fans were concerned. They were hurling all sorts at him, not just verbal abuse but coins and bottles. Thankfully there were huge fences around the ground and it was easy to see why. It was a horrible atmosphere and the kids were so ill-mannered. They'd just stick a piece of paper in front of you and demand that you sign it without a please or a thank you or any patience. I signed for one scruffy kid who promptly kicked me on the shin and ran off. I would have chased after him but he was quicker than me.

I had a similar experience when we went to Portsmouth to play a testimonial for their long-serving goalkeeper Alan Knight. It's no secret that there's no love between the two neighbours. Most of the fans restrict it to heated banter but, for a small minority, it *is* pure hatred, even in friendlies. I remember one game at Havant's ground when our goalkeeper Alan Blayney hung his towel through the back of his net only to turn round a few minutes later and find someone had set fire to it. The team coach had bricks thrown at it on the way home and that was just a Reserve game.

It might not have been a league game but the atmosphere for Knight's testimonial was evil, even though we were there to do him a favour. They fielded a lot of ex-pros, 12 of them at one point. Despite their extra man we won 5–0. Afterwards I popped my head outside to see if I could find my uncle who had come to watch the match. There was a crowd of Pompey fans, most of whom were great and I was happy to sign autographs for them until one guy spat at me and threw a right-hander. I just saw it coming and dodged it.

A few years later, during Dave Merrington's charge, we flew to Bahrain for a mid-season game. We were allowed to drink in the hotel and Dave was OK with us having a couple. He told us not to stay up late as we had a match the next day but he didn't say don't drink. Another Big Mistake. It was only an easy friendly against the Bahrain national side so a few of us had quite a lot to drink but the humidity was terrible. We'd have been struggling even if we had been in the right condition but we were all over the place. At half-time we were 2–1 down and Dave ripped into us saying, 'I hope you lot haven't been drinking.' Lew Chatterley, the assistant manager, was standing behind Dave and his face was a picture because he knew what we had been up to. Dave was quite scary when he was in full rant and none of us dared look at him or at each other. He must have known by the way we were playing that we were still drunk, but we blamed it on the humidity. David Hughes literally couldn't breathe because he had never played in such conditions and I risked Dave's wrath by telling him he had to get David off the field. The gaffer was actually quite good about it and Hughesie has been grateful to me ever since because it was due far more to the alcohol than to the heat.

DODGY REFS
AND HAT TRICKS

'COME ON MATT, DO SOMETHING – WE DON'T WANT
TO BE GOING TO EXTRA TIME!'

The 1987–88 season was a bad one for me. I only got two goals, one in the FA Cup and one in the League Cup, and I got suspended twice and missed quite a few games. I got sent off in back-to-back Reserve matches and in those days that also meant you could miss first-team games. But, not usually, I blame the refs.

We had to play Millwall at the old Den on a Tuesday afternoon. It was always a horrible place and we got stuck in traffic so we had to get changed on the team bus. One of the coaching staff had to run to the ground with the team-sheet and we eventually arrived at 2.50pm. The ref kindly agreed to put the kick-off back – to five past three. So, that helped! By 3.15 I was back in the dressing room. I got dismissed for not retreating 10 yards and then telling the ref that he was stupid. Well worth all the time and effort of getting to Millwall then.

The following week I was sent off again, at The Dell, supposedly for elbowing, although I'll never believe that a foul was committed. I was dribbling the ball when a player came in to tackle me. I stuck out an arm to hold him off and the next thing I knew the ref had produced a red card. It meant a double ban so, in all, I only started 10 first-team games that season with nine more appearances as a sub. I didn't manage a league goal but scored at Reading in a 1–0 FA Cup win and in a League Cup draw with Bournemouth. It was a really poor spell for me and maybe I was spending too much time gambling and at the snooker club where I'd spend 10–11 hours after training.

Let me tell you about David Axcell. We got off to a great start in 1988–89. We actually won our first three games, which is unheard of for Southampton. We began by beating West Ham 4–0 at The Dell, I came on as sub and scored, and as of 2008 the club have still won only one opening fixture in the 20 years since then. It meant we were top of the table and full of confidence when we went to Highbury and I scored my first goal at a big club. I had previously netted on the road at Hillsborough, Elm Park and Vicarage Road but those were my only previous away goals. It was a surreal moment. When I saw the ball in the net I couldn't quite believe I had scored at Arsenal – especially being a Spurs fan. There was a two-second gap before it dawned on me and then I went bonkers.

We played well and raced into a 2–0 lead, and were all over Arsenal but we hadn't counted on referee David Axcell. First of all he failed to see Arsenal midfielder Paul Davis punch Glenn Cockerill off the ball, breaking his jaw. I must admit I didn't see it either because I had been subbed. I twisted an ankle quite badly soon after scoring so I had to go off and, as Arsène Wenger will confirm, the view is terrible from the Arsenal dug outs. I only realized how bad the injury was when Glenn came off. He needed a plate inserting in his cheekbone and was out for about eight weeks, roughly the same length of time as Paul Davis who was hit by a nine-match ban. It had been a very sly punch but it was captured on TV and Davis was done by the FA in one of the first uses of video evidence. He also received more immediate punishment from Jimmy Case who ran over to Glenn and said, 'Don't worry, I'll get him.'

And he did. David Axcell awarded the Gunners a very dodgy penalty when the ball hit Kevin Moore's arm from all of half a yard away. There is no way he could have avoided it but the ref pointed straight to the spot. All eyes were on Brian Marwood as he ran up to score the penalty so no one noticed Jimmy standing a bit further back from the edge of the area. As players from both sides went to follow up, Jimmy took a long run-up as though he was also following up but instead he 'collided' with Davis, who went off two minutes later!

Having missed the sly punch, Axcell assumed that Glenn had been time-wasting and added an incredible nine minutes of injury-time. It was before the days of the fourth official holding up a board so it seemed as though he was just playing on until Arsenal equalized, which they did seven minutes after the game should have ended. And that point ultimately won them the title. Everyone remembers Michael Thomas scoring at Anfield to win the league for Arsenal in the last minute of the season, but if they hadn't been gifted that undeserved point against us they'd never have been champions.

I reckon we were robbed of a win, not just by Davis punching Glenn but by the ref who punished us for time-wasting when he had missed the cause of the hold-up. It wasn't the last time a David Axcell decision would influence a game I played in. In 1992 we played West Ham at The Dell in the quarter-final of the Zenith Data Systems Cup. It was the first week in January and it was bitterly cold. No one wanted to be there. That included the players, the fans and, I'm pretty sure, Axcell. With 10 minutes to go it was 1–1, and with no replays there'd have been extra-time and penalties, and the pitch was beginning to freeze.

Axcell jogged past me – I was running full tilt at the time. He said, 'Come on Matt, do something, we don't want to be going to extra-time.' Next time I got the ball I dribbled into the West Ham box. Tim Breacker put his arm on me, and I went down like a sack of spuds. Axcell immediately awarded us a penalty. I can't be sure how it looked to him, but I thought the ref was a cheat for giving the penalty; it never really occurred to me that I was the cheat for going down. After all, it was frosty and I was slightly off-balance and I was genuinely amazed to see him point to the spot. I scored the penalty and we all went home.

That set-back at Highbury seemed to stall our season and we lost our winning momentum but had a resurgence in November when Chris Nicholl won the Manager of the Month award after we beat Aston Villa 3–1. I scored with a header which I knew very little about. Nigel Spink went to punch the ball which grazed his hand; it hit me on the head and flew in. I celebrated like I had known what I was doing. That win put us third in the table, but it was our last victory until April. We went on an awful run of 17 league games without a win, diving from third top to third bottom. We didn't even look like getting a victory, apart from an away game at Newcastle where we led 3–1 with 15 minutes to go when they sent on a young lad by the name of Michael O'Neill who scored twice, and then pretty much disappeared without trace. Tim Flowers took a whack on the head with 20 minutes to go and got concussion. He

I THOUGHT THE REF WAS A CHEAT FOR GIVING THE PENALTY; IT NEVER REALLY OCCURRED TO ME THAT I WAS THE CHEAT FOR GOING DOWN.

was celebrating in the dressing room because he thought we had won 3–1.

I scored past Dave Beasant but it was my last goal of the season. I had 11 goals by New Year and then no more. The team weren't playing well and I was dropped. After 21 games without a win in all competitions, we faced a six-pointer at home to relegation rivals Newcastle on April Fool's Day 1989, with the losers looking certain to go down.

I watched from the stands and it was an awful game between two sides badly lacking in confidence. Chris Nicholl had left me out because he felt I wasn't the right sort of player for that kind of match which, in my opinion, was totally misguided. Totally. I thought as we were in serious trouble the team needed a creative spark. The match had 0–0 written all over it until injury-time when Rod Wallace skipped past the keeper who made the slightest contact. Rod was heading away from goal so there was no need for the foul but ref Gerald Ashby pointed to the spot. Derek Statham was the regular penalty-taker at the time but he was out injured, and I remember being gutted that I wasn't on the pitch to take it. I would have loved the chance to be the hero, especially as none of the other lads fancied it with so much at stake. Then up stepped the unlikely figure of 'Razor' Ruddock, who at least had the bottle to have a go in only his sixth game for the club. I swear half the crowd ducked, expecting the ball to go high or wide or both, but he slammed it home for a 1–0 win. The outpouring of relief was incredible and it turned our season around. We lost only one of our last eight to finish an amazing thirteenth while Newcastle were relegated.

I was still trying to establish myself at that stage, and it wasn't until the 1989–90 season that I became a regular. That was my first really good season and the one which made me think I had finally arrived.

We played Wimbledon early on and I scored twice, one of which was my first penalty for the club. I got behind Terry Phelan down our right and managed to lob in a cross. Alan Shearer jumped for it with their centre-back Eric Young and goalkeeper Hans Segers who punched it clear. Amazingly, the ref gave a penalty for *handball*. After scoring that spot-kick against Newcastle, 'Razor' then missed one and Paul Rideout missed against Villa so Chris Nicholl decided to have a penalty competition in pre-season. I had always felt pretty confident of scoring with a free shot from 12 yards so I lined up with 'Razor', Glenn Cockerill, Rod Wallace and a few others whose hearts weren't really in it. Chris Nicholl saw how serious I was about it and gave me the job.

A few games into that season, the club sold Danny Wallace to Manchester United, a move he memorably described as 'the icing on the jam of my career'. But it meant that the manager obviously felt that Danny's brother Rodney and I had developed enough to be able to become regulars in the side. Sadly, the move never worked out that well because Danny was plagued by injuries. At the time it just seemed that he was unlucky with niggles and strains but it turned out that he was in the early stages of Multiple Sclerosis. He has good days and bad days now, but he has done a lot of work to raise money and awareness for the charity. However his move helped me to play more games and I scored 24 goals that season. We played some fantastic stuff. Rod and I were just breaking into the team along with Alan Shearer. Tim Flowers and 'Razor' Ruddock were beginning to establish themselves and we still had the experience of Jimmy Case, Glenn Cockerill, Paul Rideout and Kevin Moore. And we also had a young Jason Dodd breaking through.

He had been signed from Bath City for £40,000 at the tail-end of the previous season, and he might as well have arrived with a piece of straw in his mouth he was that much of a yokel. He got loads of stick for his West Country roots but he dished it back, and went on to establish himself as a key member of the team for many years to come. He was a big personality, one of the loudest in the squad. You always knew when he was around because you could hear his booming laugh or his whinging – but he was a top pro and a decent player, just the kind you wanted.

He must have thought life at the top level was easy because both his first two games for the club ended in 4–1 wins. The first came away to QPR on October 14, 1989, when he was thrown in at the deep end but coped very well and we won convincingly. I celebrated my twenty-first birthday by scoring a penalty with Rod Wallace netting twice and Alan Shearer once. I decided to put highlights in my hair for the one and only time in my life. I looked shocking. A week later we were home to Liverpool who were then The Team to beat. They were top of the table and won the title at a canter that season. When they came to The Dell they were unbeaten, but it is no exaggeration to say we could have had six or seven. We hit the woodwork twice and forced some good saves as we tore the leaders to shreds. We absolutely battered them and it was one of the most complete team performances I can remember. I set up Rod Wallace for two goals and he returned the compliment by setting me up for a header. I remember flicking the ball over the head of David Burrows and crossing for Rod to volley through the legs of Bruce Grobbelaar. I got the last goal when Rod crossed from the left and I outjumped Burrows to nod in. Bruce got a hand to it but could only push it into the net. By then Liverpool were all over the place. We adopted an attacking 4–2–4 formation and had a right go, and they couldn't handle it.

There was still a real buzz about the city the following day and I remember watching it back on ITV's *Big Match* programme and wallowing in what was the best result I had ever had against one of the big teams. We had a terrific side and were probably only one or two good signings away from being genuine title contenders. Rod and I were scoring regularly and Alan Shearer was leading the line strongly, but we probably needed a couple of defenders. The midfield was getting on a bit and Chris Nicholl was under pressure to strengthen, so he splashed out a then club record of £750,000 on Alan McLoughlin from Swindon. He had done well for them against us when we played them in the League Cup. We drew up there, which was a real blow as the replay completely messed up the players' Christmas party that was scheduled for the same night. We had a tough battle to get past them at The Dell. It was 2–2 after 90 minutes but we won 4–2 in extra-time after Chris Nicholl sent on Shearer and Ruddock to rough them up. They were christened the Bruise Brothers by the local paper and the tag stuck. Alan McLoughlin was Swindon's main threat, so Chris signed him.

He was a bit of a panic buy. Although he was a decent player, he wasn't what we then needed. He was a good footballer with a nice touch but lacked a bit of pace. His best position was in the hole just behind the front two, but the only way he would fit in was if they got rid of me or Rod, so he ended up playing out of position. Having got past Swindon we really should have gone on to Wembley because we were drawn at home to Oldham in the quarter-final. We were 2–1 up going into stoppage time at The Dell but somehow referee Roger Milford found four minutes of injury-time, even though neither physio had been on the field.

Oldham equalized and we knew we had no chance in the replay because they played on a plastic pitch. We hated that surface and were beaten before we even got on the coach. We were in completely the wrong frame of mind which was highlighted when we had the chance to equalize at 1–0 down. The ball was played across the box and it was crying out for Paul Rideout to hurl his head at it. But he held back and Chris Nicholl had a right go at him. Paul said, 'You must be joking, I'm not diving on that stuff.' Chris had a face like thunder. I honestly thought I was going to see him punch a player for the second time. There was steam coming out of his ears which at least took the pressure off the rest of us because we were all crap. That plastic pitch gave Oldham a huge advantage and they beat West Ham by six in the semi-final and went on to lose to Forest at Wembley, on grass. It was a hard final to watch because we knew it should have been us in it.

We were still leaking goals but had enough firepower to outscore a lot of teams. I was feeling at home on the big stage and full of confidence, apart from an away game at Millwall. The old Den was a horrible ground, caged in and menacing. It was a great atmosphere for the Millwall players because it gave them a real lift, but away teams never felt comfortable. I was stuck out on the wing so I was close to the crowd who were giving me fearful abuse. We were losing 2–1 with a minute to go when Glenn Cockerill broke through the inside right channel and the keeper

IT WAS THE ONLY TIME IN MY CAREER I THOUGHT I MIGHT MISS BECAUSE I KNEW IF I SCORED THERE'D BE HELL.

brought him down, the ref pointed to the spot and I had the job of taking the penalty in front of their fans. It was the only time in my career I thought I might miss because I knew if I scored there'd be hell. But I came to my senses and sent Brian Horne the wrong way to get a point.

I also got a couple of hat tricks in quick succession. My first for the club came in the return game against Wimbledon at Plough Lane in a match when Francis Benali got a red card for launching John Fashanu into orbit. To this day I have never seen a player go that high. He came down with ice. Of all the people for Franny to pick on. We were losing 3–1 when we went down to 10 men, but we came back to draw 3–3. I scored another penalty after Rod Wallace fell over. It wasn't even a dive. John Scales was nowhere near him but the ref pointed to the spot, it was really funny. It was my second hat trick but I never got the ball – typical Wimbledon. My first goal took a deflection off Eric Young so they wouldn't give it to me.

Soon afterwards, against Norwich, I got my second hat trick at The Dell, which is still my favourite treble. The first goal was a tap-in from a Kevin Moore knock-down, but I really enjoyed the next two goals. I picked the ball up about 40 yards from goal and went on a dribble. I beat my old mate Andy Townsend but didn't have the pace to get away from him. I found him back in my way so I beat him again and scored with a lovely low right-footer in off the post. Then Francis Benali nicked the ball off their winger and hit it up the left wing to me. Their defender committed himself and I nicked the ball past him. I was still a long way from goal and right out on the left touchline but I saw Bryan Gunn coming out a long way and wondered what he was doing. I didn't have the energy to take the ball any further and I had the whole goal to aim at so I chipped it over him. The ball drifted and hit the inside of the far post and bounced in.

At the end of that season I won the Barclays Young Eagle of the Year award and the PFA Young Player of the Year award. The PFA was a huge honour, being recognized by my fellow professionals, even more so when I saw the previous winners. The worst thing was having to make a speech. I had an idea I might have won – or at least got close – because my agent had been told to make sure I attended. And he wrote a speech for me, just in case. I'd never done any public speaking so he offered to help – and I reckoned that if an agent offered to help free of charge I must have won. And the organizers getting Saints legend Terry Paine to present the award was another big clue. I found myself rehearsing the speech in the toilets 15 minutes before the announcements. When Rod Wallace came third it was a double celebration.

The Barclays Young Eagle award was a more low-key affair so I was able to wear an open-necked short-sleeved shirt with no jacket, although Chris Nicholl wasn't too impressed by that. It was good of him to attend to support me, but I remember getting into an argument with him because I was convinced I could be a sweeper. That would have meant playing two hulking great centre-backs to win the ball and give it to me to ping around like Franz Beckenbauer or Glenn Hoddle, making me look like a world-beater. I was always cool under pressure so I felt I could do that – although I must admit part of me was winding Chris up, getting back at him for all the times when he'd kicked me in training.

WHY I TOLD SOUNESS, HODDLE AND VENABLES TO GET LOST

'I SIGNED THE CONTRACT AND WATCHED AS IT WAS
LOCKED IN THE SAFE. IT WAS SETTLED. I WAS JOINING
MY BOYHOOD HEROES. I WAS ABOUT TO BECOME
A SPURS PLAYER.'

After those awards and those goals, people woke up to Matt Le Tissier. Especially Tottenham. I got a phone call from my agent Jerome Anderson to say Spurs were interested, asking if I'd speak to them. I wasn't going to say no, not to the team I'd always supported. Though Terry Venables was the manager I didn't speak to him, and the deal was done through their lawyers and their agent. We had a meeting at a solicitor's office in north London a couple of months before the end of the season. Saints didn't know anything about it, but I agreed terms and signed a contract which was locked away in the safe in the solicitor's office. Then it'd be brought out at the end of the season, when the clubs had agreed a fee.

Ironically our last game of the season was away to Spurs. We'd played Arsenal away a couple of days earlier and, if we'd won both matches, would have finished third. Instead we lost both and ended up seventh, but that was still my highest ever finishing position. I was due to get married (for the first time) that summer and after the Spurs game my fiancée, Cathy, announced that she didn't want to live in London, so I had a decision to make. Go or stay. I decided to stay with Saints and don't regret it at all, even though we ended up getting divorced. I made the decision, no one else. It's a waste of time thinking, what if? I phoned Jerome and told him, and he was good as gold and never tried to tell me I was making a mistake, even though he could see his commission going right out the window. He never put any pressure on me. He'd just put offers in front of me and let me make up my own mind.

I then got a message from Terry Venables saying he respected my decision, but that he'd still like to speak to me on the phone. I declined (as I did later with Glenn Hoddle) because I didn't want to be put in a position where I might be tempted to change my mind. Cathy didn't fancy living in London, so what was the point? I don't know if Terry held that against me when he was England manager. It's true he picked me, but not as many times as I think he should have done.

The good news was knowing what Spurs were prepared to pay me. So I went back to Southampton and negotiated a new contract just like the one I'd have got at White Hart Lane. I now got £1,100 per week in the first year, £1,200 pw in the second and £1,300 pw in the third, but I'd have stayed even if they'd said no. Maybe I'd have won more England caps by moving club, but I was happy where I was.

I had two other opportunities to move. The first came a couple of years later when Jerome rang and said one of the biggest clubs in Europe was in for me. He didn't want to tell me about it over the phone so I had to drive up to London to meet him in a hotel. I went up thinking it might be Real Madrid or Barcelona but it turned out to be Liverpool. Graeme Souness was the manager but again I didn't even meet him. The move never got off the ground because I didn't fancy living up north. Nothing against the north – but I preferred to live where I didn't need a translator. If I'd ever moved from Southampton then I wouldn't have gone any further than London, so Liverpool was never an option.

The only other time I came close to leaving Saints was in 1995 when Chelsea came in for me. I had a lot of things to weigh up. At that point Alan Ball was manager at Southampton and it was a brilliant time for me. He brought the best out of me and made me feel good about myself. I was happy playing for him and for Saints, I knew I'd be playing every week and I was still in the England squad. And I was in the top division. If Saints had ever been relegated then I'd have been put in a tough position. If they hadn't bounced straight back then I think I'd have been yearning to play in the top division and would have asked for a move, but fortunately none of that happened.

So did I lack ambition? That's what they said. But listen – I'd set my ambitions high when I was seven or eight. I wanted to be a professional footballer and play for England. By the age of 25 I had done both. If any of my critics could claim to have fulfilled their life's ambition by the time they were 25 then they'd be entitled to their say. But most of the negative comments were coming from people who didn't know me or who had never played the game, and definitely not to my level. So it hurt me when people said I lacked ambition because they had no idea about where I had come from or what my goals were. They certainly had no idea about my background and what an achievement it was to break away from the Channel Islands. Unless you have grown up there, you cannot begin to understand what a sheltered background it is.

Over the decades there have been very few professional footballers (Graeme Le Saux is the obvious example) from the Channel Islands, which have a combined population of only around 150,000. To come from there and play for England is a pretty big achievement in my eyes – particularly as I managed to balance that with personal happiness, which always meant much more to me than money.

A LOT OF PLAYERS MOVE CLUBS CLAIMING IT'S BECAUSE THEY ARE AMBITIOUS. DON'T LET THEM FOOL YOU; THEY ARE USUALLY AFTER THE EXTRA CASH.

And it's worth stressing that a lot of players move clubs claiming it's because they are ambitious. Don't let them fool you; they are usually after the extra cash. Nothing wrong with that, so long as they're being honest. The fans aren't stupid, they see through it – as they did when Lucas Neill chose West Ham over Liverpool claiming he was *ambitious*. Nothing against the Hammers, but how could he say that West Ham had more chance of winning cups than Liverpool? And look at the likes of Steve Sidwell, who was great for Reading. He was playing every week but then moved to Chelsea, knowing full well that he wouldn't be a regular but he'd be paid more. Is that ambition?

WHY I TOLD SOUNESS, HODDLE AND VENABLES TO GET LOST

Is a player better off getting silly money every week but sitting on the bench, or playing regularly, earning less and keeping his self-respect? I know what I chose. And earning less does NOT mean that you are being badly paid. You can't blame the players for taking that sort of money if it's offered, but there comes a time when you have to wonder how much more money someone can actually spend? If you are already on £30,000 a week, what else could you buy if you get £40,000? The only difference for the likes of Steve Sidwell is they'd have more time to spend it because they're not playing! I know times were different during my career, but the most I ever earned was just under £4,000 a week. I could never have handled sitting on the bench, week after week, and being sent on as an 'impact player', just for the extra cash. It was bad enough when I was dropped – and every manager left me out at some point – apart from Dave Merrington and Alan Ball. At least at Southampton I didn't have to worry about rotation because we never had a big enough squad for that. And I'd have hated being left out even when I was playing well simply to give others a chance. I never had a problem being dropped if I was going through a bad spell, and never went knocking on the manager's door about it. I simply waited for them to lose a couple of games, then knew I'd be back in again.

The other point which worried me about moving clubs is the number of players I saw who struggled to settle, or who found it didn't work out. I do believe certain players are right for certain clubs. If you feel comfortable, fit in and have a good rapport with your teammates then you are far more likely to play your best. There have been so many instances of players being a success at one club, taking the 'dream move' and being a bit of a flop. It isn't that they have suddenly become bad players; they just don't fit into the new team or feel comfortable in their new set up.

James Beattie was a real star for Southampton and a big hero with the fans, who loved him, but he never showed that form when he moved to Everton. If you don't get off to a good start at a new club after a big-money move then the fans can get on your back, and it can be much harder to make an impact. So was I glad I stayed at Saints.

IAN WHO?

'I'D NEVER HEARD OF IAN BRANFOOT BUT I WAS CERTAIN HE
WOULD QUICKLY APPRECIATE MY UNIQUE TALENTS AND BUILD
HIS TEAM AROUND ME, PLAYING A SLICK, ENTERTAINING
BRAND OF EXCITING ATTACKING FOOTBALL.'

By the start of the 1990–91 season I was getting a bit cocky in the
dressing room. We were a younger group of players, and I was scoring goals. I had a bit more stature, and was quicker to express an
opinion and dish out the banter. I still didn't drink but I was starting to
come out of my shell.

On the field, it took me a while to get going. The campaign began
with everyone on a high after England's run to the semi-finals at the
Italia 90 World Cup. The kick-off was delayed for our opening match
away at Aston Villa because of the crowds – a pattern repeated across
the country. I scored in a 1–1 draw and then netted a free kick at Coventry. It wasn't struck with that much power but was more of a chip which
left the keeper flat-footed, and from then on I was put on free-kick duty.

It was a fairly unremarkable campaign, we couldn't match the
previous season's results, and sadly Chris Nicholl got axed. I still
wonder if things might have panned out differently if I hadn't picked

up my first proper injury. It happened in a 3–1 defeat against Notting-ham Forest in January when I went to back-heel the ball and pulled a hamstring. I didn't even realize I'd got a hamstring muscle, let alone had torn it, but I knew right away that I was trouble. I was sidelined for five weeks and we flirted with relegation but managed to stay up reasonably comfortably.

There was a strong suggestion that Chris had tried to resign after an FA Cup defeat at Forest in March. Apparently one of his children told friends at school, and the next minute it's in the local paper. The club denied it, though it seemed more a case of him being told 'You got us into this mess, you get us out of it.' And he did. We were safe well before the end of the campaign but the writing was on the wall after a shocking display in our penultimate match, away to already relegated Derby who had gone down with a then record low number of points. They were very flat after a shocking season but still thrashed us 6–2. Paul Williams, who later joined us as a command-ing centre-back, played up front that day and got a hat trick. It came in the same week that Gerald Ratner famously described his prod-ucts as 'crap' and I remember the *Echo* said, 'If Saints could pack-age and sell what they produced at Derby, they would make a fortune – at Ratners.'

They were right, we were shocking. We weren't in the right frame of mind, our fans were in a party mood for the last away game of the season and it seemed to spread to the players. Some of the support-ers had brought musical instruments, and some of the players went into the crowd during the warm-up and started joining in. It was just a bit of fun but it wasn't right, and Chris Nicholl was rightly mad at us. I scored a penalty but I remember being very nervous because Peter Shilton was in goal. That brought my tally to 23 for the season, and since I'd missed a month being injured I was quite pleased.

IAN WHO?

We drew our final fixture 1–1 at home to Wimbledon with Jimmy Case scoring in what proved to be his last appearance for us – but it wasn't enough to save Chris's job, although we had no inkling what was about to happen. At that stage Saints had *never* sacked a manager – certainly not post-war when they enjoyed remarkable stability – although Rupert Lowe has more than made up for that with his turnover of managers* in recent years. Ted Bates had been in charge for 18 years before handing over to Lawrie McMenemy, who then had 12 years. That continuity provided the rock on which the club was built, and it should never have been destroyed.

Ted Bates was a phenomenon who joined the club as a striker from Norwich on his nineteenth birthday, and he stayed for 66 years as player, coach, manager, director and president. As manager, he guided the club from the third tier to the top flight for the first time in their history. He was a principled man, a sound judge of character and a real football man, steeped in the game. He stood for everything which made the club great, and it is so sad to see his legacy squandered by men who seemed to care more about the share price than the right way of doing things. He'd have had no time for the city boys whose approach undid all his good work and, incredibly, took the club right back to where he started. The third tier. So up until the moment when Chris was sacked, the club had had only three managers in 30 years. It was quite momentous when the axe fell. It was my first experience of losing a manager, though I soon got used to that.

---

* No one really knows how many managers Lowe has sacked to date. He maintains it is one. Technically Graeme Souness resigned, Dave Jones was put on gardening leave, Glenn Hoddle left for his 'spiritual home' at Spurs, Stuart Gray was sacked, Gordon Strachan left, Paul Sturrock went by mutual consent, Steve Wigley left by mutual consent, Harry Redknapp returned to Portsmouth, Nigel Pearson's contract was not renewed and Jan Poortvliet resigned.

I was in Guernsey and I remember reading about it on Teletext, which was how you heard about anything in those days. It came as a real shock and I have to say I was disappointed because I was just starting to get on with Chris. We had the makings of a decent side and played some good, attractive football under him. I'd scored 47 goals in two seasons, and felt I fitted in well with his style of playing. But he paid the price for us punching above our weight the previous season. In hindsight it was even more of a crazy decision to get rid of him because of what followed.

After much deliberation – and I find it hard to believe the board could take so long and still get it so badly wrong – Chris was replaced by a certain Ian Branfoot in 1991. I'd never really heard of him. I knew he'd had some success with Reading and that he'd been Reserve team coach at Southampton, but that was before my time. I also knew he had a reputation for the long-ball game which was a worry, but I was confident he would soon recognize my unique talents and adopt his style accordingly. As if.

I soon discovered that he had a set way of playing and nothing was going to change that. We had some of the brightest young players in the country with Rod Wallace, Alan Shearer, Tim Flowers, Neil Ruddock and myself. And we were held together by the experience and physical presence of Jimmy Case, who was still going strong. He was a key central cog in the team, winning the ball and getting us going. He was hugely popular with the players and the fans, so the first thing Ian Branfoot did was – get rid of him.

I think he saw him as a threat because Jim had been mentioned as Chris Nicholl's possible replacement. But Jim wasn't like that, he just wanted to enjoy his football. And he would have easily fitted in with Branfoot's style because he was capable of pinging long passes and using plenty of midfield muscle. It was sad to see him go because he was such a huge part of the team. He went to Bournemouth and carried on playing for a few more years, so I know he could have done a job for us. Although he was getting on a bit, he was a very intelligent player who read the game so well that it easily compensated for his slight lack of pace. It was a petty thing to do and was counter-productive because it got the new manager off on the wrong foot with the fans, who had loved Jim.

Branfoot replaced Jim with Terry Hurlock who was an absolute diamond and just as hard. I had played against him when he was at Millwall and he frightened the life out of me. I was much happier having him on my side than against me. With his long hair and huge muscles, he cut an intimidating figure but he could play a bit too. He was Player of the Year at Glasgow Rangers and you don't get that by being a mug. He was hard as nails on the pitch but a big softie off it, and would do anything to help you.

Branfoot looked at our defensive record and saw how many we had conceded, even though we were scoring a lot. He decided the priority was to make us more solid, which was not good news for me.

I REMEMBER READING ABOUT IT ON TELETEXT, WHICH WAS HOW YOU HEARD ABOUT ANYTHING IN THOSE DAYS.

The manager wanted a rigid 4–4–2 system with me stuck out on the wing with balls being pumped into the channels and humped into the box, which was not my idea of good football. It was a big culture shock. The new manager – and I didn't mind him as a bloke – wanted the rest of the team fighting to get hold of the scraps. Not exactly the Beautiful Game and barking mad given we had players who wanted to pass and play. Managers should employ tactics based on the kind of players they've got. But in his wisdom Ian Branfoot decided to alter the style before changing the players. And I was never going to be much use in that style. I didn't even have a long throw.

I played 31 league games but only scored six goals. I *didn't* have licence to roam, I *didn't* like that style of play and I *didn't* enjoy that season. There was an awful atmosphere off the field too because the fans didn't like what they were watching and made their feelings known. The one redeeming feature of a miserable campaign was that it provided me with my only final with the club and my only goal at Wembley. Admittedly it was only the Zenith Data Systems Cup Final, but it was still a Wembley final. I scored in every round, from when we beat Bristol City and Plymouth in two early low-key rounds to my netting a hugely debatable penalty in the regional semi-final against West Ham.

I got a hat trick in the second leg of the area final at Chelsea, including a penalty. As I was about to take it, Dennis Wise stepped up and bet me £50 I'd miss it. That was a lot of cash back then and it was easy money, so of course I accepted and scored. Unfortunately they got a penalty of their own for a late consolation goal so I felt honour-bound to offer Dennis double or quits, and he scored. But we won 5–1 on aggregate and, suddenly, a competition which began as an inconvenience meant a Wembley final. Ian Branfoot had won the trophy with Reading when it was called the Simod Cup so he knew it was worth going for. Once we reached Wembley there was a real buzz about the city and we ended up taking 32,000 fans, all of whom *booed* Ian Branfoot. That must say something. It was the club's first final of any sort for 16 years and still the manager was hated. We were warming up as the announcer read out the team sheet. Every name was cheered, even the subs, until the end when the man with the mike said, 'And the Southampton manager is Ian Branfoot'. The jeers were deafening. They even drowned out my own booing.

I was terrified I might not even play because the manager had dropped me for the two previous games, even though I had scored in a 1–0 win against Palace. He opted for the mighty Michael Gilkes ahead of me but, thankfully, he was cup-tied so I sneaked into the final. If I hadn't played I think I'd have asked for a move.

We had a great night before the match. The gaffer took us all to see the West End show *Buddy*, which was one of the best things he did as a manager, which tells you a lot about his football decisions. It was a great night and brought all the lads together. At the kick-off I was put on the left wing, which was fine because it meant I didn't have to face Stuart Pearce. Tim Flowers kept us in the match because we went 2–0 down when it could have been 7–0, but we got back into it with a goal, which was all the wrong way round as Neil Ruddock crossed for me to head home. Then I flighted a corner for Kevin Moore to nod in and it was 2–2. I was buzzing and well up for extra-time. I was young and still had some energy left, and the adrenaline rush of playing at Wembley was getting me through but we crashed 3–2.

We should have got there again in the FA Cup in 1992 because so many things seemed to point to it being our year. The first omen came when we played Manchester United in the fourth round. We drew 0–0 at The Dell and everyone assumed we'd lose the replay. But we played really well at Old Trafford and raced into a 2–0 lead with Stuart Gray scoring his one and only goal for the club. They got it back to 2–1 but we were still deservedly leading in injury-time when a freak rebound gifted them an easy equalizer. You'd have expected us to fold in extra-time – I certainly did. But we were let off the hook by possibly the only decision to ever go in our favour at Old Trafford as Bryan Robson's effort clearly crossed the line before Tim Flowers clawed it back. The ref couldn't be sure and we got away with it. So to penalties. It was the first ever FA Cup penalty shoot-out involving two top-flight teams.

Ian Branfoot asked me to go first to get us off to a good start, but I said I wanted to go last because I wanted to take the winning spot-kick, such was my confidence, so it probably served me right that I never got to take one. It was the only penalty shoot-out I was involved in throughout my whole career and I didn't get to take one shot. Micky Adams, Alan Shearer, Barry Horne and Neil Ruddock all struck fantastic penalties while Neil Webb missed for them. A lot of their senior players were conspicuous by their absence. Bryan Robson, Paul Ince and Mark Hughes didn't step up to the mark so it was left to a young Ryan Giggs. Obviously I wanted us to win but part of me hoped he would score so I could be the hero.

> **IT WAS THE ONLY PENALTY SHOOT-OUT I WAS INVOLVED IN THROUGHOUT MY WHOLE CAREER AND I DIDN'T GET TO TAKE ONE.**

But Tim Flowers made a brilliant save – and an even better celebration. Our fans were at the far end of the stadium so Tim ran the length of the field like a madman. I have never seen him run so far or fast. Mind, he couldn't have been going that quickly because Glenn Cockerill ran alongside him carrying a cup of tea and never spilled a drop. It was a wonderful celebration while I sat in the centre circle thinking, 'That was my moment.' But it was great for Tim because his first game for the club had been at Old Trafford when he let in five. I was rooming with him this time so I know he was bricking it the night before the replay.

IAN WHO?

In the fifth round we'd played Bolton away and we went 2–0 up at Burnden Park before being pegged back to 2–2. We struggled in the replay and were still 2–1 down in the fourth minute of injury-time when Barry Horne got possession just inside their half. So what did he do? He took a couple of strides and smashed it in from 40 yards. The ball flew in and all the fans who had left early came streaming back for extra-time to see us win 3–2 with another goal from Barry. That's when I felt it was our year. We'd won on penalties at Old Trafford and got out of jail in injury-time against Bolton. We now had a quarter-final at home to Norwich and our name was on the cup.

It was a crap game, a real flat, low-key, terrible 0–0. There was hardly a chance in the whole match but we fancied ourselves in the replay, especially when the semi-final draw gave us a tie against Sunderland who were then in the second tier. We were never going to have a better chance of reaching the FA Cup Final. We went 1–0 up at Carrow Road when Neil Ruddock headed in my corner, and we were comfortably in control until I lost my head and was goaded into retaliating against Robert Fleck and was stupidly sent off. I couldn't believe what I'd done. They equalized but we hung on for extra-time when Barry Horne was sent off for a foul. He was my room-mate so I reckon he came out in sympathy for me. We both sat in the dressing room feeling very sorry for ourselves as the lads battled towards penalties. They were just one minute away when Chris Sutton grabbed the winner. We were so deflated after that and I was furious with myself for being suckered into retaliating. That was the closest I ever got to the FA Cup Final. I had played in the semi-final of the League Cup in 1987 but only came off the bench when we were 3–0 down.

As a boy, reaching the FA Cup Final was the ultimate, the Big One. It has probably lost a bit of its glamour but to my generation Cup Final day was the biggest day of the year. That probably had a lot to do with the fact it was the *only* match which was televised live. The build-up would start mid-morning and I would flick between the two channels watching the interviews, the songs, the fans, the Cup Final *Question of Sport* or *It's a Knock-out*, the players leaving the hotel and the bus ride to Wembley. I would have given anything to be part of it and I had thrown it all away in one idiotic moment of madness.

In the league it was completely different. We were slipping fast and in danger of being caught in the relegation battle. We lost at Forest in mid-March and were in deep trouble, and Ian Branfoot summoned us to the club on the Sunday morning for a serious pep talk. Terry Hurlock had been out the night before and turned up still drunk. Branfoot gave a stern team talk about the consequences of relegation, what it meant to the city and the fans and stressed the importance of everyone digging in and battling. His final rallying cry was that we all had to give 110 per cent effort. Everyone was silent then Terry stood up and said, 'In all fairness gaffer, I think you'll effing get it.' Then he walked out to carry on drinking, leaving one stunned manager and a group of players trying not to laugh. But the message must have sunk in because we strung together six successive wins, a club record in the top flight.

HOW TO GET
A MANAGER
SACKED

OPPOSITION FANS:
'BIG NOSE, HE'S GOT AN EFFING BIG NOSE.'

SAINTS FANS:
'GOOD GOALS, HE SCORES SOME EFFING GOOD GOALS.'

Before the start of the 1992–93 season, the club sold Alan Shearer for a then British record fee of £3m, though with cunning to defy even Baldrick they forgot to insert a sell-on clause. We all knew Alan had the drive and the ambition to play at the top level and none of us ever felt he would stay at Southampton for too long, though we hoped we'd get another season from him. He was obviously destined to play for Newcastle at some point but they weren't in great shape at the time.

Blackburn had just been handed a wad of cash by Jack Walker and they needed a high-profile signing to confirm their status in the transfer market, just like Manchester City did when they signed

Robinho and then tried to get Kaka. Saints couldn't refuse a British record fee for a player who had cost them nothing, but they did the deal with almost indecent haste. As I said, they let Blackburn dictate the terms and we took David Speedie instead of Mike Newell. It seemed as though Speedie didn't want to be here, and he was under pressure from the moment Branfoot foolishly predicted that he and Kerry Dixon would outscore Alan Shearer.

IT WAS THE ONLY TIME IN MY SENIOR CAREER THAT I EVER MISSED A PENALTY.

He also bought Perry Groves who didn't have the best of times here. But, for all his faults, Branfoot did make one fantastic signing that summer bringing in Ken Monkou for £750,000 from Chelsea. He was a powerful, commanding centre-back who was a real presence both on the pitch and in the dressing room. He was a big threat at set-pieces and a cool head in defence – just what we needed. He was also lucky to be alive. He had been selected for the Dutch Surinam squad just before he joined Chelsea but pulled out because he felt he should join his new club on tour. The plane with the Surinam squad crashed, killing all on board.

Despite his formidable presence in the side, it was another miserable campaign. The loss of Shearer left us well short of firepower and we ended up humping the ball forward to no one in particular. Games were no fun to play in and no fun to watch. The fans grew ever more restless and their dislike intensified to ridiculous levels. One fanzine even had a picture of Branfoot on the front cover under the headline 'Hope you die soon.' That was bang out of order. Another group of fans threatened to kidnap Ian Branfoot and take him to the zoo for the day on the basis that he was treating the fans like kids. So they'd they would do the same to him. At least that had its funny side and lead to the players singing 'Branny's taking us to the zoo tomorrow, zoo tomorrow, zoo tomorrow.'

From my point of view the most memorable moment of that 1992–93 season came on March 24 – an occasion etched in my brain. It was the only time in my senior career that I ever missed a penalty. Correction, it was the only time I ever had a penalty saved. I wouldn't say I missed it. There is a difference, and to my mind it's a cardinal sin to miss the target with a free shot from 12 yards. I always knew exactly where I was going to hit the ball but I always used to watch the goalkeeper, right up to the split-second before I struck the ball, and if he went one way I'd fire it in the opposite corner. I'd never put it down the middle because I could have ended up looking stupid. I reckoned if I struck the ball with power and precision then it would have to be a very good save to keep it out.

Nigel Clough had put Forest in front at The Dell and when Neil Maddison was upended we were awarded a spot-kick and everyone assumed it would be 1–1. Not a lot of people know that I was on 99 goals for the club and I remember thinking it wasn't a great way to chalk up the ton. I liked Cloughie and Forest were struggling, so I thought I'd give Mark Crossley a chance – at least that's my excuse. I put it to his right but he guessed correctly and stopped it fairly comfortably. The most embarrassing thing about the miss was that the ball came straight back to me and, from eight yards, I put it over the bar with my left foot. I was so shocked that I had missed my twenty-first penalty that I didn't react quickly enough. It was quite a surreal moment for me because I had such confidence in my own ability. I remember staring in disbelief, along with the home fans, who'd practically started celebrating. Roy Keane put Forest 2–0 up before I pulled one back with a screaming left-foot volley from 25 yards. It was the best left-footer I ever scored and the proper way to get to 100, but it counted for nothing and no-one remembers it because it was over-shadowed by the penalty miss which was all the press wanted to talk about afterwards.

I got 15 goals that season, including a hat trick on the last day of the season when we were away to Oldham who needed to beat us and hope that Crystal Palace lost at Arsenal to stay up. I remember feeling the tension around the ground and thinking, 'Thank God it isn't us in that position.' Little did I realize how soon it would be. Our fans were in carnival mood and went in fancy dress with Francis Benali as their theme. His swarthy looks meant they all wore tea towels on their heads with false moustaches.

It was quite a low-key game. In fact, it was one of the few times I ever had a drink the night before a match. We were staying in Bolton and, as we were safe, Glenn Cockerill persuaded me it would be a good idea to nip out. It was very unprofessional really and not something I ever did on a regular basis, but I did score three the next day. The final goal was a header which brought the score back to 4–3 to Oldham after they had led 4–1. The tension around the ground was unbearable – for them. I found it quite amusing and in injury-time I almost got a fourth but my shot was blocked. At the final whistle their fans swarmed onto the pitch because Palace had lost; Oldham were safe.

Although I wasn't enjoying my football, I still didn't think about leav-ing because I was convinced Ian Branfoot's reign couldn't last much longer. So I was stunned when the club gave him a new contract that summer. Talk about rewarding failure. That wound the fans up even more, and the calls for his head grew louder and louder when we lost our first three matches. I was confident that I'd outstay him.

That pre-season brought a career highlight because, for some strange reason, we were invited to take part in a prestigious tournament in northern Italy where we faced Torino and the mighty Juventus. It was based in an amazing village in the Alps and, although there were four teams involved, we only played two matches each in order to avoid local rivals Torino and Juventus playing each other. It meant we didn't get to play Cagliari but we did get to face the two Italian giants.

We lost 3–1 to Juventus with Roberto Baggio scoring a magnificent free kick. It was absolute genius and I just stood there and applauded. But my biggest buzz came when the great Gianluca Vialli asked to swap shirts with me. I was amazed that he'd even heard of me, but he asked before the game if he could have my shirt and then he came to the dressing room afterwards saying he didn't just want to swap shirts but shorts and socks too!

In the league I scored a couple in a 5–1 win over Swindon, who had been led to promotion by Glenn Hoddle and who then quit to take over at Chelsea, leaving John Gorman in charge. I'm sure Glenn saw that Swindon were going to struggle at the top level and he decided it was a good time to jump ship and join Chelsea. For him it was a good career move. For much of the season Swindon were well adrift at the bottom of the table, and were rightly written off as certainties for relegation.

We had an awful first half to the season. We were 3–1 up at home to 10-man relegation rivals Sheffield United and only drew 3–3. Branfoot said, 'It was hard playing against 10 men because they all worked that much harder.' Three days later we were dumped out of the League Cup tie by Shrewsbury. We had won 1–0 at home but lost 2–0 away. We had Ken Monkou sent off and Branfoot said, 'We were up against it from the moment we went down to 10 men.' Get your head round that.

The next day we took a group of disabled children to a local amusement and bird park as part of the annual taxi drivers' day out.

That was always an enjoyable, humbling experience. But Ian Branfoot didn't come with us which was a disappointment for the *Echo* photographer who wanted a picture of the manager in front of the vultures. We were struggling for goals and for any sort of creative spark, so Ian Branfoot dropped me. He left me out against Arsenal and for that Sheffield United match, as well as Coventry and both legs against Shrewsbury. It made me feel pretty good to know I was being sacrificed for the mighty Paul Moody, a lovely lad who been plucked from non-league and was clearly out of his depth.

I was probably the only player who could have lifted us above the mediocre but Branfoot left me out in favour of hard-working but very ordinary players who didn't possess a fraction of my talent. That might sound arrogant but I'm just calling it as I, and thousands of Saints fans, saw it. They made their voices heard with red-card protests and marches and letters to the *Echo*. There were no fans' forums and message boards then but Branfoot came under big pressure to recall me, and that's exactly what he did for an unforgettable home game against Newcastle, which was live on Sky. It was the turning point of my career.

I remember Sky pundit Andy Gray having a full-on argument with comedian and radio personality Mike Osman, who is a lifelong Saints fan and a close friend of mine. Andy was slagging me off and saying that, in a relegation battle, the team needs someone to work hard and cannot afford luxury players like Le Tissier. Mike stuck up for me and it turned into a heated debate. I missed a chance early in the game but made up for it in the second half when the ball fell slightly behind me just outside the box, in the inside left channel. I controlled it with the back of my foot and flicked it over my own head, then over a defender, and slotted it in the bottom right-hand corner. It was a very special goal, even by my standards, although

I was slightly disappointed with the scuffed finish. I mis-hit it ever so slightly which is the main reason why it isn't my favourite goal of all-time. It wasn't quite the crisp finish I wanted! But it came at the perfect time, not only for my career but also in the match. I noticed afterwards on the television coverage that the camera panned to the dug out and Ian Branfoot wasn't even smiling. Paul Moody was warming up ready to come on and Branfoot turned to him and said, 'Sit down Moods.' I could read his lips. I'm pretty sure he was about to take me off.

Then Andy Cole equalized and, as the game drew to a close, I controlled the ball on my thigh and hit a sweet 25-yard volley for the winner. It was the best double I ever scored in a match and I was on such a high at the end. The fact that it was live on Sky made it all the better in terms of my profile, as well as sending a message to the manager. As the *Echo* said, it was one finger for each goal. It gave my self-confidence a massive boost and I began to think I might even displace the mighty Moody. He was a lovely bloke but he would be the first to admit he was surprised to be keeping me out of the team.

In the next match I scored two again, this time in a 4–2 defeat at Liverpool. We weren't helped by the uncertainty over the future of my mate Tim Flowers, who was about to leave the club. Saints had set up a deal to sell him to Liverpool with David James coming the other way. But Tim refused to speak to Liverpool because he was set on joining Blackburn so, of course, the Kop gave him all sorts of abuse and cheered madly as he let in four in his final game for us.

My two goals were the only ones I ever got at Anfield and it was another special moment in my career. I showed a neat bit of skill in the box, turning Mark Wright one way and then the other before shooting home in front of the Kop. It was only when I watched it on television that I realized a lot of Liverpool fans actually clapped.

Maybe they might not have done if they hadn't been so confident of winning the game. It was one of only two occasions in my career where the opposition supporters actually applauded one of my goals. I also noticed on TV that for some reason I was wearing a shirt with no sponsor on it. I have no idea why – it certainly wasn't because I had thrown my head in bravely and got blood on it.

Those goals against Newcastle sparked a run. I scored two at Aston Villa and really started to find my form. My confidence was high, I was enjoying my football and Ian Branfoot was still under pressure – especially after we lost at bottom club Swindon just before Christmas. They were well adrift but closed to within a couple of points of us. Their fans taunted us with chants of 'Going down, Going down' and our supporters responded by singing 'So are we, so are we!' And it certainly looked that way. The manager was desperate for anything to reverse our fortunes – including the most unlikely plan which left me stunned. He made me captain.

I was gob-smacked because he hadn't mentioned anything about it until an hour before kick-off at Everton when he suddenly told the lads, 'Matt will be leading us out today.' WHAT? He had the likes of Francis Benali, Terry Hurlock, Dave Beasant, Steve Wood and Paul Allen but he chose ME. It was probably one last desperate stab at keeping his job but it was still a very proud moment for me. Sadly we lost 1–0, but I led us to victory on December 27 when we beat Chelsea 3–1 at The Dell. Frankie Bennett, the flying waiter, got his one and only goal for the club and Tommy Widdrington scored his first senior goal. I remember the local reporter brought his six-year-old son to the match and he sat there good as gold through the press conference. Afterwards, his dad was interviewing the club secretary and Ian Branfoot's closest advisor, the lad piped up, 'Dad, now we've beaten Chelsea, do we still want Branfoot out?' His red-faced dad tried to bluff his way out of it and said, 'It's not us who want Branfoot out, it's the fans.' Only for his son to reply, 'Well, I'm a fan and I want Branfoot out.' Out of the mouths of babes ...

The club appointed Lawrie McMenemy as Director of Football, presumably in a desperate attempt to win the fans over and to avoid having to sack Branfoot. But results continued to dip. We lost at home to Norwich and had Francis Benali sent off for elbowing Ruel Fox. It was the most blatant red card and I remember Micky Adams leaping in to try and defend Franny because he hadn't seen what happened. He was trying to get to Graham Poll but Dave Beasant held him back and told him Franny had to go.

The final straw came after an FA Cup tie at home to Port Vale in front of a crowd of just 11,000. The low turn out probably had more effect on the board than the mass protest by fans holding up red cards bearing the word 'GO'. Once supporters stop coming to games the manager has no chance. If fans want the boss out, then stay away. If the club is losing money it'll act quick enough. Trust me. It wasn't a nice atmosphere to play in and we were lucky to get a 1–1 draw. My feeling was that the sooner the manager went, the better it'd be for me and the club.

I never used to buy the *Echo*, except when I had had a good game. It meant I hadn't bought a copy for about two and a half years. But I made sure I got it the day they ran the front page exclusive 'Branfoot sacked'. I remember being very relieved and thinking we could at least play our home games in a better atmosphere with the crowds behind us. It was like a huge weight had been lifted from my shoulders. As I've said I liked Ian Branfoot as a bloke but completely disagreed with him about football. I had no idea who the next manager would be and, at that point, I didn't care although I assumed that even the Saints board wouldn't be stupid enough to bring in another long-ball man.

In the meantime we lost the FA Cup replay at Port Vale under Lew Chatterley and my old mentor Dave Merrington. It was a horrible evening in driving rain, it was a rubbish game and we deservedly got dumped 1–0. The only memorable moment was Tommy Widdrington committing the highest two-footed tackle I have ever seen on a football field. It was just frustration on his part but it was a horrendous challenge which could have finished the lad's career. Tommy was sent off and was probably lucky not to end up in court for GBH.

Lew and Dave took charge again for the home match against Coventry and I was delighted we could give them a 1–0 win. Dave had a massive influence on me so I was thrilled to score a penalty for the only goal of the game. It wasn't one of my better spot-kicks. Steve Ogrizovic got a hand to it and almost kept it out but the result was everything that day. The atmosphere was much better and it felt like a fresh start but we were still waiting anxiously to discover who would be coming in as the new manager. We didn't have long to wait for the announcement. I didn't know it then, but it was about to change my life ...

GET THE BALL
TO TISS

'HE'S SHORT, HE'S FAT, HE GETS THE BEST FROM MATT
– ALAN BALL, ALAN BALL'

It was a stroke of genius when Southampton appointed Alan Ball to succeed Ian Branfoot in January 1994. It saved the club and I had my best season, ever. It was a real gamble by the club because, with the best will in the world, Bally's managerial career hadn't been anything special. He'd been in charge of Exeter City and the only real success he'd enjoyed was at our bitter local rivals Portsmouth. But he was well loved at The Dell from his two stints as a player under Lawrie McMenemy, who remained as Director of Football. They made a good partnership and, despite the sometimes heated rows, they needed each other. Bally was fiery, impulsive, full of bubble and bounce and Lawrie was the voice of reason who kept him in check.

Lawrie had won Saints their only major silverware in 1976 when, as a Second Division side, they pulled off a major shock by beating Manchester United 1–0 at Wembley, so he was nearly a god. He understood the club and its traditions, and with his knowledge and experience it was great having him around. He did seem conspicuous by his absence after some heavy defeats but when we won you could be sure the big man was ready to give an interview. I have a lot of time for Lawrie. I enjoy his company and he is a great raconteur.

I didn't know Alan Ball personally but I certainly knew all about him. As a kid growing up I had seen him play, and as a World Cup winner he had legendary status. Instant respect. He bounced in like a breath of fresh air, full of energy and enthusiasm. And right from the start it was clear he wanted to play football the way it should be played. No longer were we to knock the ball up the channels. He wanted a crisp, incisive passing game. And it got even better when he and Lawrie took their first training session and set up the side ready for the game at Newcastle.

THE GAME WAS ON VALENTINE'S DAY WHICH WAS GREAT BECAUSE IT MEANT I DIDN'T HAVE TO TAKE THE WIFE OUT FOR AN OVER-PRICED MEAL.

Bally and Lawrie set up the formation. They put three players at the back, four in midfield and two up front. I was left standing there. I hadn't been picked and I remember my heart sank. I wasn't going to be part of their plans, then I realized there were only nine outfield players. Bally walked over, put his hand on my shoulder and put me right in the middle of the lads. He said, 'This is your best player and your best chance of getting out of trouble. I'm going to put him right in the middle of the pitch and whenever you have the chance to get the ball to his feet then you have to do it. If you get the ball ask yourself, "Can I get the ball to Tiss?" He will do the rest.'

A lot of players might have panicked at the responsibility and pressure. I felt I had grown four or five inches taller. I was so proud that Alan Ball was going to build a team around me. He was a World Cup winner but he rated me as his best player and I felt fantastic. I knew I was under pressure because the other lads would slaughter me if I failed to deliver. They didn't say anything at the time but I knew they would resent me and stop giving me the ball, so I had to perform.

We went to Newcastle and set up exactly as Bally had said. I took a corner which Neil Maddison headed in to give us an early lead and something to hang on to. Andy Cole equalized just before half-time but we continued to cling on for a precious point until late on when I went on a crossfield run. I wasn't really going anywhere and eventually, after I had been kicked three times, the referee gave us a free kick 25 yards out and towards the left of the penalty area. If I say so myself, it was a brilliant free kick. The wind was in the right direction and I hit it perfectly, right-footed over the wall and into the top left corner. Mike Hooper in goal never moved an inch. There were no away fans allowed because of redevelopment to the ground so there was this amazing deadly hush. I just ran to the dug-out to jump on top of Bally.

It was the start of a good run for me. We lost at Oldham in the next match but I scored and then we faced Liverpool at The Dell in what was Bally's first home fixture in charge. There was a fantastic atmosphere around the ground. The game was live on Sky, it was snowing and it was Valentine's Day, which was great because it meant I didn't have to take the wife out for an over-priced meal. After 27 seconds we were in dreamland. I hit the cleanest half volley of my career and the ball went in like a rocket. It flew into Bruce Grobbelaar's bottom left corner. New signing Craig Maskell put us 2–0 up after eight minutes and, just before half time, he was fouled by Julian Dicks to give us a penalty.

I had previously played on the same side as Bruce in a League representative game and I took a lot of penalties against him in training, and he saved virtually all of them. He kept guessing the right way so I knew I had to do something special. I hit it harder than normal and the ball went higher than usual. It flew into the top corner, in off a post and breathed a sigh of relief. We got another penalty in the second half when Mark Wright handled, and by then it was snowing really hard. I went to put the ball on the spot but couldn't even see it. I was on a hat-trick and the last thing I wanted was a delay. The ref started to walk towards me so I just called out, 'It's OK I've found it. But in truth I just put the ball down anywhere in order to get on with it. I smashed it in and incredibly we were 4–0 up against Liverpool. They got a couple of late consolations but it meant we had got off to a great start under Alan Ball. We had a bit of impetus and a lot of belief – but we were still nineteenth out of 22.

The following week Paul Moody was transferred to Oxford, which was a huge weight off my mind, with my main rival now out the way. And that same week in training Lew Chatterley said he'd seen a free kick in Europe where the ball was rolled back and flicked up for a volley, so he suggested we should try it. We had just signed Jim Magilton from Oxford with the express purpose of getting the ball to me because he was such a good passer. He was a great lad, a real character and a good player, so we had a go. He rolled a few balls back for me to flick up and hit. Some went in the net, most went in the trees. We did that for about five minutes but thought nothing of it. It was just a bit of fun.

Next day we were home to Wimbledon. It was an absolutely dire match with very little excitement. I didn't have a good game as Dean

Blackwell followed me everywhere and I didn't have the pace to get away from him. But with 16 minutes left we got a free kick 20 yards out in a central position. I set the ball up for a normal free kick but I knew it would be tight to get the ball over the wall and back down under the bar. Jim suggested trying what we had practised the previous day so I decided to give it a go. He rolled the ball back for me to flick up. In training, I had been flicking it quite high giving me time to steady myself, but I didn't want to be closed down so I did not give it as much height and hit the volley sweet as you like. Hans Segers hadn't a hope. Afterwards he said bitterly that it was the only thing I did all match, but I just told him to look at the score.

We had a bad Easter. We played three of our relegation rivals in the space of six days and lost the lot. We were beaten 3–1 at home by Oldham who eventually went down, lost 2–0 at Chelsea who stayed up, and then were home to Manchester City on Easter Monday. Bally tried to gee us up by telling the media that if we didn't win this one then we were down. We lost 1–0 so the manager had to try and put the toothpaste back in the tube by insisting we could still stay up. But we were second from bottom with just six matches left, and only two of those were at home.

It was a real low point and we were in deep trouble when we went to Norwich and found ourselves 3–1 down with just over 30 minutes to go. At that point we were going down, no question, until I scored the only proper hat trick of my career – left foot, right foot, header. It was one of the most amazing games I ever played in. Just a couple of minutes after Chris Sutton had made it 3–1, I squeezed a left foot shot just inside the post from 18 yards. Bryan Gunn got a hand to it and should probably have saved it. Five minutes later Jeff Kenna was brought down and I scored the penalty to make it 3–3. Typically, within a minute we went behind again and things looked grim.

But with 18 minutes remaining Jeff crossed for me to head in. I say head in but actually I didn't know anything about it. I wasn't the best in the air and did have a tendency to close my eyes when I headed the ball. I wasn't sure whether the defender was going to get there first so I closed my eyes, felt the ball hit my head and was absolutely amazed when I opened them to see the ball in the net for 4–4, and that was how it stayed until injury-time. We got a corner on the right and I knew I needed to put in a decent delivery. I floated the ball across and Ken Monkou rose to head in. I had the Saints fans right behind me and I remember Ken grabbed the ball out of the net, raced across to them and belted it into row Z. We needed the fans to keep hold of the ball because if we played any longer than another 30 seconds we would have conceded again. We hung on for a 5–4 win and walked off to be greeted on the touchline by Lawrie McMenemy, who appeared from nowhere to congratulate us all. Where would he have been if that last-gasp goal had been at the other end?

That was the win which gave us the impetus to stay up. The following week we were home to Blackburn who were going for the title, but we were buzzing and played really well. The *Echo* said we 'served up a cocktail of Tizz Fizz, stout defending and a very large measure of spirit while Blackburn had a big whine.' I set up Iain Dowie and then Paul Allen to gives us a 2–0 lead at half-time but Stuart Ripley pulled one back just after the break. Then Tim Sherwood handled to give us a penalty. I put the ball on the spot and Alan Shearer came up and stood in front of me before I took it. People have often asked me what he said, but I have never really told anyone until now.

Before the game he and Tim Flowers had been discussing what I'd do if we got a penalty because Tim used to save a lot from me in training. They reckoned that I'd do something completely different and hit it down the middle, gambling that Tim would know I always went for the corners. As I prepared to take this one, Alan came across and said, 'Whatever you do, don't hit it down the middle.' I'm not sure if it was a double-bluff to try and tempt me to do that, or whether it was because he still had a lot of affection for Southampton and genuinely didn't want us to go down. I suspect it was the latter.

As it happened, it never occurred to me to put it down the centre because I always fancied my chances if I put the ball in one of the corners. I was going to put it to Tim's left, which was my favourite corner, but I kept an eye on him as I ran up. He moved a fraction early so I changed my mind and put it to his right, a sweet moment because Tim had always said I'd would never score past him. Normally when I scored a penalty I'd just salute the crowd and walk back to the centre circle – because I didn't want to waste too much energy. But as this was such an important goal and Tim had been so gobby, I really cele- brated and then waited for him outside the dressing rooms after we had won 3–1. I said, 'Unlucky. I thought you said I would I never score past you?' He looked at me and said, 'Penalties don't count.' It was like being in the school playground, which was why I took such pleas- ure when I did it for real the following season with what turned out to be the BBC's Goal of the Season.

To beat the title-challengers 3–1 was a huge boost but I was suspended for the next game at Spurs, where we lost 3–0. It was a horrible feeling not being able to help the lads and although that result knocked us back, I still felt we could get enough points to stay up. We had just three games left, and one was away to Manchester United, which basically meant we had to get maximum points from the other two. The first was our final home match against Aston Villa when I picked up the club's Player of the Year award for the second time, having previously won it in 1990. We got off to a flyer when Jeff

Kenna set me up for an easy tap-in and then Ken Monkou headed in my corner. Dean Saunders pulled one back before I got my second, which was a lot better than people think. Francis Benali hit a massive clearance – I think he was trying to trap the ball. My first touch was perfect and I controlled it on the drop with my right foot, rounded Nigel Spink and slotted in for 3–1. I scored two and made two that day as Neil Maddison headed in my corner for a 4–1 win. The atmosphere was amazing at the end and we really felt we could stay up.

We played well at Old Trafford in midweek and gave as good as we got but still got beaten 2–0. We certainly did not want to rely on other results going our way, with Sheffield United, Ipswich and Everton also in the melting pot, and knew that a draw at West Ham on the final day should be enough to keep us up. And I stress *'should be'*. It was the first time I had been through a last-day escape but I wasn't nervous. That's the surprising thing. Far from it. I actually remember relishing the occasion. I liked the pressure. I knew if I performed and scored I could be the hero. It wasn't a good start because the team coach got held up in traffic. Upton Park is a horrible place to get to and Lew Chatterley actually had to get off the bus and run to the ground to hand in the team sheet on time. We were still half-asleep as the game kicked off and went 1–0 down early on, but just before half-time we got a free kick just outside the area. I think everyone in the ground knew I was going to score. I felt supremely confident and hit it very well. The keeper had no chance and it silenced the fans who had been chanting about the size of my nose.

It was a big moment and the first thing we did at half-time was check the other scores. We started the second half much more brightly, and went 2–1 up just after the break when I crossed for Neil Maddison to head home but, true to form, we quickly conceded another goal. But within three minutes we got a penalty when Iain

Dowie was hauled down by Tony Gale, who is now a colleague of mine at *Sky Sports*. That was probably the most pressure I've ever felt taking a penalty because I knew exactly what was at stake, and the consequences of missing. I was glad it was in front of our fans and hit the ball a bit higher than normal, but it went in and we were still 3–2 up when the crowd invaded the pitch on 90 minutes, thinking that the final whistle had gone. Upton Park was about to be redeveloped and lose its terraces so the home fans were in party mood. The ref said there were still four minutes left so we had to go off while the pitch

THE KEEPER HAD NO CHANCE AND IT SILENCED THE FANS WHO HAD BEEN CHANTING ABOUT THE SIZE OF MY NOSE.

was cleared. We immediately listened to the other scores and knew we were safe unless we lost by two goals. At 3–2 up, even we were confident we could avoid that but, with our defence, you never knew.

When the game resumed, hundreds of fans were crouched on the running track behind the goals ready to run on at the end, and some were even spilling onto the pitch as the match restarted. That played a huge part in Ken Monkou bundling the ball into his own net to make it 3–3. The crowd ran on again but the ref had had enough, blew for full-time and legged it for the tunnel. The big worry was that the game might have to be replayed but, as it turned out, Sheffield United were relegated as they lost at Chelsea with the last kick of the season. It was the first time all afternoon that they had been in the bottom three – harsh! And Everton survived despite at one stage being 2–0 down at home to Wimbledon. My old mate Barry Horne had got their equalizer before Graham Stuart hit a tame low 18-yard drive which somehow evaded the dive of Hans Segers to give them an unlikely 3–2 win. A few question marks have since been raised about Wimbledon's display that day. What do I think? With my innate belief in the importance of fair play, of course I refuse to think they'd cheat.

After our match, the lads celebrated in the bar but I went and sat on my own on the team bus to savour our achievement. I couldn't have felt any more proud if we'd won the league. I was really chuffed at what we'd done. We were dead and buried on more than a couple of occasions that season and to stay up, against the odds, really felt as though we had won something. I thought, 'Let's have more last-day escapes.' I loved the thrill, the excitement. And I felt a real personal sense of achievement. I'd scored 25 goals in 38 league games, 15 of them in 16 matches for Alan Ball, which wasn't bad for a midfielder.

In the last five games I played that season we scored 15 goals. I got eight of them and set up six others, so I think I justified Bally's decision to build the team around me. I know a few of the other players were peed off that I seemed to get preferential treatment and I can understand that. Maybe it was a bit over the top the way the manager treated me and praised me, but I helped keep Saints in the top division.

12

ONE DRUNK GAFFER AND A MATCHFIXING SCANDAL

WHEN ALAN BALL DIED, HE ARRIVED AT THE PEARLY GATES TO BE MET BY ST PETER WHO SAID, 'I'M REALLY SORRY TO HAVE TAKEN YOU SO EARLY BUT I'M AFRAID WE NEED YOU FOR THE HEAVEN FOOTBALL TEAM.'

BALLY PERKED UP AND ASKED WHO ELSE WAS IN THE SIDE. HE WAS HANDED A TEAM SHEET WITH BOBBY MOORE, GEORGE BEST AND BILLY BREMNER. THEN HE SAW THE NAME OF MATTHEW LE TISSIER.

'WAIT A MINUTE, MATT LE TISSIER ISN'T DEAD,' SAID BALLY.

'NO, THAT'S GOD. HE JUST LIKES TO CALL HIMSELF LE TISSIER.'

People often ask what was it about Alan Ball which brought out the best in me. The 18 months I played under him were definitely the most productive of my career in terms of goals, assists, confidence and happiness. I've never been short on self-belief but he gave me such a lift and when he kept me captain I was on Cloud Nine.

His man-management was second to none and is best summed up by an incident on a pre-season tour of Northern Ireland in 1994. We ended up staying in the little town of Bangor, and it was immediately obvious that the secretary who booked our accommodation had never actually been there – because the team hotel was right next door to the biggest nightclub in town.

We played three games over there and after the second one the gaffer told us we could have a day off and do whatever we wanted, within reason. Inevitably I wanted to hit the golf course and I roped in Neil Maddison and Tommy Widdrington. We were sitting in reception waiting for the taxi about 11am when Bally walked past and asked where we were going. We told him and as we had 20 minutes to kill he said, 'There's a bakery round the corner lads, do you fancy a bit of breakfast?'

That sounded good so the four of us walked out only for Bally to spot a pub which had just opened up and he said, 'Never mind breakfast lads, do you fancy a quick drink?' Well it would have been rude to say no, so we trooped in and needless to say the only rounds that day were not on the golf course but in the pub. We eventually left at 6.30 in the evening, three of us walking not too badly because we were finely tuned athletes – or at least the other two were. But the gaffer was like the proverbial newt. He didn't take his drink too well and was all over the place. As we got back to the hotel, we turned right to go into the restaurant to have dinner with the rest of the lads and out of the corner of my eye I spotted the gaffer turning left and heading up the stairs to sleep it off.

I was captain at the time so of course it was down to me to take charge in his absence. I took the responsibility very seriously and immediately gathered the lads together and said, 'Good news, the gaffer's drunk and has gone to bed so we can go out for the night.' We had paced ourselves a bit better than Bally so we were up for making an evening of it and, straight after dinner, the three of us went out again joined by Dave Beasant, Jim Magilton, Iain Dowie, Neil Heaney and even Ken Monkou, which was unusual for him.

We went into Bangor and had a cracking night having a sing-along with the locals and playing silly drinking games until just gone midnight when the pub closed and ... the biggest nightclub in town beckoned. The DJ was obviously a big football fan because he recognized us and introduced us over the microphone as we walked in, which was great because it meant it was a lot easier for the lads who were trying to pull. Unfortunately, we didn't realize that the nightclub backed onto Bally's bedroom. The walls weren't very thick and he could hear every word the DJ said. He woke up and, thanks to the man on the mike, had a full roll call of who was out.

THE DJ INTRODUCED US OVER THE MICROPHONE AS WE WALKED IN, WHICH WAS GREAT FOR THE LADS WHO WERE TRYING TO PULL.

So, when we rolled in at about 2am, the gaffer was in reception waiting for us. As captain and instigator of the whole night out, I thought it was only fair that I should be the one who came in last. As I tried to sneak in unnoticed, I was greeted by one of the funniest sights

I have ever seen as little Bally delivered the mother of all rollockings to our giant of a goalkeeper Dave Beasant. There had to be more than a foot difference in height between them, and the gaffer was yapping up at Beas like a little terrier. He was laying into the likes of Jim Magilton and Iain Dowie telling them they should be setting an example – and then he spotted me!

I was trying to blend into the background but he caught sight of me under Dave's armpit and turned on me. He sent the others up to bed and said, 'I want a word with you. Upstairs. Now!' I have always wondered why hotels stick sofas at the end of corridors. I was about to find out why. Bally sat me down, plonked himself next to me and said, 'I've just had to give a massive rollocking to Dave Beasant, Iain Dowie, Jim Magilton – all senior professionals who should know better – and you are the most high profile of the lot.' I braced myself. All sorts of things were going through my mind. I imagined the headlines if I was sent back in disgrace or lost the armband. Then he added, 'You are the captain! But the way you are playing you can do whatever you want. Now get to bed.'

Of course I had to tell the rest of the lads that the gaffer had given me a right rollocking but I thought that was absolute quality, a fantastic piece of man-management. That season I scored 30 goals so I think I paid him back. But if he'd gone ballistic and taken the captaincy off me who knows what might have happened?

There's a follow-up though. I told that story at an after-dinner speech in Hong Kong a few years ago and, unbeknown to me, Dave Beasant was in the audience. He came up to me afterwards and said, 'You don't know what happened next morning, do you?' He said he went to Bally's room because he felt he should apologize. He stood at the end of the bed looking at the gaffer who had the bed clothes pulled right up to his chin. There was just a tuft of ginger hair peeking out over the top. Beas said he knew he had been out of order and he felt it was the right thing to come and say so. Bally seemed to take it quite well and said, 'No problem Beas, that's fine.' And as Dave turned to go, Bally piped up, 'Oh by the way, we are signing Bruce Grobbelaar tomorrow.'

That wasn't the only time on that tour that there were a few problems after Bally had had a few to drink. I've said that he had something of a love–hate relationship with Lawrie McMenemy, who was Director of Football. Bally was passionate, impulsive and wore his heart on his sleeve while Lawrie was the restraining voice of reason. They needed each other and worked well together but there was some rivalry and jostling for position, and that meant they did have some blazing rows – including one over dinner on that tour.

The wine was flowing and Alan launched into a lengthy rant. The gist of it was, 'You've had your effing chance, I'm in effing charge now. Why don't you eff off back to England and let me effing get on with it?' So Lawrie did just that and jumped on the first plane home while Bally went and slept it off, again. When he woke up and discovered Lawrie had gone, he picked up the phone and said, 'What the effing hell do you think you are doing? Why are you back in England? I need you here.'

They were like an old married couple in many ways, often arguing but with a deep mutual affection and respect. Lawrie also curbed Bally's impulsive excesses in the transfer market – apart from the time he made the mistake of taking a couple of days off. He got back to find Bally had signed a centre-back from Exeter by the name of Peter Whiston, a nice lad but never Premier League quality. I never quite figured out the reason for signing him, but it can't have been a footballing one.

That 1994–95 season was probably the most enjoyable of my career. I played great football and scored a lot of goals, largely without the fear of relegation. I also won the BBC's Goal of the Season for what was my favourite ever goal – largely because it was against my old mate Tim Flowers. We were at Ewood Park and I picked up the ball just outside the centre circle, beat a couple of players and spotted Tim just off his line. I hit the ball from 35 yards and it went exactly where I wanted it to go, straight to the top left corner. It was a wonderful moment, not least because Tim got nowhere near it and ended up floundering in the net. It was my second goal of the match but, even then, Tim had the last word because Blackburn won 3–2.

My form in the early part of the season was helped by the fact we'd signed a terrific player who was completely on my wavelength, both on and off the field. It was great piece of business, and it came about in the most bizarre way. After another 1994 pre-season tour, this time in Holland, we'd checked into a hotel with its own football pitches in the middle of nowhere. It was a popular venue with a lot of clubs, including Barcelona who were staying there when we arrived. They were managed by Johan Cruyff who knew Alan Ball well. They were both big stars in world football and had a strong mutual respect and friendship. Cruyff was a legend and we were in awe of him. I was the only one of our squad brave enough to ask him for his autograph.

That night Bally had dinner with Cruyff and half-jokingly asked if he had any players he could spare. Next morning Alan got up to find Barcelona had checked out but had left behind a young Danish lad by the name of Ronnie Ekelund with the message, 'Take a look at him and if you like him, he's yours.' He trained with us that morning and it was immediately obvious he was a top-quality player. He had great vision and technique, and could pick out a pass. We clicked straight away and Bally immediately set the wheels in motion for us to take him on loan, pending a permanent deal. I detected some reluctance from Lawrie McMenemy, either because the deal had nothing to do with him or because he didn't want another Peter Whiston. Lawrie was back in Southampton completing the transfer of Bruce Grobbelaar who flew out to Holland to join us.

We had a match that night and someone needed to meet the big new signing from the airport. As usual the club did things on the cheap, and instead of hiring a car, they asked a reporter and photographer from the local Southampton paper if they'd mind giving Dave Merrington a lift to Amsterdam to pick up Bruce. They were more than happy because it meant they got their exclusive and also had an excuse to upgrade their cheap run-around hire car to something befitting an ex-Liverpool household name. However, Dave did draw the line at the suggestion that they should wait in arrivals holding a piece of cardboard with Bruce's name on it. Driving back down the motorway, the photographer pulled out sharply into the fast lane without spotting a BMW hurtling up behind. He swerved back a split-second from a collision which might ultimately have saved the club a great deal of hassle and embarrassment when the match-fixing allegations were made in *The Sun*.

I was quite excited when I heard Bruce was signing for us. He was fit and agile and I thought he was a cracking keeper. I knew what a character he was so I was looking forward to hearing his jungle stories. In fact I never really got to know him that well. I got the impression that he thought his talents hadn't been properly rewarded, even at Liverpool.

As usual, we didn't get off to a good start to the season. We drew our opening game 1–1 at home to Blackburn. I set up Nicky Banger with a raking 50-yard ball which Ian Branfoot would have been proud of. I then hit a last-minute screamer from 25 yards to earn a 1–1 draw at Aston Villa before we went to Newcastle where Peter Whiston came off the bench to make his one and only appearance for the club. We lost 5–1.

Our first win came in the fifth match away to Spurs who were playing some amazing attacking football under Ossie Ardiles with Jurgen Klinsmann, Teddy Sheringham, Darren Anderton and Ilie Dumitrescu.

IT WAS THE FIRST OF THREE PENALTIES I TOOK AGAINST IAN WALKER THAT SEASON ... UNLUCKY WALKS!

All the talk was about how they were going to batter us, and sure enough we went behind after six minutes. But then Sol Campbell fouled Neil Heaney on the edge of the area. It was touch and go whether it was a penalty but the ref gave it and sent off Campbell because of the new orders to punish professional fouls with a red card. It was the first of three penalties I took against Ian Walker that season. He got a hand to all of them but they all went in. Unlucky Walks! It was still 1–1 with a minute to go when Jeff Kenna rampaged down the right and crossed low. Stuart Nethercott should have got it away but it was the worst attempted clearance I have ever seen. The ball hit me on the thigh and fell in front of me to slot in for a 2–1 win.

We drew 1–1 at home to Forest and then went to Coventry where we went a goal down inside five minutes when Dion Dublin lifted it over Bruce Grobbelaar from 25 yards. I was at the other end but I remember being really surprised to see it go in. No matter where I was on the pitch – and it was usually a long way from our goal – I always knew instinctively if a shot had a chance of going in. As the ball left Dion's foot I thought it was safe because he hadn't got enough height on it. But the ball sailed just over Bruce's fingertips and into the net. I didn't think there was anything untoward about it but it was one of the games later called into question. I'd like to think it was just a lack of concentration or judgement, but only he will know for sure.

We actually won that match 3–1, thanks largely to a terrific performance by Ronnie Ekelund who was making his first start for us after the paperwork had finally been sorted out. He was a sensation; we won three in a row and he scored in all of them. He linked up so well with the rest of the team and with me in particular, and we suddenly looked a real force, playing some fantastic football.

It was fabulous having him in the side. We had a great team spirit and beat Everton 2–0 at The Dell. I scored from the edge of the area with a side-foot curler. I ran away to celebrate and Jim Magilton came to congratulate me and give me a hug. Simon Charlton came to join in and Jim told him, in no uncertain terms, to get lost because he wanted to be the one pictured with me on *Match of the Day* that night.

Unfortunately Ronnie suffered a bad back injury which required major surgery to a disc. He felt it didn't need an operation but Saints were reluctant to make his deal permanent unless he went under the knife. I don't know if there was still some friction between Alan Ball and Lawrie McMenemy, but the club refused to budge and Ronnie went back to Barcelona. He was a big loss to us and never really recaptured his form and finished his playing career with San Jose Earthquakes, where he is now Director of Football. He is still a good friend and even flew over from the States to play in my testimonial, which was a very special moment for me. It is such a shame that his back didn't hold up because we worked so well together, never better than in a 3–3 draw at Manchester City in November when he scored twice.

A few days later the club was rocked by an explosive story in *The Sun* which accused Bruce Grobbelaar of fixing matches for money.

We were absolutely stunned; it hardly seemed real. Certainly it did not look good. *The Sun* had what appeared to be pretty damning video recordings of Bruce appearing to offer to throw games for money. That was probably the most shocking part of all and it didn't seem as though there could be any other explanation, although Bruce did argue that he was trying to gather evidence to hand to the police, and that he was trying to stitch up a former business partner with whom he had fallen out. At this point I have to mention that Bruce was tried twice and the jury failed to reach a verdict on both occasions so the case collapsed. He successfully sued *The Sun* for libel damages and was awarded £85,000. The newspaper appealed and the case was eventually taken to the House of Lords where it was found that, though the specific allegations had not been proved, there was adequate evidence of dishonesty. The damages were slashed to just £1, the lowest possible under English law. Bruce was ordered to pay *The Sun*'s legal costs, estimated at £500,000.

Incidentally, Bruce wasn't the only one implicated by *The Sun*, which also accused the Wimbledon duo John Fashanu and goal-keeper Hans Segers – both of whom were also cleared in court. Strangely enough the list of games under investigation didn't include our Boxing Day fixture at home to the Dons when they won 3–2 and Jason Dodd scuffed a 20-yard daisy-cutter which lacked any power but still went straight through the legs of Segers in goal. You could tell it was the pantomime season because it was a case of 'Hans, Easy, Ooops-a-daisy!' as the crowd cried out, 'It's behind you!' Wimbledon came back to lead 2–1 and I levelled just before half-time with a shot which I didn't quite catch right. Whenever I hit the ball, I always knew instinctively if it was going in and my immediate reaction was that I had put it too close to the keeper. I was definitely surprised to see the ball go in.

Of course, the media besieged the club. We had photographers hiding in the trees at the training ground hoping for pictures. They were taking a risk because with our shooting they were right in the firing line. It was a really bizarre situation. Bruce was such a larger-than-life character and probably one of the few people that could cope with such an intense spotlight. He just turned up for training and got on with it as though nothing had happened. It was weird. I really expected him to get the lads together and deny it all and tell us it was a media conspiracy to stitch him up, but he didn't even mention it. It was like a taboo subject which we couldn't talk about with him. He was such a likeable character we wanted to believe he hadn't done it, and none of us wanted to think our own goalkeeper might have let the ball in deliberately. Of course we talked about it amongst ourselves and that's when the Coventry goal came back to my mind, even before I knew it was one of the ones being investigated. There was no point broaching the subject with him because he'd have immediately denied it, so we just got on with things.

Lawrie McMenemy showed what an asset he was because he handled the press with his usual panache. He fed them plenty of witty quips and soundbites while actually telling them nothing. He kept them at bay without alienating them, a masterclass in media-management which allowed Bally and the rest of us to continue training in peace as we prepared for a home match against Arsenal. I was really excited going into the game because the focus of the nation was on it, and I loved that. I knew there was going to be a lot of press coverage and the chance to be the headline hero, and there was a real buzz ahead of the match.

The Arsenal fans of course were brandishing fake money, which is the sort of terrace humour which makes the game what it is. Although some of the chants can be vile, most are just funny and players have to respond in the right way. I used to laugh at the songs about my big nose and tried to answer them by putting the ball in the net. I loved it when the opposition fans sang, 'Big nose, he's got an effing big nose' and the Saints supporters responded with, 'Good goals, he scores some effing good goals'.

None of it seemed to faze Bruce and he went out to warm up as normal and he even had a bit of banter with the crowd, pretending to collect their fake fivers in his baseball cap. Jim Magilton scored the only goal of the game as we won 1–0, and Arsenal missed a penalty. It was all set up for Bruce to be the hero and his antics definitely put off Paul Dickov who missed the target. We certainly had no doubts about Bruce going into that match. After all those headlines you'd have to be pretty daft to try anything under that sort of scrutiny. As a breed goalkeepers are pretty stupid but not *that* stupid.

I have no idea how Alan Ball felt in private but he certainly defended Bruce in public, although I guess he had no choice. Bruce played virtually every match for the rest of that campaign but under Dave Merrington, who was the manager the following season, Dave Beasant played 36 of the 38 games in goal while Bruce was left on the bench. Dave knew who he wanted.

We then drew eight of our next nine league games after the Arsenal match, including seven in succession. But we made good progress in the FA Cup and fancied our chances after reaching the fifth round and earning a 1–1 draw away at Spurs. We brought them back to The Dell and murdered them in the first half, racing into a 2–0 lead which included my third penalty against Ian Walker. We looked well set for the quarter-finals only for Tottenham to throw on Ronny Rosenthal who had the game of his life. He got a hat trick as Tottenham put six past Bruce to win in extra-time. What were the odds on that result?

The run of draws saw us slip into the relegation zone following a 3–0 defeat at Nottingham Forest where the shy and retiring Gordon Watson made his Saints debut. He was sarcastically christened 'Snowy' because he took so long to settle – not! None of the lads knew that much about him, which was quite unusual, so we didn't know what to expect. When he turned up at our hotel on the Friday night a few of the lads were in reception playing cards. He sat down and the first thing he said was, 'Call me Flash.' I just thought, 'Oh my God, what have we got here?' but he was a great lad, larger than life and a big character.

He had to room with someone who didn't mind him smoking because he liked a puff. One thing I did know was that he'd had a tough upbringing and a big gambling addiction but, fair play, he has straightened himself out now and won't even play golf for money. He was definitely great for team spirit. Bally also brought in Neil Shipperley and the pair were decent additions and scored some important goals.

Having dropped into the bottom three, we certainly needed help and the season turned on its head when we hosted Newcastle on a Wednesday night. Floodlit games at The Dell were always special with a really unique atmosphere. This one was surprisingly quite flat as we trailed 1–0 with four minutes to go. At that point it looked like we might be in trouble, but the crowd stuck with us and we turned it round in an incredible finish to win 3–1 with goals by Neil Heaney, 'Flash' and Neil Shipperley. The atmosphere was absolutely amazing in those final few minutes. Newcastle must have hated playing us because we always seemed to do them. They were coasting from the twelfth minute but as soon as we equalized we just ripped them apart with the crowd absolutely buzzing. That ended a run of 12 games without a victory and then we won five out of six.

The next fixture was a Sunday televised midday match at home to Spurs. It was way too early for me, and Sky got a great shot of me standing in the middle of the pitch giving a prolonged yawn as the action flew around me. But I can't have been too sleepy because I scored twice in a thriller. My friend, and by then business partner, Mike Osman asked me to give him a sign if I scored so I signalled the letters CP, which stood for Celebration Plaza, the nightclub we had bought together. Not the wisest business decision we ever made. To use a technical financial term, it was an effing disaster.

We were very naïve and entrusted the running of it to a mutual friend but it did not work out. In fairness, Mike and I didn't spend enough time there and didn't really know what we were doing when we did. There was a lot of cash flying around and we needed to be there a lot more than we were. We paid a hefty price – to the tune of around a hundred grand each.

I almost lost another big sum in 1995 as my one and only betting scam went disastrously wrong. Spread-betting had just started to become popular. It was a new idea which allowed punters to back anything from the final score to the first throw-in. There was a lot of money to be made by exploiting it – a foolproof way to make a fast buck. We were safe from the threat of relegation when we went to Wimbledon on April 17 and, as it was a televised match, there was a wide range of bets available. Obviously I'd never have done anything that might have affected the outcome of the match, but I couldn't see a problem with making a few quid on the time of the first throw-in. The way spread-betting worked was that the bookies decided the time of the first throw would be between 60 and 75 seconds. If you thought it would be sooner than that then your stake would be multiplied by the number of seconds under the bookies' estimate. In other words, if the ball went out of play after four seconds, you'd effectively get odds of 56–1. If it went out of play between 60 and 75 seconds then it was a dead bet with no one winning or losing. The danger was that if it went over the bookies' estimate then your loss would be multiplied by the number of seconds before the first throw, and you could lose a lot of money. For example, if there hadn't been a throw-in for three minutes then your stake would be multiplied by 105, or more if it took longer for a throw. I had some mates with spread-betting accounts who laid some big bets for me. I stood to win well into four figures but, if it went wrong, I could have lost a lot of money.

CELEBRATION PLAZA, THE NIGHTCLUB WE HAD BOUGHT TOGETHER. NOT THE WISEST BUSINESS DECISION WE EVER MADE.

The plan was to kick the ball straight into touch at the start of the game and then collect 56 times the stake. Easy money. The only possible problem was if we didn't get to kick-off. I was captain at the time so I had a chat with the Wimbledon skipper and asked which way they wanted to kick. He said they liked to kick towards their fans. I told him I was happy to let them do that provided we could kick-off. Thankfully he didn't ask why otherwise I might have had to give him a 10 per cent cut of the winnings, but he thought he was getting a good deal. The plan was set up nicely. The ball was to be rolled back to me and I would smash it into touch. It seemed to be going like clockwork. We kicked-off, the ball was tapped to me and I went to hit it out towards Neil Shipperley on the left wing.

As it was live on TV, I didn't want to make it too obvious or end up looking like a prat for miscuing the ball, so I tried to hit it just over his head. But, with so much riding on it, I was a bit nervous and didn't give it quite enough welly. The problem was that Shipps knew nothing about the bet and managed to reach it and even head it back into play. I have never run so much in my life. If there had been Pro-Zone analysis back then, my stats would have been amazing for the next minute as I charged round the pitch desperately trying to kick the ball out of play. Suddenly it was no longer a question of winning money, as I stood to lose a lot of cash if it went much longer than 75 seconds before the ball went out. I had visions of guys coming to kneecap me. Eventually I got it out of play on 70 seconds, the neutral time which meant I'd neither won nor lost. Ironically we won the match 2–0 with me scoring the first, but I hadn't backed myself to get the opener. And I've never tried spread-betting since.

We lost only one of our last eight games, and that was 2–1 at Manchester United where we'd actually led 1–0 and had a perfectly good Neil Shipperley goal disallowed, and to this day I have no idea why, despite watching it again and again on the TV.

I won my third and last Saints Player of the Season trophy that year. I'm very proud to be the only person to have won it three times. It's a record which is unlikely ever to be broken as I can't see any player now staying for three seasons.

That 1994–95 season was the closest I ever came to playing in every match. I missed just one, a 0–0 draw away to Everton when I tore the tendon from my big toe to my heel. I didn't realize what that meant. From then on I had to run on the outside of my foot and, because of that, I later got problems with my calves and Achilles. I had to wear insoles which made my calves shorter and, later in my career, I ended up getting a lot of calf strains which eventually led to me having to pack up.

I was desperate to get 30 goals for the season so I played the final fixture, a 2–2 draw at home to Leicester. The moment I scored I was off, in pain. The rest over the summer did it good and I was looking forward to the new campaign. We had finished tenth, 11 points clear of relegation in a season when four went down. We lost only 12 matches out of our 42, just two more than Liverpool but we drew too many. We had 18 draws which might have been good for Bruce's pools coupon but not for our league position. And we scored 61 goals, which was more than Leeds in fifth, but conceded 63 which was more than Norwich and they got relegated.

We had a good young team, we were playing exciting, attacking football and we had a top manager whom I could relate to and one who really rated me. And then came the bombshell ...

FINAL DAY
COCK-UP

'FOR THE SECOND TIME ALAN BALL HELPED SAINTS PULL OFF
A MIRACULOUS ESCAPE TO STAY UP ON THE LAST DAY OF
THE SEASON. THE PROBLEM WAS THAT HE WAS MANAGER
OF MANCHESTER CITY AT THE TIME!'

I was on holiday in Menorca, doing the usual British tourist trick of
reading the English papers for as long as possible at a news stand
before being told to buy them or 'Get outta here'. But that day I actually paid the extortionate price for a paper because the headline said
that Manchester City wanted Alan Ball as their new manager. The link
was City chairman Francis Lee who was a close friend of Alan's. I was
absolutely gutted, but I really thought there was no way Saints would
let him go. He had transformed the atmosphere among the players
and the fans and had got us playing some great stuff. How wrong can
you be?

Next day I picked up a paper and found he'd gone. I was gobsmacked. Devastated. I knew it would be really hard to find another
manager who had the same belief in me as he did. For the first time

in my career I had had a manager who had total faith in me. I had known I was going to play every week, and play the way I wanted. That might have been selfish but it worked for the team too. Things were going so well and I couldn't understand why the club gave Alan permission to speak to City. He was unhappy about it too. Talk about sending a message that he wasn't wanted. The Southampton chairman, Guy Askham, argued that if they had refused permission then City would have approached him directly. But if that had happened then City and Bally would have been in the wrong and the board would have sent all the right signals to the Saints players and fans. By giving him permission to speak to City they were virtually saying they'd be happy to let him go. They should have fought to keep him. Alan had shown no desire to leave and they could easily have said 'No'. Alan wouldn't have kicked up a fuss, he just wanted to feel valued. If Saints had shown faith in him, he'd have stayed put.

He was the lowest-paid manager in the Premier League on just £60,000 a year. Given what he had done for the club, they should have offered him a three- or four-year contract on improved terms. Personally, I don't think that the club really rated him and they jumped at the chance of getting compensation with almost indecent haste. His track record was nothing special and he was a volatile character so it probably suited them to be able to pocket some cash and get rid of him without losing face – or so they thought.

The fans were open-mouthed, especially because that decision led to a period of instability which eventually cost the club its place in the Premier League. Three managers in 30 years had put the club on a sound footing, and suddenly here were the board changing managers after just 18 months and setting a trend which took the club on a downward spiral. Ultimately it was Bally's decision to go, but the board must take a lot of the blame. They tried to redeem the situation by appointing Dave Merrington as manager. Some said that as he had been my mentor in my youth team days, he might continue to get the best out of me as Bally had done. He was also popular with the fans. Others said he was the cheap option, and the players agreed with that one. Like Bally, he was the lowest-paid manager in the Premier League by some distance.

Personally I was quite happy with the appointment. Dave had been a big influence on me as a youngster and I knew that he believed in me, so perhaps things would work out OK. Looking back, I probably didn't give it enough thought because this was a totally different scenario now that Dave had to deal with experienced top-flight players with big egos rather than young players he could mould and cajole. I think he found it hard to make that step up. He had done a fabulous job at the club for many years as youth and Reserve team coach so, with his service, he probably felt he had earned his chance. And that was probably true. But it was a step too far because his strengths were much better suited to developing young players than dealing with established stars.

The first thing Dave did was to bring back Dennis Rofe, a larger than life character who was good to have in the dressing room. His heart was in the right place and, as his right-hand man, he was good at geeing up players. He sometimes went a bit far with the officials (like I'm one to talk) and he could get a bit heated with the players but it was only because he cared and, on the whole, he did a decent job.

I COULDN'T UNDERSTAND WHY THE CLUB GAVE ALAN PERMISSION TO SPEAK TO CITY. HE WAS UNHAPPY ABOUT IT TOO.

The opening day of the 1995–6 season gave me a lot of reasons for optimism even though we lost 4–3 at home to Forest. I got a hat trick – although looking back it was two penalties and a free kick – and I only scored seven goals in 37 league games that season as we got sucked back into relegation trouble. The ultimate irony was that on the final day of the season we stayed up at the expense of Bally's Manchester City.

The Dell had been redeveloped with a severely reduced capacity so Dave Merrington didn't have a lot of money to spend on strengthening the side. His only real signing was Barry Venison, who struggled with a recurring back problem – and an even more painful sense of fashion. It was a real slog of a season with the only light relief coming in the cup competitions. We started the League Cup with a tie at Cardiff, which was somehow inevitable under the circumstances. Despite scoring 45 goals in 64 games under Alan Ball, I had been dropped from the England squad and there had been newspaper speculation that I might actually switch my allegiance to Wales. Because I came from the Channel Islands I was eligible to play for any of the Home Countries, and having played only friendlies for England meant I could still opt for another country. I was asked about it by the media and said it had always been my ambition to play for England and no way would I play for Wales. And then of course we got drawn against Cardiff whose fans are fiercely nationalistic. I took a serious amount of abuse from them at Ninian Park but, fortunately, I had one of my better games and scored twice in a 3–0 win. At the end I felt very smug but went over and applauded their supporters just to show I wasn't upset by it, and they responded with a nice round of applause.

We beat West Ham in the next round and were drawn away at Reading who then played at Elm Park. It was pouring with rain as we turned up at The Dell for the team coach only to be told that the game was off because of a waterlogged pitch. Excellent! A night off. Except … it was a hoax call. For some reason no one at the club thought to check it out. We all went our separate ways and, in the days before mobile phones, it wasn't easy to round us all up once the truth dawned. It meant we didn't get to the ground until about half an hour before kick-off. It was still raining heavily, our preparation was non-existent and we lost 2–1.

The FA Cup brought a major highlight because we were drawn at home to the Hampshire inferiors, Portsmouth. It was the first time we had played them since 1988 when they won 2–0 at The Dell. I came on as sub that day so this was my first real experience of a competitive south coast derby. I still recalled that Pompey fan trying to hit me after Alan Knight's testimonial so I was very glad we were drawn at The Dell instead of Fratton Park – or Nottarf Krap as it is backwards.

The atmosphere around the ground was electric right from the start, quite different from anything else I had ever walked out to. The rivalry was incredibly fierce. It really geed you up. Jim Magilton was definitely on fire and scored twice as we won 3–0. I set up his second when I was given the freedom of The Dell. I picked up the ball 10 yards inside our half and ran to their area where my shot was parried for Jim to tap home. I was credited with the assist for the third when I squared for Neil Shipperley to slot in, but I have to come clean and admit I was going for goal. I was desperate to score against Poopey and my toe-poke across the box was actually a shot, but I was happy to accept the credit.

We were drawn at home to Crewe in the fourth round and a Big Freeze meant virtually every game in the country was off. Our pitch was perfectly playable but the match was still postponed on the say-so of the safety officer. The fire hoses and all the toilets were frozen with blocks of ice preventing them from flushing, which just goes to show you can't beat the cistern. I couldn't see the problem. If there had been a fire and there were 15,000 people dying for a pee, they could surely have put it out themselves.

We were taken to a replay and were coasting at 3–0 up before they pulled two back and the last 20 minutes were frightening as the home side mounted wave after wave of attacks. We began to think it might be our year until we drew Manchester United away in the quarter-finals and lost 2–0.

Things weren't great in the league, despite the fact I was happy to be working with Dave again. I was struggling for goals and as a result I asked Dave to take the captaincy off me. I had been skipper for two years, during which time I had played some of my best football, but I'm not a shouter by nature. I tried to lead by example and when I was playing well I felt I could captain the team, but when I went through a bad spell I didn't want that responsibility and hoped it might free me up to play better. I think the fact I had been dropped from the England squad also affected my form. There was part of me that thought if 45 goals in 64 games are not good enough then what's the point?

It also didn't help that Dave changed the shape of the team a bit. With things not going well I think he felt he needed to keep things tight. I played a bit deeper and didn't feel I was getting into great forward positions. I don't think the team created that many chances because I don't remember missing too many sitters – but it was April before I scored my first goal in open play. I'd netted two free kicks and four penalties but that goal came against Manchester United at home in the infamous 'grey shirts' game.

We were hovering on the brink of relegation when the champions-elect came to The Dell four games from the end of the season. We had only won seven matches all season but that afternoon, for some reason, we really turned it on. The atmosphere was electric and we ripped into them from the start. Ken Monkou lashed in from close range on 11 minutes and 12 minutes later we were in dreamland as Neil Shipperley put us 2–0 up. Two minutes before the break Peter Schmeichel decided to drop a cross at my feet, and I reacted quickly to hook in from a tight angle to make it 3–0 at half-time. We couldn't quite believe what we'd done. It was one of those days when everyone seemed to be on top of their game. Normally to win a match you need seven or eight of the 11 to be on decent form. You can afford to carry one or two, usually me. But to beat United it needs everyone firing on all cylinders, and we blew them away.

At the start of the second half the United players came out in a completely different kit. In the first half they had worn their all grey strip, but after the break they changed to blue and white stripes. To be honest I never noticed, even when the crowd laughed. We held out strongly but conceded a consolation two minutes from time to the annoyance of one fan who had backed a double, with Ken Monkou scoring first in a 3–0 win at huge odds.

There were no organized post-match press conferences in those days, reporters just grabbed players for interview in the car park. I was surrounded by journalists wanting my views on United changing their shirts and I had to say I really hadn't twigged. Graham Poll was the ref and our club secretary Brian Truscott gave him a lot of abuse for allowing United to change their kit because it wasn't allowed.

Fergie said afterwards that his players couldn't pick out the grey shirts against the crowd which just seemed like an excuse – and not a very good one. The fact is we played them off the park. It took a little bit away from our victory because of course the press focused on the change of kit rather than our performance. Although he isn't noted for being magnanimous, I thought Fergie could have been a little bit more gracious, especially as I got him his job.

We lost at Newcastle and then went to relegation rivals Bolton for the penultimate match of the season. Lawrie McMenemy wanted us to play safe and go for a point but Dave wanted us to go all out for the victory which should make us safe. Most of the lads spent the morning in the local Ladbrokes and, to the casual observer, it might have looked as though we weren't taking the match seriously but, as we arrived at the ground, there was a hard look of determination in every face. We won 1–0 when I latched onto a suicidal pass from Jimmy Phillips and scored what proved to be the last ever goal at Burnden Park as Bolton moved to the Reebok afterwards. We celebrated wildly on the pitch at the final whistle thinking we were safe until news came through that Man City had won at Villa of all places, while Coventry had won at Wimbledon.

MOST OF THE LADS SPENT THE MORNING IN THE LOCAL LADBROKES ... IT MIGHT HAVE LOOKED AS THOUGH WE WEREN'T TAKING THE MATCH SERIOUSLY.

It meant that our fate was still in our own hands on the final day, we simply had to equal or better what Man City did. We were at home to Wimbledon who had nothing to play for but they were notoriously competitive, while City were at home to Liverpool who not only had nothing to play for but were in the FA Cup Final the following week. Of all the last-day escapes, this was the most horribly tense and the closest we came to going down during my time at the club. We had put ourselves in a decent position knowing we only had to match City's score – and there was still the chance Coventry could slip up at home to Leeds. Nothing against Coventry, but I was hoping they would be the ones to go down simply because of my high regard for Alan Ball. I didn't want him to be relegated but, obviously, if it was a choice of City or us then I was desperate for us to survive. In the end it was City who went down in slightly bizarre circumstances, and with Bally taking a lot flak for a bad miscalculation.

Nowadays *Sky Sports* are all over the final-day fixtures, keeping everyone updated almost as soon as the ball hits the net while mobile phones and text alerts keep fan bang up-to-date. Back then information was a little more sketchy, with supporters taking portable radios to the game to keep in touch with the other scores. Word would filter through to the players but, quite often, rumours would sweep through the stadium and the crowd's reaction could be quite a distraction. We expected to beat Wimbledon but it was one of those games where we never looked like scoring, so it was just as well that we heard City had gone 2–0 down at home to Liverpool. If it stayed like that then we were safe no matter what happened at The Dell. But with the Merseysiders having nothing to play for and keen to protect players for the Cup Final, they took their foot off the gas and City fought back to 2–2. Suddenly we were in deep trouble. We didn't know whether to stick or twist. We could go all-out to try and win our game to guarantee safety but risk leaving gaps at the back knowing that if Wimbledon scored we were down. Or we could focus on holding what we had and hope that City didn't score again. It was horrible.

The crowd were edgy and that got through to the players, but we were saved by strange developments at Maine Road where the rumour spread that we were losing. In the confusion Alan Ball sent word to his players that a draw was enough for them, so Steve Lomas took the ball to the corner flag to waste time when in fact they needed another goal to stay up. With the way the game was going they might well have got it if they had pushed against a disinterested Liverpool side, but they played out a 2–2 draw. It finished a few minutes before our match so we knew we just had to see it out at 0–0 to stay up. We did but it was sickeningly close. I felt so sorry for Alan afterwards when I heard how he had got his facts wrong but I was still relieved that we'd stayed up. But then it was all put into stark perspective as rather more grim news reached the dressing room.

A couple of days earlier Dave Merrington's wife Pauline had been rushed to hospital with a brain haemorrhage, but he'd never said a word to us about it. He didn't want to add to our stress so he kept quiet about it, that's the kind of guy Dave is. He wanted to shield us from all distractions so we had no idea she was even remotely ill. She was in a bad way and it would have been entirely understandable if he had stayed with her. Instead, he left her bedside on the moming of the match not knowing whether she would still be alive afterwards. He came to The Dell, guided us to safety and then rushed back to the hospital without joining in the post-match celebrations or even doing the usual press conference. Thankfully Pauline pulled through and Dave's reward for that selfless sacrifice? He was sacked!

14

SUBBED BY A FISH UP A TREE or

PEOPLE CALLED RUPERT SHOULD NOT RUN FOOTBALL CLUBS

'IT IS SOMETHING I WILL NEVER LIVE DOWN. I WAS SUBBED FOR THE NOW INFAMOUS UNKNOWN CHANCER BY THE NAME OF ALI DIA. THE SHAME OF IT ...'

I was stunned when I heard Dave Merrington had been axed as manager. I was shocked at the way he had been treated after so many years of loyal service. OK, it hadn't been a great season and maybe it was a step too high for him. But he hadn't had a lot of money to spend and it had taken him time to adapt to his first real job in management. He was very much Old School with a belief in discipline and hard work. Those of us who had come up through the ranks really rated him, but maybe he found it harder to win over some of the more recent signings. Whatever the footballing merits of the decision, after all his years of dedication, it seemed a very harsh way of doing things, especially given the situation with his wife. I will always regret not being able to produce my very best form for him but it's great to see him regularly at St Mary's, working as a pundit for local BBC radio where he speaks with all the trademark honesty he showed as a coach.

Dave's departure meant we were now looking for our fourth manager in two and a half years. Next in line was Graeme Souness, a close ally of Lawrie McMenemy who remained Director of Football. In some ways I was quite pleased because I thought it showed ambition, and if someone of his stature was prepared to come to Southampton that had to be a positive sign. It looked as though we were ready to take the step to the next level. It was a high-profile appointment, particularly by Southampton's standards. Souness had plenty of experience and I knew he'd tried to buy me in the early nineties when he was Liverpool manager, so I was quite upbeat. Mind, he hadn't had a great managerial career, though he'd enjoyed some success at Rangers where they always had a 50–50 chance of winning the league.

He joined us from Galatasaray where he'd hit the headlines for marching into the centre circle after a Cup Final victory, away to their hated rivals Fenerbahce, and planting a club flag in a hugely provocative gesture. That took real bottle. It showed nothing would faze him but then to get to the top of this profession you need a touch of arrogance – and he had more than a touch to be fair. I also knew what a fantastic footballer he had been and that is how I tended to judge people. He was one of the best of his generation in his particular role, and he had looked after himself well. I have got to say he was still in great shape. He spent a lot of time in the gym and loved to join in training just to show he could still play a bit. He was still an aggressive so-and-so. I couldn't get the ball off him. The sad thing is our manager was probably our best player.

He came with quite a fierce reputation and I must admit I wasn't looking forward to it. But he was much more placid than I expected. I don't know if that was because of the heart operation he'd had a couple of months before. He was on medication which may have calmed him down although he was still incredibly sure of himself. He had that arrogance you normally get from players who know they are good. He had a great sense of his own worth – and probably with good reason. He had a presence about him which commanded respect from the minute he walked into the room. And his reputation meant a lot of our players were probably in awe of him. I certainly was – at least until he dropped me. Then, like any player who is left out, I thought he was a muppet, until he put me back in again.

I got on OK with him until an incident towards the end of the season. We were having a bad run, I had lost my place and Souey called a team meeting in the canteen. He went round each of the players in turn and – in front of everyone – asked them, 'Do you think Tiss does enough for the team?' All the lads said 'No'. I'd like to think that a lot of them were just too scared to oppose him and said what he wanted to hear. Souness certainly didn't ask Francis Benali because he'd have stuck up for me. I was absolutely stunned that the manager would do such a thing and in front of everyone. After all I had done for the club; I felt I deserved better than that. I have no idea what he was trying to achieve. Maybe he was trying to fire me up but I lost a lot of respect for him.

I came out of that meeting absolutely fuming with him and with my teammates who hadn't stuck up for me. I still think it was a really strange piece of man-management to single me out like that. While

Bally made me feel special and got the best out of me, Souey just made me resentful. I came away steaming with anger and with my chin on the floor. I couldn't believe he'd done that. If he had a problem with me, it would have been better to take me aside and explain that was why he was dropping me instead of picking on me in front of everyone. I didn't talk to anyone. I just went home, gutted that none of my so-called mates had stuck up for me. That was the lowest point I can remember under Souness.

He hit the ground running and made sweeping changes to the coaching staff, and I have to say they didn't improve things. Like most managers he brought in his mates, but these were people who didn't fully understand the club and its traditions, and the importance of bringing through home-grown players. Phil Boersma, Ray Clarke and Alan Murray came in but it seemed to me they didn't have the same dedication, commitment and coaching knowledge as those they replaced. But he did bring in Terry Cooper who was a great character to have around. He had a wise head and spoke a lot of sense. I liked him and I was surprised he didn't manage any higher. He had a good sense of humour and was very good company. He also had a very cushy number later on as the club's chief European scout. He lived in Tenerife and just jetted off wherever. Terry played a key part in the signing from Bristol City of Richard Dryden, or 'Trigger' as he was known after the somewhat dim character in *Only Fools and Horses*.

He was a great lad but not the sharpest tool in the box, and that image wasn't helped by his West Country accent. He was the stereotypical journeyman player in the nicest possible way, an honest hardworking pro who spent all his career in the lower divisions but suddenly got a crack at the top flight. He arrived with a ringing endorsement from Mark Lawrenson who was then a pundit for ITV in the Bristol area, and who apparently said if Richard Dryden was in the Saints team at the end of the season then he would present the show stark naked. He was – and he didn't.

'Trigger' was so thick that he actually revelled in his nickname, which was well deserved. He once drove to the supermarket and then spent 20 minutes looking for his car, and was just about to report it stolen when he remembered he had taken his wife's car, not his own. And when he was in digs he wasn't allowed to use the phone so he had to go to the call box down the street. One night he walked back and found the car was missing from the drive so he rang the police and reported it stolen – and then realized he had driven it to the phone

'TRIGGER' WAS SO THICK THAT HE ACTUALLY REVELLED IN HIS NICKNAME, WHICH WAS WELL DESERVED.

box because it had been raining. It was still parked there. The clever thing would have been to keep quiet but he told everyone and got merciless stick. 'Trigger' might not have been the most high-profile signing but he was solid and dependable and never let us down, good value for the £150,000 fee which was worth paying just for the entertainment value.

Souey had good contacts and picked up some quality players on the cheap. We went on pre-season tour to Scotland and were joined by a slight figure by the name of Eyal Berkovic. It was obvious right away that he could play but the only question was whether he could withstand the physical demands of the Premier League. Souey was keen to play him in a pre-season friendly at Dunfermline but the club didn't have international clearance. Souness suggested sneaking him on as a sub towards the end, and gave the local press strict instructions not to mention him. He was asked what they should do if the Israeli midfielder scored and he told them to credit it as an own goal. As it happened he put Berkovic on midway through the first half – and sure enough he scored. The problem was it was a solo run, taking the ball round the keeper and slotting into an empty net. Around 200 travelling fans were bemused to read the description in the paper – probably the best own-goal ever.

Typically Southampton didn't want to commit themselves to signing him, and left options open at the end of the season which meant we lost him to West Ham, with Souey's departure giving him the perfect get-out. He was a cracking player but his command of the English language seemed to vary according to whether he liked what was being said. He rarely seemed to understand requests to help with the club's many community projects, but knew all right what was being said when we were given time off.

Other signings included Uli Van Gobbel, a man-mountain Dutch defender who had plenty of strength but not enough stamina. The only time he ever went on a run was when he retired; he fled from Holland after he was jailed for four months for buying cars on credit, then selling them without paying the car company. Souey obviously had a lot more money to spend than Dave Merrington and, apart from signing Graham Potter, he used it wisely, digging out a couple of gems from Norway.

He arranged a special practice match at Staplewood to give a trial to two strikers by the names of Egil Ostenstad and Tore Andre Flo. Both were outstanding. Egil quickly signed and went on to be a big success but the Flo deal got complicated. His club Brann Bergen had to pay something like 50 per cent of any fee to his former club Tromso and, according to the Saints board, they kept putting up the price. I think once again it was a case of the club not wanting to fork out too much money and failing to back the manager – a costly error given how well Flo did for Chelsea, who nipped in to sign him.

Egil proved himself a deadly finisher and got some vital goals before being snapped up by Blackburn who seemed to take most of our good players. For a while it seemed like we were their feeder club with Alan Shearer, Tim Flowers, Jeff Kenna, Kevin Davies and Egil Ostenstad all moving there with varying degrees of success. Egil did really well for us but I always wondered how much better we might have fared if we had signed Tore Andre Flo as well. That would have been some partnership. Egil was an excellent signing and had a great first season despite the fact he must have been knackered. He had played a full campaign in Norway and then came over here and had virtually another full season with us. It is a shame he didn't stay longer but he turned down a new contract and seemed to stop trying as hard in his third season, before moving to Blackburn where things didn't really work out too well for him. But we did land a top-class Norwegian in Claus Lundekvam, who went on to become Souey's legacy to the club. We snapped him up from Brann Bergen for a bargain fee of just £400,000. He stayed for 12 years.

I remember it well. I had been away on England duty – Glenn Hoddle still liked me at that time. I came back to the training ground and walked into the dressing room to find a tramp had wandered in. I was about to offer him a cup of tea and show him out when he introduced himself as our new signing. But he turned out to be one of the best bits of business we ever did. He was a phenomenal centre-back although no help whatsoever in terms of goal-scoring, in fact I'm surprised he didn't get booked for time-wasting whenever he went up for a corner. But in defence he was superb, strong in the air, good on the ground and calm under pressure – sometimes too calm. In the early days we'd be screaming for him to belt the ball in the stand but he insisted on bringing it out of defence, earning him the nickname 'Silky' because of his skill on the ball. He revelled in the nickname and even named his boat *Silky*. Sometimes that tendency cost us the odd goal but he quickly learned when to play the ball and when to launch it.

We also called him 'Dave' because he looked like Rodney who was called that name by Trigger in *Only Fools and Horses*. Claus loved that series and could recite episodes virtually word for word. It was a sign of how well he adapted to life in England. He completely got that humour, our banter and the drinking culture. The best tribute I can pay him is that he was the most English foreigner we ever had. His partnership with Michael Svensson was one of the best in the Premiership, right up there with Tony Adams and Steve Bould or Steve Bruce and Gary Pallister. It was such a shame when injury forced him to retire in 2008 but I was proud to be chairman of his testimonial committee.

It came as a complete culture shock though when Silky made his debut in a 2–2 draw at home to Nottingham Forest. I equalized in the last minute as we came back from two down but Claus was breathing out of his backside, and looked stunned by the pace and power of the game. That was one of only two points we gained from our first seven matches as another poor start left us firmly in the relegation zone – unchartered territory for Souey.

Our first win came at home to Middlesbrough. I scored two in a 4–0 success, the first direct from a corner. And yes, it was intended. I often used to shoot from a corner knowing I could whip the ball in with enough bend so that even if I didn't score directly there was a strong chance it'd fly in off a defender or one of our strikers – or anyone except Claus. That victory gave us a lift and we drew 1–1 on TV at Coventry where I got one of my top 10 goals with a 30-yard shot which curled away from a flat-footed Steve Ogrizovic. Eyal and Egil made their debuts from the bench and we let in a last-minute equalizer. Then we thumped Sunderland 3–0 before Manchester United turned up, fresh from a 5–0 drubbing at Newcastle, with most neutrals predicting we would suffer the backlash. After that match Magpies' manager Kevin Keegan said it would be a long time before another side put five past United – so we hit them for six.

United finished seven points clear of Newcastle that season to win the title at a canter, but we smacked them 6–3 at The Dell, and they couldn't even blame the kit. In fact a lot of people mistakenly think this was the 'grey shirts' match because it was such a remarkable score. It was certainly one of the best games I ever played in. The only slight blemish was that Roy Keane got sent off on 21 minutes for a crunching tackle, which he later admitted was designed to jolt his teammates out of their comfort zone as we were already 1–0 up through Eyal Berkovic.

After 34 minutes I got the ball about 30 yards from goal, wriggled past a couple of challenges to create space and I remembered that the previous week Philippe Albert of Newcastle had lobbed Peter Schmeichel from a very similar position. I had watched that game on television and just took a gamble that Schmeichel would be off his line again. Without even looking I sent a perfect chip over his head for 2–0. David Beckham pulled one back but Egil Ostenstad made it 3–1 just before the break. David May scored just after half-time which made it a bit nervy but, seven minutes from time, Eyal hit a cracking volley for 4–2, quickly followed by Egil's second for 5–2. By now it was getting silly as goals were flying in all over the place. Paul Scholes netted for them and in the last minute Egil completed his hat trick, and yes it was a hat trick. The bloody silly dubious goals panel took it off him reckoning it was an own-goal by Gary Neville, even though the shot was virtually over the line before the diversion. I bet they wouldn't have reached the same conclusion if it had been a United goal. It was a top-quality hat trick in my book – and Egil still has the match ball to prove it.

But things never went smoothly for long at Southampton. Two weeks after beating Manchester United 6–3 we lost 7–1 at Everton. We had a few injuries and then Simon Charlton got hurt early on so our left winger, Neil Heaney, had to go to left-back. He had never played there before, had no idea what the role entailed and was up against Andrei Kanchelskis in full flow. It wasn't pretty. We were 5–0 down after 35 minutes and I seriously feared it could be double figures. We had Chris Woods on loan in goal and it was embarrassing. Thankfully the manager had a cunning plan for the next match at home to Leeds. He unleashed a secret weapon by the name of Ali Dia. So secret that no one had ever heard of him – but everyone in Southampton knows his name now and it will forever be etched in Souey's memory.

Ali Dia was recommended to him in a hoax phone call from someone claiming to be the cousin of World Footballer of the Year, George Weah. Or maybe the caller said that Ali Dia was the cousin of George Weah. It was all very confused and I don't think anyone really knows who made the call but the upshot was this lad turned up for training ahead of a home game against Leeds. He played in a five-a-side and looked like a fish up a tree. He was awkward and gangly and I remember thinking he would never make it. I confidently expected that that'd be the last we would see of him. How wrong was I? Having seen him train, it never occurred to me that he would play, even less that he'd actually come on as sub in place of me. I thought he had no chance of making at top level or indeed any level. I was amazed when I turned up before the Leeds match to find that not only was he in the squad but actually on the bench.

After training on the Friday before the match I was practising penalties and felt a slight tweak in a thigh. I didn't know whether to say anything to the medical team, and I thought it'd be OK with a night's rest so I kept quiet. After about 20 minutes of the game against Leeds I went to cross the ball with my right foot and felt the thigh tear where I'd felt the pain the previous day. I knew right away I'd have to come off – and to my astonishment Souey decided to put on Ali Dia. Oh my God, it was embarrassing. The kid hadn't got a clue. He tried hard enough but just ran about like a headless chicken and ended up being subbed himself. He was on for 53 minutes. I can't believe it took that long for Graeme to realize he was rubbish. I suspect he didn't want to lose face and was desperately hoping the lad might fluke a goal. It was the most bizarre debut in Premiership history. I was watching from the dug-out as we lost 2–0 and honestly I was waiting for Jeremy Beadle to turn up with the *You've been Framed* crew. Certainly it was a set-up of some sort but we never found out who was responsible. Why was it always us who fell for these hoaxes? Ali came in for treatment on the Sunday and was expected in for training on the Monday but he left that night. Next thing he surfaced at Gateshead playing non-league football, but he'd had his 53 minutes of fame.

THANKFULLY THE MANAGER HAD A CUNNING PLAN FOR THE NEXT MATCH ... A SECRET WEAPON BY THE NAME OF ALI DIA.

No one was brave enough to give Graeme any stick, especially as results weren't helping his mood. We lost the next three and then came news of a bizarre reverse takeover by a little-known company called Secure Retirement. Their main asset appeared to be the fact they were listed on the Stock Exchange, which was necessary for the club to finance the move to the new stadium, apparently. They injected the princely sum of £3m. Big deal. We could have raised that amount simply by putting in a sell-on clause for Alan Shearer.

As players we didn't take too much notice of what was going on behind the scenes, but it had a huge impact on the whole fabric and foundation of the club. Secure Retirement were run by a man called Rupert Lowe who had never even seen a football match until we played Lincoln City in the League Cup that season. His arrival immediately got Souey's back up. To be honest I think the mere fact he was called Rupert should have been enough to sound alarm bells. People called Rupert should not be running football clubs. His background was rugby and hockey, and Souness was quoted saying it wasn't the future he had been promised when he agreed to become manager. The talk was that Graeme had a wealthy group of Israeli backers lined up to come in and provide a significant cash injection which would have lifted the club to a new level. But the club opted for a deal with Secure Retirement which meant the directors all maintained their involvement – and benefitted financially overnight. I don't have any problem with directors making money provided it's also good for the club. The takeover didn't directly affect the players. We just knew we had a new chairman who talked posh and didn't know much about football.

We spent £500,000 of the new funds on a goalkeeper, Maik Taylor from Barnet. Maik was a lifelong Saints fan who became an instant crowd favourite. Almost immediately we recouped the half million by selling Gordon Watson to Bradford, so it was hard to see how this cash influx was actually helping us. In fact we were still second from bottom going into 1997. The New Year began badly as we went out of the FA Cup at Reading, again, and once more the weather played a big part. This time it was not rain but ice. There was another Big Freeze and virtually every game in the country was off. I think ours was one of only three which survived, but it shouldn't have done. The pitch was iron hard and the ref was a young Graham Poll who recently admitted to me that he cocked up and the game should never have been played. But, on the day, quite inexplicably, he passed it fit. He told us we would be OK provided we only went at it 90 per cent. I said I wasn't going to raise my work-rate for anyone.

How he could possibly imagine that teams would be happy to play at 90 per cent in an FA Cup tie? There's no way it should have been played and we lost 3–1. Claus got caught in possession for the opener and although Egil Ostenstad levelled we bombed out in the second half, finishing with nine men. Francis Benali was sent off by Poll for the second time and then Robbie Slater got a red card supposedly for abusing the linesman. An angry Graeme Souness had to be restrained by stewards as he tried to get to Graham Poll at the final whistle. Personally I think they should have let him – it would have been more entertaining than the match.

We bounced back winning 1–0 at Middlesbrough, and then mounted another one of our late come-backs against Newcastle coming from two down to snatch a draw at The Dell with two goals in the final minute. Tony Gubba was commentating for Match of the Day and got a little carried away with the excitement. Neil Maddison had just pulled one back, the crowd were at fever pitch, we were piling forward and I smashed one in from 25 yards. It was the hardest I have ever hit a ball. John Beresford told me he heard the whistle as the ball flew past him. It was a little too close to Shaka Hislop but he was beaten by the sheer power leading Tony Gubba to describe it as 'Goal of the Century'. It didn't even win Goal of the Month. I think the timing caused him to get a bit over-excited.

Certainly the fans were beginning to get a bit hysterical as results continued to stutter and we won only one of our next 10, 1–0 away to Newcastle. They must have really hated us at that time. A 2–2 draw at home to Leicester saw us go bottom with just seven matches to play, although four of those were six-pointers against sides just above us in the table. We were five points adrift of safety and three behind our nearest rivals and next opponents Nottingham Forest. We travelled there knowing defeat would all but put us down, a point which was reinforced as we listened to the radio on the team coach and heard the experts say that Southampton had gone and it was just a question of who else would be relegated. That was a wake-up call.

We were incredibly focused on what we had to do and pulled off a 3–1 win. We got off to a flyer with an early goal from Jim Magilton, but I was having a shocker and was replaced by Mickey Evans who scored two good goals. He had just signed from Plymouth. He was a real West Country yokel who made the Wurzels look sophisticated. He wasn't the most naturally gifted but he was strong, brave and committed – an inspired signing, just what we needed. He showed all those qualities at home to West Ham when Robbie Slater slung in a deep cross from the left wing. Mickey was running in full tilt but the only way he could possibly squeeze the ball home at the back stick was by colliding with the post. He knew he was going to get hurt but you know what they say – no sense, no feeling. He clattered into the post and was unconscious before the ball hit the net. But that selfless determination just summed up the spirit in the side. Jason Dodd also took one for the team that day when he committed a professional foul which could only lead to a red card. But it prevented us from conceding a goal and we won 2–0.

It was so tight and tense that Graeme Souness decided he couldn't risk the luxury of playing both me and Eyal Berkovic away from home

– and for some inexplicable reason he decided to go with Eyal. He was a super footballer with a brilliant touch but, when it came to tackling, I was like Norman Hunter compared to him. And he wasn't exactly a team player in terms of his character, as he showed when we went to Sunderland. It was the classic six-pointer, a real colossal clash with the losers almost certainly going down. And for some reason the fixture computer determined we should make that long trek on a Tuesday night, which was a big ask for our fans. It wasn't even as though it was a re-arranged match. It had been on the calendar right from the previous summer, although it still came as a surprise to our Director of Football, Lawrie McMenemy. Apparently he thought the game was on the Wednesday and therefore organized a doctor's appointment for the Tuesday. It couldn't possibly be rearranged and so he had to stay behind. Obviously it had *nothing* to do with the fact he'd have faced a hostile reception from the Sunderland fans who still remembered his spell in charge which led to their being relegated to the third tier.

Being a midweek match we flew up on the day. I was injured and not in the squad but I had split up with my wife Cathy two days earlier so Graeme suggested I come with the team, just to get away from everything. We got to Southampton airport and the tarmac was deserted apart from one rickety old plane which looked more like an Airfix kit – without the glue. It was little more than a flying box and Eyal said, 'We are not flying in that are we?' We were sure our plane would be arriving soon so we wound him up and jokingly said yes, until we got called for departure and it was still the only plane in sight. Eyal freaked. He said, 'I'm not flying in that. I will drive to Sunderland.' And he did. We just sat open-mouthed as he legged it out of the airport. He never moved that fast on the football field.

He jumped in a car with Malcolm Taylor, our kitman, and set off for the north-east. Bearing in mind it was mid-morning, it was at least a five-hour drive and the game was that night, it was hardly ideal preparation. He got there at 5pm for a 7.45 kick-off. It was the last ever floodlit game at Roker Park and there was an intense atmosphere. Their fans are passionate at the best of times but we quietened them with a 1–0 win, and they ended up going down, one point behind us.

It was a long midweek trip but there was no chance of a lie-in next morning as the phone went crazy. The press had got hold of the fact that I had left Cathy and wanted a statement and pictures. It was a pretty stressful, wretched and emotional time for both of us and for the kids, and the last thing we needed was that kind of intrusion from the media. Some celebrities court publicity so they can hardly complain when they get it in the neck, but I always kept my private life to myself. I just happened to be good at football and fame was a by-product of that. It wasn't something I ever sought for its own sake. I never regarded myself as a 'celebrity' and I always resented intrusion by the press. I was always happy to talk to them about football but my family were off limits. Even in this book, I'm not going to talk about my private life, except for the impact these troubled times had on my game. I knew the press would have a field day

VILLA BARELY THREATENED, NEITHER DID WE – ALTHOUGH THAT WAS NOT UNUSUAL.

once news leaked out but even so I was surprised just how much interest there was – and that was before the days of 24-hour news channels. It was painful enough without having to spell out the reasons to ghoulish reporters who were making money on the back of my misery.

And when the news broke about my going out with Angela – now my wife – I found myself on the front page of *The Sun*. I was thinking, 'Surely there must be some global crisis which is more important than a footballer having a new girlfriend?' Thankfully I had already told Cathy before it came out in the papers which was at least one small mercy. I wasn't the sort to play around so I was never the victim of a kiss-and-tell story, despite the best efforts of the national press who sent photographers to follow us on a club trip to Tenerife just after I left Cathy. They were hoping for pictures of me with another girl but I was – and still am – very much in love with Angela so they got nothing. A few of the lads were pretty fed up with me, though, because it meant they couldn't go on the pull because of all photographers lying in wait.

Thankfully the break-up didn't affect me on the field. We beat Blackburn 2–0 at The Dell. I came off the bench to get the second but any hopes that that win might mean safety were dashed as bloody Villa let us down again, losing to a last-minute Middlesbrough penalty. But it meant that even a narrow defeat in our last game would be enough to save us. It looked perfectly set up. We needed a point to be absolutely safe, and Villa needed a point to get into Europe. Plenty of fans plumped for a 0–0 draw. It looked a cert. Only we could manage to lose 1–0 to an own-goal.

There was no pre-arranged deal, but both teams knew a point suited us both. Villa barely threatened, neither did we – although that was not unusual. Then 'Trigger' turned the ball into his own net. I told you he was thick. But both teams were happy with that result and it was one of the more low-key, last-day escapes.

The celebrations from the manager were certainly very muted at the final whistle. He gave a brief wave to the fans and disappeared down the tunnel. I didn't think too much of it at the time because he never got too close to the players. He didn't hug any of us after a good win. And he didn't join our post-match jubilation. I presumed it was simply that he didn't feel survival was something to celebrate, which showed he didn't really know our club that well. All his career had been spent challenging for honours at the other end of the table so this probably came as quite a culture shock. But I wonder now that if by then the writing was already on the wall because he left soon afterwards.

However, he did leave a legacy. Just before the Villa match he signed a young lad by the name of Kevin Davies from Chesterfield for what proved to be a bargain fee of £750,000. He was ineligible to play at Villa Park but was in the dug-out as we stuttered to safety. By full-time he was probably wishing he had stayed at Chesterfield.

The feel-good factor continued two days later when Francis Benali staged his testimonial. It was a great night for him as a host of former Saints stars came back including the likes of Alan Shearer, Tim Flowers and Jimmy Case. Apparently it finished 8–7 to the ex-Saints but no one was too sure. I have watched the video and still can't keep track, it was one of those nights with a couple of very memorable moments.

Franny had never scored for the first-team and of course we were all expecting him to net the obligatory debatable penalty. No one expected him to curl in a genuine goal with a peach of a shot into the top right corner – and with his right foot. And it was a great night for me because I have always been a bit of a frustrated goalkeeper so I got a go between the posts. I was up against Alan Shearer and Tim Flowers who were playing up front for the ex-Saints. Of course both were desperate to score past me, even in a testimonial. Tim did beat me with an angled shot which was a decent finish. And he sent me the wrong way from the penalty spot which gave him a lot of pleasure. But I made a decent save from a volley to deny him a hat trick. That was nice as he had denied me a hat trick at Blackburn when I went through one-on-one. But I had great fun against Al, making a string of fantastic saves even if I do say so myself. There was one at point blank range. He really thumped it but I managed to get in the way and I loved seeing his frustration. Then a cross came in from the left and Alan absolutely thundered in for a header but I just got there first, caught the ball one-handed, lobbed it over his head, darted round, caught it again and cleared it.

A lot of it was pantomime stuff. Dave Beasant also played outfield and, after conceding a goal, the ex-Saints stuffed the ball up his shirt and charged up field and into the net. The ref wasn't sure which law he had broken so he just let it stand. It was that kind of night. That was followed by a trip to Elat in Israel but I refused to go. I had just left Cathy, was still in emotional turmoil and I had a lot to sort out both personally and from a practical point of view. I met with the manager and he told me I had to go on the trip. I tried to explain to him about my personal situation and that it wasn't right for me to go but he said I had to. Maybe it was part of the deal that I had to play in the game out there? I said I wasn't going so he told me he would fine me. I said fair enough, thanks very much. I should have lost two weeks' wages, which would have been around £5,000, a small price to pay considering how desperate I was not to go. But the fine was never enforced because Souness left soon afterwards. It is just as well Rupert Lowe has now left Southampton otherwise he would probably have tried to enforce it now – with interest.

15

LAWRIE OUT, DAVE JONES IN

'THERE WAS ABSOLUTELY NO WAY I WANTED TO SPEND
THE REST OF MY LIFE WITH A FLOPPY ARM! IT WOULD HAVE
RUINED MY GOLF SWING.'

I don't think anyone knows the full story behind the departure of
Graeme Souness. There had been rumours for months that Torino
were chasing him, and I know he found it difficult working with Rupert
Lowe who had taken over as chairman towards the end of the season.
In his arrogance Rupert made out that he was almost reluctantly
accepting the post, like he was doing the club a favour, and I think he
genuinely believed that. But I'm right there with Souey in thinking that
a hockey-loving ex-public schoolboy by the name of Rupert is hardly
likely to be on the same wavelength as the fans, or have an understanding of the club, its history and traditions.

But it still came as a shock when I heard that Souey had resigned
while he was on holiday in Israel. Even more unexpected was the fact
that Lawrie McMenemy followed a few hours later. The public decla-
ration was that Lawrie felt honour bound to go because he was the

one who'd brought Graeme to the club. But if that was true, why didn't he go when Alan Ball resigned to go to City or when Dave Merrington was sacked?

My reading is that it was a tactic on his part. I think Lawrie thought that the club would panic at losing him and beg him to return and help them appoint a successor, or even take charge. Did Lawrie gamble, thinking the inexperienced new chairman wouldn't be able to manage without him and that he'd end up increasing his power base? That seems the only logical explanation. But it backfired spectacularly. He reckoned without the arrogance of Rupert who jumped at the opportunity to get rid of him. They were always going to clash. Lawrie was the traditional manager, steeped in the game but disparagingly dismissed by the new breed as 'old football'. Lawrie might have been regarded as a dinosaur and he certainly had his faults, but he knew the game, the club, the players and the fans. He was always going to be a rival to Rupert who wanted to call the shots, and if Lawrie made a mistake it was by underestimating the size of the new chairman's ego.

Rupert thought he could do the job and that he didn't need Lawrie's help, so he promptly accepted his resignation. I'm not sure it was even formally submitted but Rupert couldn't get him out the door quick enough, which was the start of a rift which is still as deep as ever. It's incredibly petty that there is nothing at the new stadium named after Lawrie who, remember, is the only man to have won Southampton any silverware. It is an absolute disgrace to cut him out like that. When the stadium was built, the club held a poll among supporters who were asked to vote for four legends who'd have suites named after them. I never saw the votes but Lawrie came fifth – behind FA Cup winning goalscorer Bobby Stokes, Terry Paine, Mike Channon and me. The players' lounge was named after Ted Bates – fair enough because there's no bigger legend in the club's history. And a hospitality bar was named after club president John Corbett who'd bailed the club out financially when it had been on the brink of going under, and the directors' room was named after former chairman Alan Woodford. But did Lawrie get a mention? No. It was so ridiculous that Mike Channon said they should name the toilets after Lawrie because that was how Rupert was treating him.

The local paper came up with a good idea, naming the media suite after Lawrie because one of his great strengths was dealing with the press, and he certainly gave the club a much bigger media profile than it often deserved. But the board

MIKE CHANNON SAID THEY SHOULD NAME THE TOILETS AFTER LAWRIE BECAUSE THAT WAS HOW RUPERT WAS TREATING HIM.

steadfastly refused to acknowledge his achievements with any kind of lasting tribute. When Rupert Lowe returned for a second spell as chairman, he even ordered a picture of Lawrie with the FA Cup to be removed from the boardroom. It was replaced by a picture of a train presented to the club by *Doncaster Rovers*. How out of touch can you be?

I was sorry to see Lawrie go but not overly disappointed to be losing Graeme Souness, especially after the way he had humiliated me in front of my teammates. I lost a lot of respect for him over that. So there was yet another search for a new manager, which was about to become a recurring trend. The new man was Dave Jones. We knew all about him because his Stockport side had knocked us out of the League Cup quarter-finals a few months earlier. We thought that we'd done the hard part by drawing 2–2 up there in difficult conditions, thanks to a late equalizer from Egil Ostenstad. Stockport were two divisions below us, albeit on their way to promotion. Alan Neilson played left-back despite being right-footed, and I told him not to be afraid to cut back onto his right foot and I'd time my run accordingly. It was a rare moment where one of my tactics actually paid off. He whipped the ball in with his right foot and I chested it down and volleyed in to put us 1–0 up. We were cruising towards the semi-finals but they outplayed us and deservedly won 2–1, so I thought Dave Jones was a decent appointment.

I was even more encouraged when he took the time and trouble to phone me before the first day of pre-season. It was the first time a manager had ever done that to me, and I met him at the Hilton Hotel because he wanted to pick my brains and get a feel for the club, which seemed very sensible. It was a clever move too because I immediately felt he was on my side. Things seemed to be going very well – and then I broke my arm. Before his departure Graeme Souness had landed us with a 10-day pre-season tour of Germany. He must have known he wouldn't be coming with us because we were based in the middle of nowhere. We played Carl Zeiss Jena, again, and it was interesting to see how much the place had changed since the Berlin Wall had come down. And then we went to the tiny town of Ansbach. I remember scuffling for the ball and falling. It was a nothing challenge but I put my left arm out to break my fall and heard two little clicks. I thought it was weird but I didn't feel any pain – until I went to push myself back up. It was agony.

I wasn't sure what I'd done but I knew it hurt like hell. I sat on a stretcher in a corridor waiting for an ambulance which took an eternity to reach this club house in a remote forest. The blood had drained from my face because of the pain. The journey to the hospital was a shocker because the country roads were packed with bumps and potholes, and the pain was like being plugged into the mains. Our physio Jim Joyce gave me a couple of painkillers but they made absolutely no difference. The x-ray showed I had shattered the elbow joint; the ball of the elbow had broken into three pieces and the specialist recommended immediate surgery. He wanted to remove the joint.

I said if he did that it'd leave me with a floppy arm and he agreed. I panicked and told Jim to get me out of there immediately. There was no way I was going to be left with a dangly arm. I was beginning to doubt whether this guy was even a real doctor. I couldn't believe it and said I didn't care how much pain I was in, I wanted to go home. We couldn't get a flight that night so I had to get a taxi back to the hotel and somehow try and sleep. At least I had company on the flight. Simon Charlton had pulled a calf muscle so he volunteered to come back with me. I think he just wanted to get away from the boredom of the tour.

I went to see a specialist and he was absolutely gobsmacked at the diagnosis I'd received in Germany, and he reassured me I wouldn't be left with a floppy arm. He said there were two options: he could put it back together with screws and wire, his first preference; but if that failed he would need to insert an artificial joint, except that would have to come from France and would take a week to arrive. He wanted to have one just in case, so that meant I had seven nights of trying to sleep with a broken arm. I still remember rolling onto it in my sleep and screaming with the most excruciating pain I have ever felt in my life. As it turned out, of course, he didn't need the artificial piece so I had gone through one week of agony for absolutely nothing, but it was still better than having a floppy arm. The screws and the wire are still inside me.

When I came round from the anaesthetic, the first thing I did was to ask when I would be able to swing a golf club again. That was far more important to me than when I'd be able to play football. And I was actually back on the driving range before I was back on the pitch. I missed the first six games of the season but came back for the match against Liverpool at The Dell. I was expecting to be on the bench but about an hour before kick-off Dave Jones told me I would be starting. I was a bit nervous about my arm but he didn't give me much time to think about it.

I suspect the Liverpool lads were under orders to test me out because within two minutes one of their players took me out on the edge of the area. I fell onto my arm and there was a sharp intake of breath around the ground and an eerie silence as I lay on the ground for three or four seconds waiting for the pain to kick in. But it was fine and I breathed a huge sigh of relief as I got up. However, I still paid a price for missing most of pre-season because I tweaked a hamstring just before half-time. That was unheard of for me, but it only happened because I'd not had the right preparation, and it was the first of many niggling injuries.

HE LOOKED LIKE HE HAD MUGGED A TRAMP ON THE WAY TO TRAINING, WHICH TOOK THE PRESSURE OFF ME.

Dave Jones went back to Stockport to sign two of their better players, goalkeeper Paul Jones and left-back Lee Todd, who was the scruffiest dresser I've ever seen. He looked like he had mugged a tramp on the way to training, which took the pressure off me. He certainly showed plenty of ability in training but couldn't transfer it to the pitch. He seemed to lack the right mental attitude to make it as a player. Paul Jones was under pressure from the start because the fans loved Maik Taylor, but gradually won them over with some fantastic displays and won our Player of the Year trophy.

Dave Jones then sold Jim Magilton to Sheffield Wednesday for £1.6m and spent £1m of it on Carlton Palmer, who was the only player I knew who could trap a ball further than I could kick it. He wasn't the most naturally gifted talent but he was awkward to play against because he had these great long octopus legs. He was incredibly loud and very, very confident and quickly dominated the chat in the dressing room. You couldn't say anything without him butting in with an opinion, even when he knew nothing about it.

Carlton was unbelievable. How he remained so skinny was beyond me, he must have had a freakish metabolism because the amount of alcohol he could put away was amazing. He'd have a right skinful followed by two hours sleep and then next morning leave everyone for dead in the sprints. How did he do it? He was amazing in training – provided there wasn't a ball involved.

He also tried to stamp his personality on the club. We were on the same team in a five-a-side and I gave the ball away and didn't chase back, as usual. He had a real go at me, trying to embarrass me in front of the others. I snapped, 'Carlton, your job in the team is to win the ball back – and when you get it, you give it to me because *I* can play.' There was steam coming out of his ears but we left it at that. He realized that if I had the balls to stand up to him then maybe I wasn't such a softie. The first few weeks were a bit fraught but we actually got on OK after that. I think he was just testing me to see how far he could go. We even socialized a bit because I was living at Ocean Village at the time, not far from Carlton and our new £2m club record signing David Hirst. It's fair to say those two liked the odd beer.

I got on well with Hirsty. He had a very dry sense of humour, we shared a similar outlook and had a pretty good understanding on the pitch. He'd been struggling with an injury before he arrived and I always thought it was a real shame we couldn't have got him earlier. He was a terrific finisher and a very good footballer, prompting Alex Ferguson to try and break the British transfer record for him. He made his England debut at the same time as Alan Shearer and, at that stage, was ahead of him in the pecking order. It would have been awesome if we'd got him in his prime but, even so, he was a great signing and a good lad to have in the dressing room – and on a night out.

The arrival of those two helped us turn around our typically bad start, when we lost seven of the first nine, with just one win immediately putting the new manager under pressure. But then came the new arrivals and we won four out of five, which also coincided with my wearing red boots for the first time. We'd won 2–1 at Barnsley in the League Cup but our kitman Malcolm Taylor forgot to pack Carlton Palmer's boots. As he wore size 9, the same as me, he asked if I had a spare pair. I had the red ones with studs and a pair of black mould-eds, which I was just about to put on. I decided it would be kinder to let him have those, so I wore the red ones. After about 15 minutes I could sense the ball drop behind me so I flicked it over my own head and that of Arjan de Zeeuw, ran round the other side and as it dropped I hit a sweet 25-yard volley which flew in off the underside of the bar. I turned to Carlton and said, 'That's why I can wear red boots and you can't.'

After those four quick-fire victories we then lost the next three and really needed a victory at home to Leicester, and it came from the most unlikely of sources. December 13, 1997, is a day which will live long in the memory of all Saints fans and especially mine. It will go down as the day I provided the assist for Francis Benali to score his one and only league goal. After 11 years and several hundred games without a goal, the Leicester defence probably thought there was no point marking him as he stood 15 yards out waiting for my free kick. He was screaming for it and I remember thinking, 'He's completely free … but it's Franny.' I expected him to nod it across goal for someone else. It never occurred to me he might actually score but he met the ball with a thumping header which flew into the top right corner. He assures me he meant it – and Franny wouldn't lie. It was a terrific goal followed by a second of stunned silence and then a volcanic roar, very similar to the last ever goal at The Dell.

It was a special moment for both of us, having played up front together for the youth team. He did score a few at that level so I'm not sure why it took him so long to get off the mark, but I was pleased to have been part of such a special moment. He was a schoolboy at The Dell well before me and brilliant for the club. He is still a great mate and one of the loveliest men you could meet – except when the red mist descends. Then there's no getting through to him. As his captain and friend I immediately knew when his eyes had gone. I'd try to calm him down but there was nothing you could do. Launching John Fashanu into orbit probably made his reputation as a tough tackler, as Nicky Barmby would have testified from row C following another trademark challenge which led to another early bath. He was aware of the problem and did his best to try and curb it, culminating in his ninth and final red card at Bolton. Jamie Pollock was a niggly, narky wind-up merchant and he was targeting Franny who quickly reacted. As the red mist descended, you could see him struggling to control it. He knew it was wrong as he drew back his fist. In the end it was neither one thing nor the other, but his powder-puff slap was still enough to get him sent off but not enough to hurt Pollock. Franny would have felt better if he'd decked him.

His incredible will-to-win was a big factor in all our relegation escapes. People always say my goals saved us but we'd never have survived without someone like Franny in the side. You need players like that. He wasn't the most naturally gifted but his commitment was awesome. That comes from a local lad playing for his home club. I still remember one goal-line clearance in an end-of-season Great Escape at Wimbledon. Any other player would have given it up but not Franny. He'd never give up, no matter what the score – and somehow he got the ball to safety, and we got the points and stayed up.

Over the years a succession of players were bought to replace him – Lee Todd, Simon Charlton, John Beresford, Micky Adams, Stuart Gray and more. And he saw them all off. He epitomized the spirit of Southampton, shown by the lads who came through the youth team such as Tommy Widdrington and Neil Maddison. They seemed to care that bit more. We could certainly have done with them in 2005 when we pathetically went down without a fight on the final day.

We had no big-time Charlies in our side. We were aware of our limitations and it helps in the dressing room when you don't have any prima donnas. I always regarded myself as just one of the lads, which is all I ever wanted. People say I played as an individual but I loved being part of a team, which had lots of different components. I was acutely aware of my deficiencies as a player, and I know that I needed other players to make up for that. I got almost as much pleasure from setting up a colleague as I did from scoring, and I really enjoyed being part of a tight-knit group whose collective spirit kept us up for so many years, often when we had no right to stay up. If you look at the resources we had compared to the budgets of our rivals, we consistently performed well above our weight by surviving on gates of just 15,000. There were times when I'd look at the squads of the clubs who did get relegated and wonder how the hell that

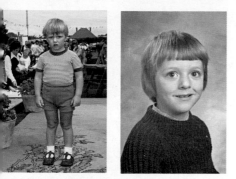

Far left And you thought Simon Cowell started the trend for high waistbands. This is me looking every inch a footballer of the future.
Left Even at an early age I was showing a penchant for dodgy hairstyles.

Above Dedicated followers of fashion. Purple and orange were very big in Guernsey in the Seventies. Mum used the same bowl for all four haircuts before Uncle Ray and Auntie Sue's wedding in 1975. I am front right.

Above I am back row, third left, wearing a T-shirt saying 'Up the Spurs'. Maybe it should have read, 'Turn down the Spurs'?

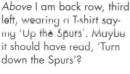

Above Howzat? I was Guernsey Under-14 Cricketer of the Year for hitting so many boundaries – because saved me having to run.

Right Calm down, calm down! I'd just heard Liverpool were in for me.

Above Le Tissier hat-trick – me, Carl and Mark prior to winning the Methodist Association of Youth Clubs National Five-a-sides at the Royal Albert Hall.

Right Called to the headmaster's office for all the right reasons. This is me signing schoolboy forms for Saints with headmaster Alan Gray and my dad.

Guernsey goalkeepers' gain was England's loss. Phil Parkes might not have been smiling so much if he had known how many goals I would put past his fellow keepers.

Athletes lunch at The Dell social club. Andy Cook and I tuck into sausage, beans, egg and chips with a glass of Cok‹ – before the dieticians ruined the game.

Home from home with the Ford family, Pete, Pat, Stuart and Martin.

I was so desperate to play for England Under-17s that I even wore a tie.

See, I was skinny once. It was March 1986 and we were playing Luton.

Saints youth team 1985. Back row: (left to right) Francis Benali (complete with caterpillar under his nose), Phil Parkinson, yours truly, Ian Hamilton, Steve Davis, Keith Granger, Chris Wilder, Allan Tankard, Dave Merrington (coach); front row: Greg Llewellyn, Peter Spargo, Mark Blake, Robbie Carroll, Craig Maskell, Paul Johnson, Ian Down.

I'd love to say it was a baggy shirt – bu‹ it was skin tight. And no, I have no ide‹ what I was doing. Probably copying the snooker players and removing a piece of fluff for a clean contact on the ball.

Right If you want to save 35-yarders at Ewood Park, you need to be over here goalie.

This shows the great team spirit we had at Southampton. I have just equalised at West Ham, in the first of many Great Escapes, to silence the home fans who had chanted about my big nose as I lined up the free-kick.

Can someone please give me the ball?

A caricaturist's dream. Saints legend Ron Davies's take on my rugged good looks.

Look Shorty, you can't book me, we're at The Dell.

Well, you can tell by the way I use my walk, I'm a woman's man, no time to talk.

The chiropractor is on standby as Jim Magilton jumps on my back.

Me and an ugly-looking beast – and a dinosaur.

Matty, Batty and Fatty. A proud moment as the first Guernseyman ever to play for England replaces Paul Gascoigne.

Two outstanding goalscorers – and Alan Shearer.

Pair of posers. Alan Shearer copies my all-action style.

An all too rare sight – not the fact that I'm playing for England, but that I'm running.

Saux annoying! Jersey boy Graeme Le Saux beat me by just 64 minutes to become the first Channel Islander to play for England.

I wonder why I didn't play for England more often. Training session before the game in Ireland. I think Alan Shearer is telling me about creosoting his fence again.

Taking a well-earned rest during a game at West Ham. I chat to the fans taking the mickey over my playing bingo.

Getting a shot away in the ZDS Cup Final.

Carrying Alan Shearer – as always!

Goal of the Season: Tim Flowers picks the ball out of his net, November 1994. Unlucky Tim!

The last goal at The Dell and the last goal of my career, what a time to do it.

It's amazing what adrenaline can do as I outpace James Beattie in celebration. I moved faster here than I ever did during the match.

With the legendary Ted Bates at the official opening of St Mary's.

Receiving the Freedom of the City of Southampton, November 2002.

With my painting on the side of a FlyBe passenger plane.

Making my entrance onto the pitch at my testimonial.

What a line-up!

Another reminder why I should never wear a cap.

Facing the final curtain.

Making it on to the leaderboard on the European tour.

Walk? You must be joking.

Relaxing with the legend Alan Ball in his back garden.

The best grandparents in the world.

I'll get more caps than you, Dad.

Three generations – Grandad, Dad and brothers.

Thank heavens Ava has got her mother's looks.

Walking with Angela on a beach in Mauritius on our wedding day.

My two little girls Keeleigh and Ava.

A miracle in itself, getting Mitchell to look at the camera.

Sadly, I never spent enough time as a player in the dressing room at St Mary's.

Saints concede again: Gillette Soccer Saturday.

Me with Jeff Stelling at his 50th some time ago. Someone gave him a box to stand on.

I used to love trying to score direct from corners.

happened because, man for man, they were better than us. But what we had was a collective belief, a unity and spirit. We had players who'd come up through the system and knew what the club was about, and we brought in others who'd fit into that mould.

A prime example was John Beresford, who was a big name when he joined in January 1998 for £1.5m, which was a lot of money for us. He was a great character in the dressing room, chirpy and great for a laugh. I got on really well with him, to the extent that a couple of years ago I took him to see Shania Twain in concert. I know how it sounds but I had been a big fan long before she became famous. I was given a ticket to see her at Wembley Arena but I was right near the back. So I bought a couple of

HE WAS ABOUT THE ONLY BLOKE I KNEW WHO SHARED MY LOVE OF MALIBU AND COKE.

tickets to see her at Sheffield but couldn't find anyone to go with me. Bez lived up there so I asked if he fancied going. He was always up for a night out so I went up and stayed with him. We got to the arena a bit early so we stopped off in a bar. He was about the only bloke I knew who shared my love of Malibu and Coke, which isn't exactly a manly drink. The look on the barmaid's face was priceless as two guys walked in and ordered this girly drink – and when we told her we were going to see Shania Twain you could see 'What a pair of gays' stamped across her forehead.

Bez made his debut for us in a 3–2 win at Liverpool, the only time in my career that we won at Anfield, and I wasn't playing. We even got a penalty there, which was quite a rarity, but even the most biased of refs couldn't have failed to give that one. In fact David James was lucky not to be done for GBH as he raced from his goal and cynically took out Matthew Oakley who was clean through. It was the most blatant penalty you'll ever see and it could have seriously injured Matt who was stretchered off. But, of course, as it was a Liverpool player at Anfield he only got a yellow. David Hirst grabbed a couple of goals in a well-deserved victory and it followed hard on the heels of our now annual home win against Manchester United who were beaten 1–0 by a goal from Kevin Davies, who was carving out a big reputation for himself. He was on a terrific goal-scoring run but his season was ended by an injury in that game.

We were looking a decent team and stayed up comfortably, finishing twelfth. I ended up with 11 goals from 25 games, which was OK considering the amount of matches I missed through injury. Seven of them came in my last nine appearances and it seemed as though I was hitting top form just at the right time for the World Cup … For France 98. But we know why I wasn't in that.

16

LAST-DAY ESCAPE

'LE TISS, LE TISS, MATT LE MATT LE TISS ... HE GETS THE BALL
AND TAKES THE PISS, MATT LE MATT LE TISS!'

I was very optimistic before the 1998–99 season. We had a good young manager who brought in six new players giving us a blend of youth and experience. At the older end we signed David Howells, Stuart Ripley and Mark Hughes to complement emerging youngsters Mark Paul, Scott Marshall and a certain James Beattie. Mark was picked up from non-league football with King's Lynn, though it was a step too far for him, while Scott came from Arsenal and played just two matches, scoring an own goal in both. But he looked a decent enough player when he was fit. However, James Beattie was an excellent signing.

The three older players had been around the block but they were all big names and hopes were high. It was a tactic successfully used in the past by Lawrie McMenemy, who would bring in players towards the end of their careers and extract a few more good years out of them. But David Howells struggled with injuries and it was clear his best days were behind him, and the same could probably said for Stuart Ripley who didn't really do it for us. Mark Hughes did OK but didn't score that many from a new deeper role in midfield, and he never really threw himself heart and soul into the club, although you couldn't question his commitment on the pitch. Just count the bookings. Refs had been ordered to clamp down and issue more cards but Hughes was too long in the tooth to change his game. He was very quiet and didn't join in with the banter, although not in a way that made you think he was miserable. Like Francis Benali, he'd change completely the moment he stepped over the white line. He was quietly spoken and wouldn't hurt a fly off the field but was an amazing competitor on it. I had a lot of respect for Mark and for what he achieved in the game. He had great presence and when he spoke everyone listened. You could see he'd be a good manager.

The three experienced players were probably the biggest names the club had signed in a long while and, just before the new season, we also signed Scott Hiley on loan from Manchester City. I liked him. He was a steady player though not blessed with great pace, like myself. But he passed the ball well, made a string of fantastic and crucial goal-line clearances during the season and became a good friend.

Even by our usual standards it was a shocking start because we lost seven and drew one of our first eight games to find ourselves marooned at the foot of the Premiership. We weren't helped by a massive blow in our opening game when we lost John Beresford with an injury which eventually finished his career. But it did mean an early opportunity for a promising youngster by the name of Wayne Bridge, who started out as a left-winger but was moved to left-back by the manager in a stroke of genius. I still vividly recall thinking Dave Jones was talking rubbish though when he said Bridgey would go on to play left-back for England. For once, I was happy to be proved wrong.

Having lost 2–1 at home to Liverpool, we went to newly promoted Charlton who were back at the Valley which was still being re-built as we arrived. The match was in doubt because the safety certificate was only granted just before kick-off. I wish it hadn't been – we lost 5–0. We were woeful, and the biggest disappointment of all was that I missed out on my one and only chance to go in goal. We were 2–0 down and had just used our final sub when Paul Jones was sent off for a professional foul on Clive Mendonca. David Howells, probably realizing we were in for a hiding, pulled an old pro's trick and imme-diately took the gloves before I could get there. I had always wanted to go in goal, even more so after my exploits in Franny's testimonial. It would have made sense because whenever we went down to 10 men I was always the 'luxury' player to be taken off because the team needed extra energy. I'm convinced I would have saved their penalty and that would have given us the momentum to go on and win. Instead we just fell apart, and continued in the same vein by losing our next three. It was the club's worst ever start to a season.

P 5   **L** 5   **F** 2   **A** 16   **Pts** 0

We got our first point in our sixth match at home to Spurs when Mark Hughes played a long pass from midfield and I volleyed it in. It should really have been the other way round. But then we lost at West Ham and you could tell things were really bad when we failed to collect our usual three points at home to Manchester United, who won 3–0. We did get a 1–1 draw at Arsenal where I set up David Howells for our equalizer. As a former Spurs man that goal meant a lot to him and us. We finally got our first victory at the tenth attempt, beating Coven-try 2–1 at The Dell, but even at that early stage of the season we were being written off as relegation certainties. We still only had 10 points by December 19 when we hosted Wimbledon. Dave Jones told us we would have to win virtually all our remaining home games if we were going to stay up – so we did. In fact we won nine, drew two and lost only one of our last 12 at The Dell, starting with a 3–1 victory over the Dons with two goals from Egil Ostenstad and one from new Moroccan midfielder Hassan Kachloul, who had come on trial. In his first training session he smashed into me with a late tackle. I got up, lifted him up and said, 'If you want a contract here, I'm not the one to start kicking.' It was tongue-in-cheek but he got the message. He did well though, scoring four in his first six games to give us new impetus.

It was the most remarkable revival. We spent the entire season in the bottom three until the beginning of May when we finally climbed out. We won our last three games, which was incredible because we hadn't even won two in a row up to then. Incredibly we stayed up by five points, which had been unthinkable before that home game against Wimbledon. Even I was beginning to think that we had gone. I had felt like that at Easter under Alan Ball but this was the first time I had felt so despondent in December. Apart from the arrival of Hassan Kachloul, there were a couple of other crucial signings. First we got Chris Marsden, who was your typical journeyman footballer, a good honest, unspectacular pro who had made a solid career in the lower divisions. He was an excellent signing, someone who would roll up his sleeves and get stuck in, leading by example.

Towards the end of the season we also got an unknown Latvian by the name of Marian Pahars who didn't even have proper boots and didn't speak a word of English, not even 'Yes' or 'No.' But bloody hell he could play. If he'd had as much heart as ability he'd have been a world-beater. It was a big struggle to get his work permit but once that came through he gave us a real lift with three goals in four starts. It was clear right away that he could play. He had a great ability to turn defenders. He would feint to shoot and, when a defender tried to block, he'd check back and could finish with both feet. I will always remember him nutmegging Jaap Stam to score a great goal at Old Trafford the following season. I just laughed because not many players ever did that. If only he'd stayed fit for longer. Then he began to pick up niggling injuries and wouldn't play with them. He wasn't the bravest and you do wonder how much of it was a mental problem. But when he played he gave us a real lift. We won four, drew three and lost only two of our last nine, starting with a 1–0 win at home to Sheffield Wednesday when I headed in a Matt Oakley cross. It was special because it was the first time my son Mitchell had ever seen me score.

Towards the end of the campaign James Beattie began to emerge. When he first arrived he was fairly quiet and shy, but he came out of his shell as he began to play well and score some goals. He might now come across to some as brash and arrogant, unless you really know him. But that is a front he puts up because basically he's quite a shy lad. And when he is full of confidence and on a roll, he is a real handful.

IT WAS SPECIAL BECAUSE IT WAS THE FIRST TIME MY SON MITCHELL HAD EVER SEEN ME SCORE.

Three games from the end of the season, James swept home a superb cushioned volley from a tight angle on the right of the penalty area. He swears he meant it and I'm inclined to believe him. That gave us a 2–1 win over Leicester and lifted us out of the bottom three for the first time. Then came one of the most memorable matches I ever played in, away to Wimbledon who were then playing at Selhurst Park – or Dellhurst Park as it became known that afternoon. We took more than 11,000 fans; it was incredible, they were everywhere. There was a long convoy of coaches and they took over the whole stand along one side of the pitch. They turned it into a home game and we knew there was no way we could let them down.

I had pulled a calf muscle in the win over Leicester and normally would have had no chance of being fit but the Hampshire athlete Roger Black had recommended a muscle tear specialist to me when we did *Question of Sport* together. He told me that Mark Zambarda would get me fit quicker than any club physio. The treatment was very intrusive and unbelievably painful but it quickened the healing process. We had just two games left to save ourselves and I was desperate to play so I called him up. He had worked with the likes of Linford Christie, Steve Backley and Kris Akabusi as well as Roger, and was fairly confident I'd play. Dave Jones didn't think I had a chance of being fit, but I spoke to him the night before the match and told him I knew it sounded weird but I had so much confidence in Mark that I felt I would be OK. Dave said he'd stick me on the bench and bring me on if necessary.

He sent me on at 0–0 and I put a free kick onto the head of James Beattie to put us in front 18 minutes from time and then, with six minutes remaining, I scored direct from a corner. The idiots on the dubious goals panel put it down as an own-goal because the ball may have taken the faintest touch off Robbie Earle. The only reason they took it off me was because it was direct from a corner so they thought I couldn't possibly have been shooting – but I was. I had a definite plan to whip it in knowing I had the ability to score direct or, failing that, get the slightest touch from a defender or forward leaving the keeper with no chance. That should have put us safe but 10-man Charlton got a last-minute winner at Villa, who never did us any favours. Blackburn lost at home to already relegated Forest and then drew in midweek, so that meant the final place was between us and

LAST-DAY ESCAPE

Charlton on the last day. They were at home to Sheffield Wednesday and had a better goal difference than us, so if they won and we drew at home to Everton, we were down. We had to win.

In the end it was surprisingly comfortable as Everton gave a low-key display. Chris Marsden rattled Olivier Dacourt early on and that set the tempo for a straightforward victory. There was a fantastic atmosphere. The crowd were really up for it and Marian Pahars scored twice to give us a 2–0 win. Charlton lost so we stayed up by five points. Comfortable really. I don't know what all the fuss was about.

SAINT AND SINNER

'I EVEN MANAGED TO GET BOOKED WHEN I WASN'T PLAYING. I WAS WARMING UP AND THOUGHT IT MY DUTY TO POINT OUT AN ERROR TO THE LINESMAN. BUT MAYBE I SHOULD HAVE PHRASED IT A LITTLE DIFFERENTLY? I WAS LUCKY NOT TO BE SENT OFF. AGAIN.'

Throughout my career I was often in trouble with refs – not for tackling, obviously. But I picked up numerous bookings for dissent because I hated the feeling of being cheated, deliberately or not. If someone was blatantly being unfair I'd lose it. I'm still the same. I'll take any criticism or decision as long as it's fair, but if decisions went against me as a player that were blatantly unjust I couldn't help myself. I'd let the ref have it. If there was a 50–50 decision which I lost, fine. As long as I could see why the ref came to his conclusion I'd let it go. But if he got it badly wrong …

I agree that in most cases refs aren't being deliberately dishonest but, the fact remains, that a lot of decisions do go in favour of the big teams, especially at Old Trafford and Anfield. Why? Are refs subconsciously swayed by their high-profile managers or the big crowds; do they want to be liked by them (and refs are human, not robots)? I don't know. But clearly there's a problem. Examples? How long have you got.

Neil Shipperley had a goal disallowed for us at Old Trafford in 1995 and to this day I have no idea why, even after watching it on countless replays. It was the most bizarre decision. The ball was crossed in from the right and Neil rose to nod in. It was a completely clean header but the ref decided it was against the rules for

IN FACT IN ALL THE TIME I PLAYED, OVER 16 YEARS, WE NEVER GOT A SINGLE PENALTY AT OLD TRAFFORD OR AT ARSENAL.

Southampton to score at Old Trafford, so he ruled it out. He must have been so embarrassed when he watched the replay because there was nothing wrong with it. It was a disgusting decision, one of the worst I've seen.

In fact in all the time I played, over 16 years, we never got a single penalty at Old Trafford or at Arsenal. Admittedly we didn't get in their box that often but you can't tell me there wasn't one single infringement in all that time. We did get one spot-kick at Liverpool, as I've said, but only because it was the most blatant offence I have ever seen. David James came hurtling off his line and took out Matthew Oakley. It was GBH and Oaks was carried off, and there was no way a penalty couldn't be given, although obviously it wasn't serious enough for a red card. Heaven forbid.

So while it's incredibly rare to get a marginal penalty at a big ground, the refs are very quick to spot even the slightest contact in the away team's box. I have never looked at the stats but I'm willing to bet that over the last 10 years Manchester United, Liverpool, Arsenal and Chelsea have conceded far fewer penalties at home than any other team in the Premier League. And you've got to ask if refs are worried about getting on the wrong side of Fergie, who sometimes likes to make it very clear who he thinks should take charge of United's games. Would you want to risk upsetting him? I'm certainly not criticising him for that because he's paid to look after the interests of United – and he is very good and very clever at it – but isn't it time the authorities told him to stop trying to interfere with their decisions?

When I began playing there was a points system for bookings, and you'd get, say, two, three or four points depending on the seriousness of your offence. Dissent didn't get as many points as fouls, and that suited me. It meant I could accumulate seven or eight cautions before I had to watch my tongue. I usually knew where to draw the line, and also which refs I could give some stick to. I could tell by their body language and demeanour how much they'd take before they'd get the card out, although I often over-stepped the mark. I'd push it as far as I could because to me a yellow card was neither here nor there. And I was never suspended that long.

I remember once getting booked for dissent when I wasn't even playing. It was at Highbury and I was warming up as sub when the linesman gave a blatantly wrong decision. I called him a cheating ****. He immediately flagged and I really thought I'd be sent off but the ref only booked me. I looked down the touchline at Glenn Hoddle, who was our manager at the time. He had a face like thunder. The ref might as well have sent me off because I knew then there was no way I was going to get on the field after that. But despite my willingness to argue the toss, I was never sent off for dissent. Both my first-team red cards were for physical offences.

The first was for violent conduct in an FA Cup quarter-final replay at Norwich in March 1992. We were 1–0 up and cruising towards a semi-final against second-tier Sunderland. We had a great chance of reaching the final that year – until I lost my head and was goaded into retaliating against Robert Fleck. I clipped the ball down the line and I felt his studs raked down my Achilles so late that neither the ref nor the linesman saw it. Stupidly, I took matters into my own hands and walked aggressively towards him. The crowd could see I had lost my head and was going to do something stupid. The ref reacted to their yells and turned round just in time to see me give Fleck a forearm smash and a right foot across his shins. I didn't even wait for the red card, I just kept on walking.

The second red card came in October 1995 in a live Sky game against Liverpool at The Dell. I probably only made two tackles in the whole of my career, and both were in this match. Dave Merrington came up with the brainwave of playing me as the holding midfielder. I know – it surprised me too. The theory was that I'd sit in front of the back four and spray killer passes around. The flaw was that I was required to do some tackling.

My first yellow that night was for a foul on Ian Rush. Normally I wouldn't have gone anywhere near him except perhaps to compare noses. On this occasion we were 1–0 up and I went to put in a tackle and mistimed it. It wasn't vicious or nasty – I just wasn't very good at tackling. It didn't injure him but Dermot Gallagher felt it was worthy of a yellow card. He said I was late for the ball, and I told him I'd got there as fast as I could. In the second half we were 2–1 down and chasing the game. I decided we needed to push forward and chased the ball a bit more than necessary. I went through their centre-back just after he had got rid of the ball, Dermot Gallagher showed a second yellow and I was on my way. I met Dermot at a dinner last year and he told me he was absolutely gutted to send off the local hero and he was dreading walking through the car park afterwards. But I've no complaints. And to be honest, he was one of the better refs.

One of the big problems now is that refs are often too quick to give a red card and that they panic under pressure from the crowd. And most, if not all, have never played the game at any decent level so they can't distinguish between a nasty tackle and a mistimed attempt for the ball. (Most officials are lads who were not very good at football, and the only way they can get involved is by becoming a ref.) I also think the fourth official should be an ex-player who can quickly look at a video replay and make a judgement. Refs can't officiate on their own. They can't see every incident. They need help. It doesn't have to be a high-profile former star; in fact most of them have so much money that they don't need the hassle. But there must be plenty of ex-pros who still need the extra cash. The match would only need to be halted for around 30 seconds – less time than it usually takes for teams to argue their case. And it would ensure the right decision is made, especially when refs got a goal decision wrong.

The worst one I can remember was an 18 yard shot from Mark Hughes at home to Leeds. It was hit with such power that it flew back out but the ref thought it had hit a post and waved play on. I'm not sure if it hit a stanchion or the advertising boards behind the goal, but the ball definitely went in. That could have proved very costly. It would have put us level at 1–1 and might have given us the platform to go on and win the game. Instead we lost 3–0, and that could have had a major knock-on effect at the end of the season – as it did for Bolton who went down when they had a goal ruled out in similar circumstances a few years ago.

And refs should also be prepared to change a decision, even if that means losing face. That's why I was full of admiration for Steve

Bennett in 2008–9 when he gave Hull City a penalty for what he thought was a handball against Aston Villa when in fact the ball had clipped the bar. It took a big man to change his mind when he realized it was a mistake – and of course the home crowd went mad. But he actually gained more respect for admitting he got it wrong than he'd have done if he had just refused to change his mind.

I didn't like Steve as a ref when I was playing, I felt he lost control of his emotions, he used to get the same glazed look in his eyes as Francis Benali did when he was losing the plot – but I did salute him for that decision. He had the bottle to go to the linesman and, whether it came from the fourth official or not, the right decision was made, which makes a mockery of what I was told all through my career, that there was no point arguing with officials because they never change their mind. It just shows I was right to keep shouting at them.

There are some refs you can have a bit of banter with, although FIFA have done their best to try and stamp that out. And they don't want officials to use their commonsense; everything has to be set in stone. My favourite was Paul Durkin because he did have that human touch and a sense of humour. He'd take a bit of stick and dish it back. I remember we were playing Everton and it seemed to me that in the first 20 minutes he gave every throw, every free kick and every 50–50 decision to them. I was getting fed up so when he did it again I thought it was only fair that I should enlighten him as to what he was doing wrong. I said, 'For F***'s sake Paul, are you going to give us anything?' He just looked at me and said, 'Have you actually touched the ball yet?' He said it with a smile on his face but, 'Fair enough' I replied, he'd made his point. That banter and rapport is what's now missing from the game. Refs think they should be the stars of the show.

Not all of them are like that but certainly a few are very 'up themselves'. I'd include Uriah Rennie and Rob Styles in that bracket.

Graham Poll had a tough time when he first came on the scene but he improved quite a bit with experience. He loved himself but he was a decent ref and it's a shame his career ended up with him being remembered for the fiasco of showing three yellow cards to the same player.

Generally I didn't have too high an opinion of refs who are right down there with traffic wardens in my estimation. Perhaps part of the problem is that players have very little contact with them. Even when I was captain I don't remember ever meeting refs before the game, although I believe that has now changed. There was never any contact with officials after the match – unless you count me yelling at them as I walked off the pitch.

I DIDN'T HAVE TOO HIGH AN OPINION OF REFS WHO ARE RIGHT DOWN THERE WITH TRAFFIC WARDENS IN MY ESTIMATION.

And the problem doesn't end there. I only appeared at an FA hearing once, after I had been sent off twice for the Reserves in 10 days. It was a bit like being made to stand on the 'naughty step' at school as they talked down to me. I didn't really say anything. Ian Gordon, one of the club directors, did most of the talking – which was probably just as well otherwise I'd probably have ended up in more trouble. The panel consisted of councillors from regional football associations. I've said for years that they should have ex-pros on the panel, not necessarily high-profile stars but people who have at least played the game to a fairly decent level and understand it. But that will never happen because the FA councillors do not want to lose their power.

The whole system needs a radical overhaul.

GLENN, CHIPS AND FRY-UPS

'GLENN HODDLE IS A BIG BELIEVER IN REINCARNATION.
I MUST HAVE DONE SOMETHING REALLY BAD IN A
PREVIOUS LIFE TO GET HIM AS MANAGER TWICE.
WHATEVER IT WAS, I HOPE I ENJOYED IT.'

After the hurt and disappointment of being left out of the England squad for France 98, you can imagine my deep joy when Glenn Hoddle became the new Southampton manager in January 2000. I've often felt that Saints were a footballing soap opera with each episode becoming more unreal. First we lost a very good manager following ridiculous allegations of child abuse and then in walked my old mate Glenn. No scriptwriter could have come up with that.

Having narrowly avoided the drop with three successive wins at the end of the 1998–99 season, we managed to maintain the momentum at the start of the new campaign winning three of our first five, which was quite remarkable for us. And we were comfortably mid-table when we went to Old Trafford on September 25 for a game which still gives a smile to all those who love to see Manchester United embarrassed.

It was bad enough for the champions when Marian Pahars put us in front with a sublime goal, cheekily nutmegging Jaap Stam before slotting in. I just laughed. As if that weren't humiliating enough, it got worse for United with a moment to feature on any DVD about football bloopers. I had got injured in a 4–2 win over Newcastle but I came back for this match at Old Trafford. Dave Jones put me on at half-time but I didn't even touch the ball for the first six minutes until I got it 25 yards out. I remember thinking I had to get it onto my right foot and smash one. That's not quite what happened. I stubbed my foot on the ground just before I kicked the ball. I hurt my ankle and it turned into a really feeble shot. I turned away in pain – and disgust. I was worried about my ankle and annoyed with myself for cocking it up, until I saw our fans cheer. I had no idea the ball had gone in and, until I saw it on TV that evening, didn't even realize their keeper had let it through his legs. Massimo Taibi had a 'mare. It was a simple take but he somehow missed it altogether. He blamed his studs getting caught in the turf according to his translator, who was probably doing him a favour. What he really said was, 'I'm a crap keeper.' That was the beginning of the end of his career at Old Trafford.

That brought us level at 2–2 and typically we went behind again before Mikael Silvestre cocked up. Marian Pahars robbed him and squared for me. I was waiting for the pass and was ready for a simple tap-in, but he actually smashed the ball quite quickly. I instinctively stuck out a side foot and the ball flew in making a much better-looking goal than it should have been, and we hung on for a 3–3 draw.

Two days later the club was rocked to its core as Dave Jones was charged with child abuse. He had gone to the police station voluntarily and everyone, including him, expected it to be a case of providing them with information from his days as a social worker in a Liverpool care home. He had worked there for a while after he finished playing, before he got into coaching and management. The police had leaked his name to the press a few weeks earlier saying he was being investigated for abuse. None of us could believe it when he was charged with nine offences of indecent assault and child cruelty. Instinctively I knew he couldn't possibly be guilty. You trust your instincts with a person, and Dave was as decent and honest a guy as you could wish to meet.

Never in a million years would Dave Jones have been capable of sexual abuse. And that view was reinforced by the way he conducted himself throughout what must have the most horrendous ordeal. I cannot think of a worse crime to be falsely accused of – and Dave felt the same. He said he would rather be charged with murder. Legal restrictions meant he couldn't even defend himself in the press, although the local paper did take his side. They knew he was a decent, innocent man.

There was a stunned atmosphere at the training ground but Dave was very open with the players, and with anyone who spoke to him about the case. He said he was totally innocent, had nothing to hide and was looking forward to having his say in court, although I don't think he really believed it would go that far. He answered questions honestly and easily, never got defensive or evasive and never cracked under the pressure, and I never had a moment's doubt about his innocence. The fact that he was charged was bad enough – but for the case to go all the way to court was an absolute scandal. And it was no surprise that it collapsed the moment it got in front of a jury.

Two 'victims' pulled out just before the case went to court, one failed to turn up and, after four days of flimsy evidence, the judge had had enough and pulled the plug. It turned out that the Crown Prosecution

Service had contacted a lot of the former residents at the care home asking if they had suffered any sort of abuse – adding if so they might be entitled to compensation. Half of them were in prison when they got the letters and suddenly saw the chance to earn easy money. What other answer were they going to give? And with Dave being a high-profile figure, they had the chance to make a name for themselves.

How the CPS didn't see through that will always be a mystery. Dave must still be burning with anger and resentment. It cost him several hundred thousand pounds to clear his name, money which he didn't fully recover through the court. Worse, his father died through a stress-related condition soon after Dave was charged. I hope the people who falsely accused Dave – and particularly those who relentlessly pursued the case when all the evidence pointed to his innocence – can live with themselves. It also cost him his job at Southampton. He didn't let the court case affect him at the training ground – in fact he described working with us as his salvation. If that was the case, then things really must have been bad!

HE DESCRIBED WORKING WITH US AS HIS SALVATION. IF THAT WAS THE CASE, THEN THINGS REALLY MUST HAVE BEEN BAD!

Dave took it all in his stride but results on the field weren't that good. Our form wasn't helped by the fact that I was starting to pick up niggling injuries. I would play a few and miss a few. I played in a 2–1 home defeat by Chelsea on Boxing Day and then Dave played me again at Watford two days later, even though I had been struggling with a few knocks. It was too much and I suffered one of the worst muscle injuries I ever had. I ripped the back of a hamstring and the back of a calf at the same time. I went to see Mark Zambarda and he said he had never seen such a complicated series of pulls.

It kept me out for a long time, which wasn't good timing as we changed managers in mid-January. We had slipped to seventeenth and there were fears of another relegation battle, though that was nothing new. As Dave said, it was business as usual. The final straw was probably a 5–0 defeat at Newcastle in a live Sky game. We had a lot of injuries, so all the crocks went down to the casino to watch the match on television. We were a goal down after just two minutes and, embarrassingly, I jumped up and cheered because I had drawn Duncan Ferguson in the sweepstake. I remembered myself and sat down but I got a lot of stick off the lads. It was a case of the team being hammered but hey, it's not all bad; I won a *tenner*.

Another goal followed almost immediately and we were three down after 15 minutes, four behind on the half hour and statisticians were thumbing the record books for our heaviest defeat. The local paper was full of letters from fans saying there should be a change of manager with most calling for the return of Alan Ball. We then beat Dave Jones' old club Everton 2–0, but it was too late to save him. He was placed on 'gardening leave' with chairman Rupert Lowe announcing it would free him to concentrate fully on his court case. In came Glenn Hoddle as a 'temporary' replacement, although it was never made clear what would happen after Dave was cleared, as we all expected. Would he get his job back? We couldn't imagine Glenn meekly making way to allow Dave to pick up the reins. It was never said, but we all knew he was not coming back.

I hadn't spoken to Glenn since he left me out of the World Cup squad. It wasn't that I was blanking him, just that our paths hadn't crossed – apart from one slightly surreal moment in the summer of

1999. I was having dinner with a friend at the Chewton Glen, a top hotel in the New Forest. Gradually the restaurant emptied until there was just us and a couple behind me. They were arguing and, at the sound of raised voices, I stopped my own conversation and listened in. The more I heard, the more I recognized one of the voices. I turned round and saw Glenn with his wife. He didn't see me so I had a little chuckle and called the waiter over and said, 'Can you ask that couple over there if they'd like a drink?' It was my way of subtly letting them know I was there and had heard them arguing. When Glenn saw me, his face was a picture. He must have thought of all the people to have overheard, why did it have to be me? But he did accept the drink.

The next time I saw him was when he walked into our training ground as manager. I had mixed feelings. Obviously I was unhappy at the way I had been treated with England, but I still rated him as a good coach even though his man-management skills clearly left something to be desired. I actually thought it was a good appointment for the club. And because we were similar as players I was hoping that by working with me on a day-to-day basis, Glenn might bring the best out of me. I was ready to put the past behind me but I'm not sure he felt the same.

It was exciting for the fans to have a big-name boss, a former England manager who put the club in the spotlight. There is no doubt the players were excited. But it wasn't long before I realized that Glenn and I weren't going to see eye to eye. There were a few clues in training. People would make mistakes the whole time and get away with them but if I did something wrong he was very quick to get on my back. He didn't do that with anyone else. Maybe he had higher expectations from me because I was the most naturally talented player, or maybe he thought I was 'swinging the lead' because I was injured when he arrived and it took me a long time to get fit. I don't think he fully realized the extent of my problem. It didn't help that my eventual come-back from that injury was as a sub away to Spurs in a game which obviously meant a lot to Glenn – and we lost 7–2 – despite twice taking the lead. Whoops!

Anyway, Glenn singling me out for criticism went from bad to worse and I'd had enough. I turned round one day in training and told him to eff off. He couldn't believe what I'd said. He was too stunned. Besides, he didn't like confrontation. He'd shy away from it so he let it go. I'd have had more time for him if he had sent me off.

Working with him at Saints made me understand why he had a problem with me. He does have a large ego, and many times during my career I was compared to him because of the way we both played. We were often spoken about in the same sentence but I don't think he liked that. He felt he was in a different league to me. Talk about petty. He certainly loved to look the best player when he joined in coaching sessions – and in fairness, he often was. He might have hung up his boots long since, but it was obvious that he could still play. It reminded me exactly why I had

HE CERTAINLY LOVED TO LOOK THE BEST PLAYER WHEN HE JOINED IN COACHING SESSIONS – AND IN FAIRNESS, HE OFTEN WAS.

idolized him as a player but there were times when I wasn't sure whether our training sessions were for our benefit or his.

I probably lost more respect for him while he was at Southampton than I did when he was England manager. It should have been a fruitful partnership but I found him incredibly arrogant and extremely stubborn. It didn't matter what we were talking about, he had his opinion and he was always right. And I never felt his heart was in the job.

It was a stepping stone to a bigger club – and the Tottenham job was probably always in his sights. He needed Saints to get him back in the game. His reputation had been tarnished after the World Cup and his comments about the disabled. He didn't seem to have learned anything from that or to have developed any kind of human touch.

There was an inkling or two that he was never going to be part of the community. It was a shame because tactically he was the best manager I ever played under. From knowing the opposition's weaknesses to setting up his own team to counter that, he was top-class. I remember him physically moving defenders on the training field to show them exactly where they should be for set pieces. He knew how to change things on the pitch if the match wasn't going well, and he certainly tightened up our defence.

Being a manager encompasses many things. It isn't just about coaching and one of the biggest ingredients is the ability to man-manage people and get the best out of them. You need to be able to get players to want to play for you and, as good as Glenn was as a coach, he was just as bad at man-management. Now there's nothing wrong with being aloof, because you can still get the players' respect, but arrogance doesn't work. Hoddle wasn't a particularly warm person and he never really dealt with people on a human level, whether it was players, club staff, fans or the press. I know he probably felt very bitter towards the media after the way he lost the England job but the local press in Southampton were obviously on the club's side. Their job was to promote the team wherever possible, but he treated people as though they were inferior.

But for all that, he certainly had a positive effect on our performances. The players' touch got better and the training sessions definitely improved the lads' ability on the ball. Chris Marsden developed a lot under Glenn and Dean Richards flourished. He forged a strong partnership with Claus Lundekvam and we suddenly looked a lot less vulnerable. We had picked him up on a free transfer and ended up selling him for £8m – to Glenn when he was at Spurs.

Glenn brought a lot more professionalism and sports science to the club, particularly in terms of diet and nutrition. He sent me to see a French doctor to speak about diet. All I remember is that I was advised to eat poached eggs on toast before training. Sadly they weren't on the menu at McDonald's, which had become my regular stop-off in the morning. At one point we got a dietician who asked me to write down everything I ate for the next fortnight. I was too honest for my own good and wrote down everything, the burgers, the chips and the fry-ups. Her jaw hit the ground when I showed her the list. She questioned how I was still alive let alone playing at the top level. I did try the poached eggs on toast for a fortnight but it didn't make a bit of difference, so I went back to what I liked.

Results did improve and we saw out the rest of the campaign free from the threat of relegation for once. The last game of the season was at home to Wimbledon who needed a win to stay up, a reversal of the situation five years earlier. Glenn didn't like the way Wimbledon played. He felt they didn't belong in the Premier League and thought we would be doing everyone a favour if we sent them down, so we were under orders to show no compassion. I was injured but the team won 2–0 with Wayne Bridge curling home a free-kick for his first goal for the club. Wimbledon went down and have never recovered. We finished fifteenth, the same position we'd held for the final 10 games of the season. It was normal for me not to move – but not the whole team.

MATT OUT OF DELL

'I ALWAYS FELT I WAS DESTINED TO SCORE THE LAST GOAL
AT THE DELL BUT I WAS TOTALLY UNPREPARED FOR THE
EMOTION OF THE MOMENT.'

Glenn Hoddle's departure was as sudden and as controversial as his arrival. And it was made worse by the fact we were doing so well at the time. It was no surprise because we always felt he was using Saints as a stepping stone, but it was still a shock when in March 2001 he left to manage Spurs. I have to be honest and say he had made us a much better side, and the whole club looked ready to step up to the next level amid the excitement of the pending move to a new ground.

There had been talk of a new stadium ever since Southampton won the FA Cup back in 1976. There had been many false dawns, the biggest being a planned move to Stoneham – an absolutely perfect site on the outskirts of the city, right next to the airport, Parkway train station and the M27 and with enough space to park 5,000 cars. It couldn't have been better so of course the politicians refused to grant permission. The land was controlled by two planning authorities – Southampton (Labour) and Eastleigh (LibDem) – and was owned by the County Council (Conservative). So no agreement there. Instead the new ground was situated almost right in the city centre, with hardly any parking or room for expansion. Terrific.

No one really believed it would actually materialize until well after building work had begun. At that point we began to realize that finally we would have a ground which would enable us to compete with the bigger clubs. We had been outpunching our weight for years by staying up on crowds of just 15,000, and knew that couldn't continue. If you keep playing Russian Roulette, sooner or later you get the bullet. The Dell was a wonderful homely ground and a big advantage to us in many ways because visiting teams hated playing there. The crowd was right on top of the pitch and the dressing rooms were cramped. By the turn of the Millennium visiting clubs were also squeezing five subs, other squad members, the coaching staff, physios, kitmen and masseurs into the tiny visitors' dressing room which had just enough room for 11 players and a manager, with the heating stuck on high.

As the new stadium took shape, so did the team and by March we were flying high in eighth place on the back of five successive wins. There was genuine talk of a realistic push for Europe, and that is why there was so much anger at the timing and manner of Glenn's departure. If he'd waited until the end of the season people would have understood. The media suggested that Tottenham were prepared to wait and if Glenn had held on here until then he'd have gone with the thanks and best wishes of everyone at the club. But Spurs were in the semi-finals of the FA Cup and I think he was swayed by that. What would he have done if we'd still been in the competition?

We had looked set to reach the quarter-finals where we had been drawn home to Liverpool who, in August, had been three up at The Dell with 15 minutes remaining only to draw 3–3 as we staged a famous fight-back. But that was eclipsed by Tranmere's fight-back against us in the fifth round. We had drawn 0–0 at The Dell and, for once, the replay was held the following week rather than the usual 10 days later. It didn't suit us because we had Jason Dodd and Matt Oakley injured from the first tie and Tahar El Khalej away on international duty. All of them would have been available a week later. And I was sidelined by injury, which saved me from one of the most embarrassing nights I can remember.

The replay at Prenton Park was live on Sky, and viewers must have switched off in their thousands at half-time thinking there was no chance of an upset as we cruised to a comprehensive 3–0 lead. It looked like the game was over. Glenn even felt confident enough to take off Marian Pahars at half-time to rest him. But Tranmere had a good giant killing record, particularly in evening matches. I watched it on TV in a bar with a few mates, and thought I was in for a good night as the drinks flowed and we took charge of the game. But it proved to be one of the great cup come-backs of all time.

Even watching on TV I could sense the change in atmosphere when they pulled one back early in the second half. Their crowd were fired up and I could sense we were uneasy. The lads said it was even worse being there because they panicked under pressure. To add insult to injury it was our former striker Paul Rideout who scored a 21-minute hat-trick as Rovers pulled back to 3–3 with 11 minutes remaining. At that stage the only question was whether they would get a winner or whether we could hang on for extra-time, not that I fancied our chances of making it to penalties. Inevitably they scored again to complete a collapse which eclipsed anything we had previously suffered. I just put down my drink and walked out. I knew we didn't have it in us to recover.

I must admit I'm glad I didn't have to travel back that night. Apparently Glenn's face was like thunder. As the coach driver switched on the engine, the radio came on and Glenn snapped at him to turn it off. They drove to the airport in silence and, as the lights were dimmed for take-off, no one dared switch on their reading lamps, so the plane took off and landed in silence and darkness. But Glenn did get a second crack at the FA Cup with Spurs. How come managers are not cup-tied like players?

We then beat Everton at The Dell, and strangely enough that was also Dave Jones' last match. And then the most bizarre thing happened. We were given a week's holiday. *In March.* In all my time in the game, I never knew a manager give the squad a complete week off at any stage of the season, let alone towards the end of it. We had a two-week break for internationals, and we thought maybe we might go abroad as a squad for a bonding trip but we never expected to be given free rein. As a professional it was very rare to get two consecutive days off during the season let alone a full week, so we should have guessed that something wasn't quite right. It was really odd that someone as meticulous and as controlling as Glenn should give everyone a holiday for no reason.

IT WAS REALLY ODD THAT SOMEONE AS METICULOUS AND AS CONTROLLING AS GLENN SHOULD GIVE EVERYONE A HOLIDAY FOR NO REASON.

Almost as soon as we reported back, Spurs put in a request to speak to Glenn, who said he wanted to go. It caused a lot of bitterness between the clubs with Rupert Lowe expressing surprise at the speed with which negotiations were concluded, from what was supposed to be a standing start. I felt Glenn owed it to us to stay until the end of the season after we had given him a route back into the game when no other club would touch him. If he'd done it properly then there is no question he'd have got the Southampton job again when Gordon Strachan left a few years later.

Results dipped after he left. Before his departure we had won five in a row and lost only one in 11, and that was away to Liverpool. Glenn was replaced by our first-team coach Stuart Gray, who was put in temporary charge until the end of the season. I liked Stuart. He was an excellent coach and good with the lads. He was able to mix easily with the players, and was a good link between them and the manager. That was his niche and he was very good at it, but that probably made it difficult for him to become Number One. It would have been easier for him to become a manager at another club where he would have walked in as the gaffer and been in charge right from the start. It is much harder to go from being the players' friend to their manager.

Football is littered with similar appointments where clubs take the cheap option and promote the first-team coach. You only need to look at England replacing Sven-Goran Eriksson with Steve McClaren, Bolton did it with Sammy Lee, and the only time it really worked was when Liverpool promoted Bob Paisley. I don't think clubs really take into consideration the authority a manager needs. Saints had tried this previously with Dave Merrington and again later with Steve Wigley. You'd think they would have learned.

A manager needs to generate a certain amount of fear. Players have to be slightly in awe of him, but we still called him Stuart rather than 'gaffer'. It didn't really work and the results weren't good. We lost five and drew two of the next seven, and there didn't seem to be any way Stuart would get the job full-time, but the board were probably swayed by the wave of emotion as the season reached an unforgettable climax.

We beat an under-strength Manchester United 2–1 and then came the long-awaited last ever league game at The Dell against Arsenal. And I will be eternally grateful to Stuart for showing there is still room for sentiment in football by naming both me and Francis Benali on the bench for a match which meant so much to both of us. I had missed the United game through injury but I had recovered by the Tuesday. I wasn't fit enough to play 90 minutes but Stuart told me I would be on the bench with Franny, and promised that we would both be on the field when the final whistle blew. It was great of him to do that and to let me know because I stopped worrying about it. I had spent my whole career at The Dell and it would have been heart-breaking if I had missed that last match. And it was nice to be alongside Franny on the bench. We had shared so many special moments down the years and for us both to get on was special.

There was a lot of excitement around the city that week, and tickets were like gold dust because everyone wanted to be there. I spent most of the week imagining that I would get the winning goal. I honestly believed that that was my destiny. And the game was perfectly poised when I came on with about 15 minutes to go. Arsenal were going to finish second whatever happened at The Dell, but they were definitely not taking it easy and twice took the lead. Each time it was cancelled out by Hassan Kachloul who scored two on the opening day of the season and two on the last day, with none in between.

Arsenal didn't want to lose, that's for sure, and they were actually pushing for a winner when Stuart sent me on. He told me just to enjoy it. I was really relaxed and had a few good touches as the game seemed to be petering to a draw. Unusually, James Beattie was play-ing on the right – and Stuart left him there and put me up front with Marian Pahars so that if anything dropped there was a good chance it would fall to me. It was tactical genius. With a minute to go Beatts flicked on a Paul Jones clearance, and Martin Keown half cleared. The ball dropped just behind me on my left foot and it was quite a difficult chance, made harder by the fact Chris Marsden was coming in trying to take it off my toe. Even with my left foot I had more chance of scoring than he did. And with little time left there was no way I was going to let him have it.

As soon as the ball left my foot I knew it was going in. Alex Manninger had no chance – and the explosion of noise was incredible. Even now it sends a great shiver down the spine. I knew what it meant to everyone, not just me. I heard afterwards that even hardened newspaper hacks who thought they had seen everything were struggling to dictate their copy with voices breaking up through the surge of emotion. Many said they found it hard to find the words to describe the enormity of the moment. It was amazing.

Everyone had been willing me to score the last goal at The Dell, although Chris Marsden again tried to spoil it with a 20-yard shot in injury-time. If that had gone in I'd never have forgiven him, but Alex Manninger tipped it over and I almost joined in the congratulations. I would have tipped it over myself if I could have done. The atmosphere was electric as the final whistle blew. The fact that I had scored the last goal and that it was the winner made it an afternoon which no one there will ever forget. The Dell held 15,200 but I swear there were twice as many in the ground judging by the number of people who have since come up to me and told me that they were there. I know a lot of people without tickets stood outside just to be part of it, and they managed to get in when the gates opened 10 minutes from time. There were so many lovely stories to come out of that day. Hampshire Cricket Club had a home match and apparently there was a big cheer there when they announced the score and the scorer.

As luck would have it, I had agreed a new contract the previous week. At the final whistle the players were presented with commemorative silver salvers by the chairman. As Rupert Lowe gave me mine I told him he was lucky because if I'd waited another week to negotiate my contract I'd have been in a much stronger position. My goal lifted the club a couple of places up the league so that we finished tenth instead of twelfth, getting half a million pounds in prize money. My goal more than easily paid for my new contract. And finishing in the top half also triggered a bonus in some players' contracts, including Claus Lundekvam who made several thousand pounds. When I got up the next day there was a crate of 12 bottles of Malibu and 24 bottles of Coke on my doorstep from him as a thank you.

It took a while to come down from that incredible high – and from the post-match celebrations. My son Mitchell had come over from Guernsey for the game with my parents which made it hard to go out to celebrate so we stayed in. At 10.30pm there was a knock on the door and Hampshire Cricket Club chairman Rod Bransgrove turned up with the Hampshire team. The neighbours didn't get much sleep that night but I think they could forgive me after the day we'd had. I was on a high for much of the summer and wore out the video recorder replaying the goal, and hoped that'd be the turning point for me from the niggling injuries I was starting to pick up. But it did not work out like that.

20

END OF THE ROAD

'I SAT IN THE DRESSING ROOM AND CRIED AS THE
REALIZATION HIT ME THAT IT WAS ALL OVER.'

I didn't have my testimonial at The Dell because I had been promised
the first match at the new stadium, St. Mary's. But, as the ground took
shape, it became increasingly difficult to get the club to commit to a
date. In the end it was decided that I could not have the first game –
which would have been madness – because the stadium needed a
trial run without a full house. My testimonial was put back to the end
of the season and, as things turned out, I was delighted. I'm a big
believer in fate and it turned out to be the last game of my career,
which made it all the more special.

On the Wednesday before the new season started, I pulled a calf
muscle in training – it was the first of five separate calf strains that
season which made it a nightmare. I made only one appearance as
sub at St Mary's and three away from home, and not one single start.
I felt even more frustrated when the team made the usual crap start to
the campaign. We struggled at the new stadium. The crowd had been
close to the pitch at The Dell which gave us a big advantage, but it
took us a while to adapt to the new atmosphere.

Stuart Gray had got the manager's job full-time. Rupert Lowe made 'no apologies for giving a bright young English coach a chance', but his track record as caretaker wasn't brilliant. It was clear he was struggling and, in October 2001, we went to West Ham who were also having a bad time. Gordon Strachan was spotted in the crowd and everyone assumed he was being lined up to take over as the Hammers' new manager. But they won 2–0 and the following day he was our new boss.

It's fair to say he wasn't everyone's choice. He'd been sacked by Coventry that summer but he was the best appointment Rupert ever made. Gordon was short and ginger, just like Alan Ball, and I reckoned we only got him because we had a lot of leftover 'GS' (Graeme Souness) tracksuit tops.

I felt sorry for Stuart because I liked him. I saw him on the day he left and it was clear he'd taken it badly. It had been his big chance and he didn't feel he was given a fair crack of the whip. He was very emotional and close to breaking down. It was horrible to see because he had worked his way up through the coaching ranks from the club's community officer to manager. Looking back, it was probably the right move because Strach was an inspired choice. He was certainly a character.

I had heard he enjoyed putting the media on the back foot and I'll never forget his first press conference broadcast live on Sky and local radio. The local reporter was so desperate to ask the first question that he didn't think it through. 'So Gordon, do you think you are the right man for the job?' 'No, I'm rubbish. I think they should have got George Graham.' Ouch. Talk about an instant put-down.

Gordon was also great value in post-match press conferences. If reporters asked a stupid question they'd get an even more stupid answer. It was TV gold.

I know there was one occasion when Terry Cooper recommended a full-back and Gordon went to watch him. Gordon said he didn't fancy him but he quite liked the look of one of the strikers. He went back to watch the big lad up front and decided he wanted to take a chance on him. He brought the player over and left him with Rupert Lowe to sort out the contract. Agreement on salary couldn't be reached. The player's name? Emmanuel Adebayor.

There was certainly a big question mark over who brought in the other notable new face who arrived at the same time as Gordon. The club spent what remains its second highest transfer fee of £3.25m on an Ecuadorian striker by the name of Agustin Delgado. Rupert was so keen to extol his virtues that he showed a video of some of Delgado's goals on the big screen before our home game against Ipswich. Good job he didn't make a video of his goals for us when he left because it would have lasted two seconds.

The transfer happened at almost exactly the same time that Gordon arrived. Stuart Gray is adamant he didn't sanction it and Gordon says the deal was set up before he arrived, and was too advanced to cancel. It's a real conundrum. I know a lot of South American deals offered opportunities for some shady payments but I can't imagine Rupert would have allowed anything untoward to go on. It just seemed a strange transfer at a strange time when we didn't have a manager.

I'm still not quite sure why the club bought him, and why they paid so much for a player who arrived with a knee problem which never got any better all the time he was with us, except when he was on international duty when it mysteriously cleared up. We also bought a compatriot to keep him company, just as we'd bought Imants Bleidelis to help Marian Pahars settle. Kleber Chala was a nice enough bloke and did try but he wasn't very good. There is no doubt he put a shift in but he just wasn't up to it. Delgado did show ability on the rare occasions he was fit but that was about as often as a Francis Benali goal.

Between them, Delgado and Chala were probably the biggest waste of money in the club's history – and there is quite a lot of competition for that trophy. Delgado's nickname was the Tin Man, probably because he had no heart. He came up with a bizarre series of excuses as to why he couldn't play. On one occasion it was toothache. Another time he went AWOL because the club forgot his birthday. I remember after that Gordon went round every table in the canteen wishing every player a happy birthday. Delgado would drive him to distraction and he got fed up being asked by the press whether the absent Ecuadorian was fit. At one point he came up with the memorable reply, 'I have far more important things to worry about. I have a yoghurt on its sell-by date and that is far more important than Agustin Delgado.'

I can barely remember training with Delgado and, as I was injured so much of the time, you'd have thought that I'd get to know him in the treatment room. But he didn't seem to be there either. God knows where he was. He did, however, pop up in the 2002 World Cup Finals where he played all three games for Ecuador and became the first Saints player ever to score in the World Cup.

Meanwhile my injuries were becoming more persistent and prolonged and, by February, I knew it was going to be my last season. I was just coming back from my fourth calf strain of the season; I played a Reserve game at St Mary's and it went again. I went into the treatment room, sat on my own and cried. I decided there and then that was it. I gathered myself together and then Strach came in to see how I was. I just said, 'It's no good. I can't do this any more. I'm hanging up my boots at the end of the season.' He was really good about it. He said I was very fortunate that there were video recorders in my era and that I should be very proud of what I had done in my career. Then I cried again.

Strach was brilliant. He was really respectful of the senior players and he was great to me. Although I spent most of the season injured, he always asked how I was and tried to gee me up by telling me I would get a chance as soon as I was fit. It's a real shame I didn't get to play more under him because he was a top manager. I liked him as a player and as a character, and I was touched that he tried to do the right thing by me – even if it didn't

DELGADO'S NICKNAME WAS THE TIN MAN, PROBABLY BECAUSE HE HAD NO HEART.

quite work out. He put me on the bench for the final league game of the 2001–02 season at home to Newcastle. I wasn't fit enough to start and, being honest, probably wasn't fit enough to be a sub, but we were safe from the threat of relegation. The intention was to give me the last 15 minutes, just so I could say a proper goodbye and maybe – just maybe – sign off with one last goal. But events made it impossible for him to do that.

First of all Marian Pahars got injured – there's a shock. Jo Tessem came on, so that was one sub down. Then Tahar El Khalej got himself sent off. It was one of the clearest red cards you could ever wish to see as he took a long run-up and launched himself into a flying tackle to bring down Kieron Dyer who looked likely to miss the World Cup Finals as a result. It was a horrendous tackle and I knew it was going to be very difficult for Gordon to put me on with the team down to 10 men. I was always the one taken off when we were a man short – and that was when I was fully fit. We were leading 2–1 at the time and then Anders Svensson picked up a knock with 25 minutes to go. There was no way I could have lasted 25 minutes. My calf had only just recovered and, although it might have held up, the manager couldn't take that chance. With £500,000 a place in prize money, Gordon couldn't take any risks – and I don't blame him. We ended up winning 3–1 which lifted us from fifteenth to eleventh and made the club a lot of money. I certainly don't hold it against him for not putting me on. It could have cost us the match, or my calf could have gone and I'd have missed my own testimonial a few days later.

By a quirk of fate, Paul Telfer got the sort of goal which had been my trademark. I've no idea where it came from because he wasn't noted for his goalscoring, but he hit a superb 35-yard dipping volley in the last minute. If I'd been on the field it might well have fallen to me, but it is no good thinking about what might have been. At least I'd got that last goal at The Dell. And now I had a chance to say a proper goodbye at my testimonial a couple of days later.

It was a superb and very emotional evening for me with a great turn out by all the lads. It was Saints v England and I played one half for each. I wanted the crowd to be entertained so I asked former team-mates like Alan Shearer, Tim Flowers and Neil Ruddock as well as some of those I had played alongside for England including Paul Gascoigne, Chris Waddle and Peter Beardsley. And there were England legends Stuart Pearce and Kevin Keegan. It would have been very easy for them to have said no or to have made an excuse, but they all made a fantastic effort to come. All my former managers wrote tributes in my match brochure – with the notable exception of Glenn Hoddle. And Ronnie Ekelund flew in all the way from California because I wanted to play alongside him for one last time. That made the night even more special. And, as the finishing touch, my brothers got themselves fit. Kevin and Carl both played while Mark refereed. And then, totally unplanned, my son Mitchell decided he wanted to play. He was only 10 but when he saw the game wasn't that serious he asked if he could come on as a sub. A lot of youngsters would have been scared, especially in that company and in front of a capacity crowd of 32,000, but he was fearless and showed a lot of confidence, even a touch of arrogance. I wonder where he gets that from?

One of the funniest moments came when a penalty was awarded and Ian Wright tried to help Mitchell by putting the ball on the six-yard line. Mitchell was having none of it. He put the ball on the proper spot and stepped up cool as you like to fire it right into the corner of the net. I couldn't have been more proud. I'm not sure Neil Moss would have saved it even if he had dived the right way. The crowd loved it and chanted, 'Sign him up!'

It finished 9–9, Carl scored a couple, Kevin got one and one of the ball boys scored after being sent on by Kevin Keegan.

At the final whistle they set up a video montage of some of my best goals set to Frank Sinatra singing 'My Way'. I told the fans, 'I always did things My Way – but I like to think I also did them Your Way.' It was off the cuff but I was quite proud of those words which struck a real chord with the supporters.

I didn't know that montage was going to be shown and I stood in the centre circle welling up with Mitchell by my side and Keeleigh in my arms. It was a really emotional moment not just for me but for the whole crowd. Many people have asked how I held it all together. That was down to Keeleigh. She was only six so she had hardly seen me play because Cathy and I had divorced when she was two, and injuries meant I didn't play a lot during the years when she was old enough to watch me. She was glued to the screen as I started to fill up. I was just about to break down when she said, 'Daddy, you were quite good when you were little.' You couldn't have scripted that. I realized I had put on a bit of weight but that was priceless!

It is fair to say my weight fluctuated over the years – but never more so than then. I was weighed as normal the day before the Newcastle match. I was 14 stone. I weighed myself on the morning of the testimonial, three days later, and was 14 and a half stone. Even by my standards that was pretty good going. Within two months of my retirement, I had put on two stone.

FROM FINAL
TO FARCE

'JUST MY LUCK. I GIVE MY ALL TO THIS CLUB FOR 16 YEARS
AND THEY REACH THE SODDING CUP FINAL THE YEAR AFTER
I RETIRED. I WONDER IF THE TWO ARE CONNECTED?'

I must admit it hurt like hell when Saints reached the 2003 FA Cup
Final against Arsenal, the first season after I retired. It was Sod's Law
it'd happen the moment I packed up.

It had been another good solid season under Gordon Strachan
who assembled a good unit of quality players. And they also had the
luck of the draw. They were drawn at home to a disinterested Spurs
side in the third round and won easily 4–0 – and did not face any
Premiership opposition again until the final. Strach ensured there were
no slip-ups against Millwall, Norwich, Wolves and Watford.

The final at Cardiff was a real bitter-sweet occasion for me. I was
working for Sky and the atmosphere was absolutely incredible. I know
pundits often say that – in fact Chris Kamara says it every game – but
this really was something else. I reckon the whole of Southampton
must have been in Wales that day. One end of the stadium was a

great wall of yellow. With the roof closed the noise was deafening and I'd have given anything for one last match. There was a real lump in my throat but I managed to hold it all together until the pre-match show went to the adverts just before kick-off. I went out and stood on the balcony as 'Abide With Me' was played. Tears were in my eyes. I was so proud of the team and the fans but I was also sad, not just for myself but for Francis Benali and Jason Dodd who'd also spent so many years at the club but had to miss out on the big one through injury. And my big mate Claus Lundekvam almost missed out on the final even though he played. He was very nearly sent off in the first minute when he clearly fouled Thierry Henry in the box. It should have been a penalty and a red card but, to his great credit, Thierry stayed on his feet allowing the referee to play the advantage. It was not exactly a classic final and Saints lost 1–0 but … what an achievement.

With Arsenal qualifying for the Champions League, it meant Southampton were guaranteed a UEFA Cup place whatever the result of the final. Things were looking up. And at Christmas 2003 they were in fourth place in the Premiership – yes, fourth place. And on merit. No one seriously thought they would actually qualify for the Champions League but nor did anyone foresee a cataclysmic decline. That began when Gordon Strachan abruptly left in February 2004. The whole thing was a shambles, badly handled from start to finish. Gordon had planned to go quietly at the end of the season but it was leaked to a national paper who plastered it all over the back page. That put Gordon and the club in a very difficult position.

As I've said, his hip operation sounded a bit strange. Whatever the real reason, Gordon had given Rupert Lowe plenty of notice about his intention to go at the end of his contract, giving Saints plenty of time to find the right replacement. But when the news leaked out it created a problem. It undermined the manager's authority in the dressing room. He could no longer shout at players because they'd just turn round and say your opinion doesn't count, you won't be here much longer. It meant, in effect, that Gordon had to go almost immediately. There was a lot of tension and stress around the club and among the fans – heightened by reports that Rupert was lining up a sensational return for Glenn Hoddle.

If you think that the departure of Dave Jones was handled badly, I believe Rupert made an even bigger mess of this one. The Hoddle story split the supporters right down the middle. A few were prepared to forgive and forget his quick exit to Spurs but most didn't want him back at any price. It showed how out of touch Rupert was with the fans. He thought he could just re-appoint Glenn and everything would be sweetness and light. I must admit I didn't think he deserved a second chance with Saints. How could we be sure he wouldn't do exactly the same thing again if another bigger club came calling?

IF YOU THINK THAT THE DEPARTURE OF DAVE JONES WAS HANDLED BADLY, I BELIEVE RUPERT MADE AN EVEN BIGGER MESS OF THIS ONE.

The only way Glenn could have come back was with a touch of humility. But that was not in his nature. He needed to apologize to the fans, say he'd made a dreadful mistake and promise to be fully committed to the club. But I could not see him doing that. Rupert wanted to press ahead regardless, but some of the board were wary of losing the fans' goodwill and they abandoned the plan. After that Rupert just made one mistake after another. First Steve Wigley took over briefly as caretaker manager before Paul Sturrock was unveiled as the new boss. I think Rupert hoped it would be another appointment in the Dave Jones mould, and there was no doubt he'd done well to take Plymouth from the bottom of League Two to the threshold of the Championship. I didn't know him as a person but I am in favour of giving a chance to managers doing well in the lower leagues, so I definitely felt it was a good move.

Paul was a decent guy and he knew the game but he didn't look like a Premier League manager. It seemed a bit much for him. His comfort zone was in the lower leagues, and he proved that when he eventually returned to Plymouth and did very well again. Some people just suit certain clubs. But Paul did not help himself. He was forever going back to Plymouth and talking about Plymouth. In pre-season, he took the players for a week to a training camp in Austria and then immediately to Sweden for some friendlies. The lads hadn't seen their families for almost a fortnight by the time they got back and thought they'd get a day off. But the next friendly was away to Plymouth, and Paul wanted his new team to put on a good show so he ordered the lads in for two days of training followed by an overnight stay. Before the match he was given a massive welcome on the pitch while our lads stood sweltering in the tiny tunnel on a baking hot day. They lost 3–1 and I suspect it was a bit of a two-finger job. Then they gave a shocking display at Villa on the opening day and Sturrock went by mutual consent. I think he knew things weren't right and he was struggling to cope with the pressure.

Steve Wigley again stepped in and everyone assumed he was the caretaker – until he announced he had got the job. I'm not entirely sure that was what Rupert planned. His endorsement seemed less than whole-hearted and no one really knew what was going on. Steve is a lovely guy and a good coach but, like Stuart Gray before him, he found it very difficult to step up from being the players' friend to their boss. His team selections were sometimes puzzling to say the least, particularly his exclusion of summer signing Peter Crouch, who is a much better footballer than he is often given credit for. Coming from Villa I think he was tarred with the same brush as their previous lanky striker, Ian Ormondroyd, who was just gangly. But Crouchy can really play. He is probably not quite as good in the air as he should be for a man of 6ft 7in, but he is much better on the ground than his frame suggests.

Things went from bad to worse under Wigs and, eventually, the club was forced to make yet another change – and nobody saw this one coming. Of all the managers to walk through the door, the last person I expected was Harry Redknapp. He'd left our big rivals Pompey just a couple of weeks earlier, but that wasn't the biggest reason I was taken aback. He just never struck me as Rupert's type. Rupert is like a city toff, full of himself to the point of arrogance while Harry is what Rupert would call 'old football'. He is down-to-earth, a man of the people, a bit of a wide boy and a wheeler-dealer who knows the game, and I thought it was a good appointment. With all his experience I thought he'd have enough about him to get the club out of trouble. We were third from bottom but I was confident he'd sort it out.

I don't think Rupert ever wanted Harry but he was over-ruled by the board. The two of them were like chalk and cheese and they were never going to hit it off. The thing about Harry is you have to let him do things his way. Sometimes that means turning a blind eye to the way he works; you just let him get on with it. What you can't do is tie him down and tell him how to operate. If you want someone just to coach the players and do things strictly by the book then get a Glenn Hoddle. Harry is a law unto himself – but he gets the job done. If he had been allowed to do that then I think he'd have kept Saints up. But it was clear that he hated the environment and having to work with

Rupert. He said all the right things publicly but his body language said something else.

The opening game set the pattern. Saints were 2–0 up at home to Middlesbrough on 90 minutes but only drew 2–2. If the game had gone on another minute, they'd have lost. It was a real body blow after the team had played so well. A major problem that season was the injury to Michael Svensson, who battled hard for years in a bid to recover before finally conceding defeat and hanging up his boots at the end of the 2008–09 season. He was a top, top player, a fantastic centre-back who won everything in the air and was a perfect partner for Claus Lundekvam who struggled without him. Harry brought in Calum Davenport but he did not look very confident at that stage of his career. He has improved since then but he had a shocking time with us. Harry also brought in Henri Camara who started well but faded, as he tends to do. He signed Nigel Quashie who gave the midfield more bite, and he brought Peter Crouch into the side. But it was not enough. The writing was on the wall as the team raced into a 3–0 lead at home to Aston Villa but in the end could only draw 3–3. We were still in with a chance of survival on the final day – and being brutally honest we should have stayed up.

Our fate was not in our own hands. If Norwich won, we were down. But they lost by six at Fulham. All we had to do was win at home to Manchester United. That was not as tough as it sounds. They had nothing to play for and had the FA Cup Final the following week, and gave a very half-hearted display. They were there for the taking. Saints teams of old would have got stuck in and rattled them with a few meaty challenges but there was nothing. At half-time it was 1–1 and I actually wondered if there was an unspoken agreement that we would not injure any of their players before the Cup Final if they went easy. It was like a training match for them because they missed countless chances with half-hearted finishing. And we never got at them. In the end they pretty much put us out of our misery with a second goal, and the game just petered out.

That was the saddest thing of all. When I looked back to all our Great Escapes and the effort and passion, when relegation did finally happen we went down so tamely without a fight. That was unforgivable, and that hurt more than anything. That would never have happened with the likes of Francis Benali, Jason Dodd, Tommy Widdrington and Neil Maddison. It was scandalous.

But if I had been stunned by the arrival of Harry Redknapp, the next twist left me utterly gobsmacked. Even allowing for the fact that Saints had turned into a soap opera, no one could see this one coming. A scriptwriter would have rejected it as totally implausible. Rupert, in his wisdom, appointed as Technical Director Sir Clive Woodward. That's right, the man who led England to World Cup glory – at rugby. A man with a wealth of experience and knowledge ... none of it in football.

But look at the context. Relegation had cost the club £50m so it just didn't have the money to make quirky appointments. All the available cash should have been directed at getting us back in to the Premier League. Then you bring in extra backroom staff and improve the gym. Ted Bates, in his wisdom, used to say, 'You win nothing with bricks and mortar.' He was so right. All the money should have been channelled into bringing in players who would get us promoted. Instead Rupert was star-struck by Sir Clive and by the idea of revolutionizing the game. All the values which had served the club so well for so many years were dismissed out of hand as 'old football', and he opted instead for Sir Clive and the likes of Simon Clifford who was so far up his own backside that he needed a glass bellybutton to see out. He came from the mighty Gosforth Town, a non-league club that he'd pledged to take to the Premier League within 10 years. That was in

2005. He will have to go some. Last time I looked they were towards the bottom of the second tier of the Unibond League, five divisions away from the Premier League.

Bringing in Simon Clifford was one of Clive's biggest mistakes. He came in with a big ego and inflated ideas of his own importance, all through making his name from Soccertots coaching courses. Dealing with hardened experienced pros was totally different. He had no real experience of the game at the top level but talked like he was God's gift. Clive brought in other medical and coaching staff, instantly alienating many of the club stalwarts who had been there for years, important people who knew and understood the players. Clive did do some good things and left a legacy of improved training and medical facilities, it's just that Saints couldn't afford it. The money should have gone on players. His offhand manner also rubbed people up the wrong way and, of course, his very presence made the club a laughing stock. If Clive had stuck to the sports science it wouldn't have been so bad, but it worried me when I heard him say he wanted to be a top football manager and that his ultimate ambition was now to win the World Cup for England at football. To be fair, he couldn't have done much worse than Steve McClaren.

So, you had Sir Clive Woodward with all his forward-thinking emphasis on sports science sharing an office with Harry Redknapp, a

> **CLIVE DID DO SOME GOOD THINGS AND LEFT A LEGACY OF IMPROVED TRAINING AND MEDICAL FACILITIES, IT'S JUST THAT SAINTS COULDN'T AFFORD IT.**

traditional old-fashioned football man. I'd have loved to have been a fly on the wall in that office when they were together – and it was only for a few months – or to have witnessed one infamous meeting which degenerated into a slanging match. I heard it was straight out of the school playground with Rupert and Harry going toe to toe, yelling, 'Eff off!' 'No, you eff off!' 'No, YOU eff off.'

But Sir Clive did try to get me onto the coaching staff. He wanted me to coach the club's strikers from the youth side to the first-team. I had Sky commitments but I was definitely interested. I thought I could work around those and come in Monday to Friday and then see whether I was needed on match days. Clive was keen on the idea and told me to meet Rupert to arrange financial terms. The only question was whether the package would compensate for my loss of earnings with Sky.

And what was I offered? Rupert offered me less for working five or six days a week than Sky were paying me to work five or six days *a month*. I heard afterwards that he thought it was very reasonable for someone with no experience. Obviously 17 years playing in the top flight didn't count. In fact the money wasn't really an issue for me – but the amount being offered did tell me exactly what Rupert thought of the idea. He didn't want me working at the club. It would have been a huge PR coup for him but either he saw me as a threat or feared I might take away some of his glory. Or maybe he still had a grudge because I'd publicly said that Glenn Hoddle should not get the job when Gordon Strachan left.

Anyway, by December 2005 Harry couldn't take any more. You could see from his body language that he'd had enough. He quit to return to Pompey, remarkably. You couldn't make it up. You would've got good odds against that happening but it left us looking for a ninth manager in nine years under Rupert.

Francis Benali and I had long discussions with Sir Clive Woodward about the idea of our taking over as a managerial partnership. We had a very serious meeting with him at his flat in Bassett and spoke in depth about the job. I think he wanted to be manager with Franny and me as coaches, but neither of us were happy with that. I suggested it would be better if he was Director of Football with me and Franny as managers. Clive was all for it and phoned Rupert to get the ball rolling. But we did not get a call, let alone an interview. He felt it would be wrong to employ someone with no coaching badges.

In fact I did start taking my coaching badges but I thought they were a complete waste of time. They were designed for novices, not players who had been at the top of the game for 17 years. The Level 2 badge was incredibly simplistic. I was being told how to teach someone to pass the ball 10ft with their side foot. If that was Level 2, what was Level 1? The only possible reason I could see for those courses was that they're a massive cash cow for the FA. They must rake in a fortune from them. It costs thousands to get your Pro Licence. And it certainly has not helped us find an English manager for the national team. Steve McClaren was a disaster, another example of what happens when you promote from within on the cheap. Thankfully Fabio Capello is doing well, considering he looks like Postman Pat.

At that time, I would have fancied a crack at coaching because the club had fallen so quickly. I did not think things could possibly get any worse. We were two thirds of the way down the table when Harry left so I thought it was a chance to do something about it. Management had not really appealed until then but, suddenly, I was up for it. I had seen the decline and I wanted to make MY club better. I wouldn't have been interested in managing anywhere else or working my way up through the lower leagues – far too much like hard work. But the chance to help Southampton was very tempting and for Rupert not even to reply to us showed just what he thought of us, and of the fans who'd have loved it. Instead he appointed George Burley, 24 hours after appearing to offer the job to a Dutch unknown by the name of Mark Wotte.

There was a huge clear-out of players but George kept us clear of relegation trouble though there was increasing unrest on the terraces culminating in a revolution which ousted the board. The problem was that the chairman had alienated the fans so much that there was now a mood for Anyone But Rupert. So what happened? A tax exile in Jersey by the name of Michael Wilde bought a large chunk of shares, including a substantial number from existing board members. That enabled him to call an Extraordinary General Meeting to vote out Rupert and the rest of the board – at least those who did not switch allegiance to his camp. Michael didn't have quite enough shares to oust Rupert on his own, and he needed the support of local business-man Leon Crouch who was temporarily cast in the role of Kingmaker.

Mike needed to win the PR war so he dipped into the club's heritage and recruited Lawrie McMenemy and Mary Corbett, the daughter of former club president John Corbett who had kept the club going when it faced financial meltdown after the war. He'd paid the players' wages out of his own pocket and, in the Sixties, with remark-able foresight, bought a seemingly worthless piece of land just outside the city. Jacksons Farm would now be worth millions if planning permission were ever granted for housing. So, property developer and Liverpool supporter Michael Wilde, what attracted you to Southampton Football Club?

I like Michael but I have to say he did not do a great job with the people he brought in to run the club – with the notable of exception of Lee Hoos, who is now chief executive at Leicester. Because

Michael did not have any experience of operating a football club he brought in Jim Hone as chief executive. In addition they brought in Ken Dulieu who was supposed to be a non-executive chairman for the PLC board. But that soon became a salaried executive role with expenses that would make an MP blush. Likewise, I gather Jim Hone lived in the De Vere hotel for several months when he arrived at the club. Rupert Lowe and Andrew Cowen received pay-offs when they were ousted. Eventually, Hone, Dulieu and Hoos were kicked out in the next power struggle so they all got pay-offs – on top of their big salaries. Then we wonder why we had no money. I must be the only person in Saints' recent history to leave the club and not receive a penny for going.

Meanwhile, it was becoming increasingly unpleasant behind the scenes with so many power struggles that I never knew who was speaking to whom. In a nutshell there were two boards – the PLC board of the holding company and the football club board. At the start, the power was held by the non-executives and two share-holders, Michael Wilde and Leon Crouch. But, almost by stealth, the executives increased their power base. The balance of power shifted and they forced Michael Wilde out on the basis that he had not delivered the investment he had promised when he took over the club. The sole business plan seemed to be to gamble on spending a lot of money they did not have on buying players to win promotion. But when that failed, there was no plan B.

Saints did reach the 2007 play-offs to get back into the Premier League but lost to Derby on penalties. After going down 2–1 at St Mary's the team produced an awesome display to win 3–2 at Pride Park. This is about the only competition where away goals don't count double so it went to spot-kicks and, again, I would have given anything to have been able to take one. We had massive away support and transformed one end of the ground into a wall of yellow, showing once again what a great fan base there is at this club. But Derby won and then beat West Brom in the final to reach the top flight, only to bomb out abysmally being relegated with a record low number of points. That hit Saints hard because it meant the club now lost the parachute payment which had effectively sustained it for two years. The board had to scrape around to try and find investment, something none of its members had been expecting to do when they came in.

The big problem now was all that in-fighting and backbiting meant that no serious investor would touch the club. By all accounts Paul Allen, one of the co-founders of Microsoft and one of the world's richest men, was interested in coming in but he took one look at all the political wrangling and backed off sharply. The best offer the board could attract was from the Hedge Fund SISU, which ended up taking over at Coventry. I think that is the only time that Rupert Lowe (who was still a sizeable shareholder),

I THINK THE CLUB HAS HAD QUITE ENOUGH SELF-SATISFIED, ARROGANT, EGOTISTICAL SMUGNESS TO LAST A LIFETIME.

Michael Wilde and Leon Crouch have ever been on the same side when they all voted against it. That led to Jim Hone, Ken Dulieu, Commercial Director Andy Oldknow (now back at the club as Chief Operating Officer) and Lee Hoos walking off into the sunset with handsome settlements while Leon Crouch stepped in as chairman.

Leon is a true Saints supporter, someone who makes decisions based on what is best for the club rather than for his own pocket. He might not have the polish of Rupert Lowe but his heart is in the right place. He's a bit rough and ready but I think the club has had quite enough self-satisfied, arrogant, egotistical smugness to last a lifetime. And unlike Lowe and Wilde who merely spent money on shares, he put his own cash into the club. I believe that at the first board meeting after Michael Wilde came in, Leon said he would put a million in if the others did the same. It went very quiet. More recently he has kept the club alive by paying the monthly wage bill to the tune of £1m.

When he took over as chairman at the turn of 2008, it seemed the club at last had someone in charge who was prepared to make decisions for the good of the club. The biggest of those was the appointment of a new manager after George Burley was lured away to become manager of the Scotland team. I think that was something which suited both parties. George could not turn down such a great opportunity and, by then, his body language was suggesting that he'd had enough of the bickering at the Southampton circus. Saints got some compensation and made a fresh start. They bought time with the caretaker pairing of John Gorman and Jason Dodd, but a shocking 1–0 FA Cup defeat at Bristol Rovers showed it was not working and Leon Crouch took swift and decisive action. He brought in Nigel Pearson who immediately won over everyone at the club with his strong, likeable personality, commonsense and knowledge of the game. He was a breath of fresh air and for once it seemed as though everything was geared up for a bright future.

He used his contacts in the game to bring in some good loan signings and he instilled a real fighting spirit and togetherness in the players – and the stadium staff loved him. To his eternal credit he led the team to another last-day escape from relegation. I really thought those days had gone, the moment we were relegated to the Championship. Never in my darkest nightmares did I think we would be battling to avoid the drop to League 1.

I was in the Sky studio and went through hell on that final day at home to Sheffield United. We had to win and hope other results went our way. It was a real rollercoaster of emotion that afternoon as Saints went behind but fought back to take the lead only for the Blades to level. Remarkably Stern John put us back in front before being sent off. It was a horribly tense finale knowing that if we conceded or Leicester scored at Stoke we'd be down. But we got away with it and the future looked rosy. We had a passionate, committed, caring chairman and a knowledgeable, respected, talented manager ... what could go wrong now?

Re enter Rupert. Of all the episodes in the Saints soap opera, this probably surprised me most. Forget Bruce Grobbelaar being charged with match-fixing, Dave Jones being wrongly accused of child abuse and Harry Redknapp arriving and leaving – they were nothing compared to this bizarre alliance. Michael Wilde – the man who spent around £3m of his own money specifically to get rid of Rupert Lowe – suddenly teamed up with him to get rid of Leon Crouch. You couldn't make it up. Between them they had enough shares to regain control of the club. And since Nigel Pearson had been a Leon Crouch appointment, he was never going to last.

He must have known the writing was on the wall when Rupert rejoined. This is Southampton and one of the reasons we got into such a mess was that we'd had eight managers in 10 years under Rupert Lowe. So what is the first thing he does when he returns to the club? He gets rid of the manager. Brilliant. Not just any manager but the best manager we'd had for some time.

Rupert said he had to cut costs but getting rid of a quality manager and bringing in a couple of Dutch guys who did not know the Championship wasn't just a false economy, it was crazy. Yes, their combined wages were less than Nigel's but he had indicated he would take a pay cut. If Nigel Pearson had stayed I'm sure we would not have been relegated.

22

LOWE DOWN

NEVER IN MY WORST NIGHTMARES DID I EVER THINK WE WOULD DROP INTO LEAGUE 1 ....

Having overseen Saints's relegation once, Rupert Lowe forced his way back into the club and did it *again*. What on earth possessed him to return? He says it was because he loved the club and wanted to help – but to my mind the best way that he could have helped was by staying away.

We'd just found a bit of stability after a couple of traumatic and turbulent years. In Leon Crouch we had a chairman who was a bit rough and ready, and quite impulsive. He let his heart rule his head. But that heart was definitely in the right place. He cared deeply about Saints and was probably the only chairman I have known who has actually put his own money into the club. Even in the Spring and Summer of 2009 he persistently put his hand in his pocket to bail out the club, and without his major contribution Saints probably wouldn't exist any more. I don't think the fans really know the full extent of his generosity. He even got the support of the bank, engaging with them amicably (not arrogantly), and was well liked by the club's staff because he talked to them on their level. For all his wealth, he had the common touch and he didn't talk down to people or at them.

We also had a top manager in Nigel Pearson, who was popular with everyone at the club. The finances weren't great, but everyone was pulling in the same direction. Then Rupert's return caused a massive upheaval. It looked like he was on a personal quest – and had a few old scores to settle. I know there were some staff, not on the football side, who feared for their jobs when they heard he was back. And, yes, they were among those made redundant. They were good people, long-serving employees who had worked above and beyond their job description because they loved the club and were determined to help it succeed. I know the finances dictated that cut-backs had to be made, but there are decent ways of doing it.

On the football side, it looked to me as though Nigel didn't keep his job simply because he was a Leon Crouch appointment. Rupert had obviously previously thought about bringing in Dutch coaches and now saw his chance. Though Jan Poortvliet and Mark Wotte were on lower wages than Nigel Pearson they can't have been that much cheaper, especially as a large chunk of Nigel's salary was a bonus for saving the team from relegation. Talk about a false economy. And what's the point if it all ends in relegation and costs the club a heck of a lot more in the long run?

Jan would be the first to admit he was surprised to get the job, and he was so desperate to take it that he paid his own compensation to leave Helmond Sport. I've never known a manager do that before. That left Rupert in a stronger position to implement his own ideas. I think he had long favoured the kind of continental structure where the club president signs the players and employs someone to coach them. How many British managers can you think of who'd accept that system?

He also took great pride in the Academy which he set up, though I think that Lawrie McMenemy might argue that he had created a pretty good youth system which produced the likes of Mike Channon, Steve Moran, the Wallaces, Alan Shearer and myself among others. Anyway, Rupert thought that playing the youngsters was the way ahead and he made a point of telling people they'd rip through the division. And they did, straight out the bottom. In fact when Rupert told me his plans at the start of the season, he said he thought the kids were good enough to make the play-offs. But whatever their individual strengths, collectively they just weren't up to it. They gave everything and put up a real fight but you can't field seven or eight youngsters each week and expect consistent performances. There's too much pressure. If you're going to blood kids then you slip them into the team, say one or two at a time, and let them gradually learn from the more experienced players. And to make things worse, the new manager didn't know the division. The Championship is a very physical league and you simply can't play 'total football'. The nail in the coffin was the very poor scouting system. How could a foreign manager who didn't know the English game (a) find new players and (b) know the best way of playing the opposition? He didn't know enough about them.

I realize we had to unload some of the higher earners, either permanently or on loan, but we shipped out Stern John who had been among the division's top scorers the previous season and Grzegorz Rasiak, a proven marksman, and so of course we struggled for goals. You could see early in the season that we were heading for relegation, but nothing changed. It was as though it would have been an admission of failure to start using more experienced players.

To this day Rupert seems to have absolved himself of the blame but, as the person at the top, he *has* to take most of the blame. He was there for longest and, from the moment Gordon Strachan left, everything started to unravel. It was a mistake to appoint Steve Wigley and then to replace him with Harry Redknapp and not let him manage his way and bring in Clive Woodward when the club couldn't afford it. Then in came Michael Wilde but he didn't deliver and was forced out. The new board promptly rejected a potential take-over from SISU. But why? SISU took over at Coventry and look where they are. Saints would jump at the chance to be in Coventry's position.

Leon Crouch tried to steady the ship but made the mistake of not involving Michael who, as the largest shareholder, still held a lot of power. To be fair, neither Leon nor anyone else could ever have envisaged that Michael and Rupert would actually team up. And the downfall of the club lies mostly in the boardroom politics – the egos, the infighting, vindictiveness and petty bickering. But the various managers also have to take some blame because they are the ones who picked the team – with the possible exception of Jan Poortvliet. And you can't forget the players who failed to perform, particularly against Manchester United who were well below their best and there for the taking on the day when we were relegated in 2005.

Never in my worst nightmares did I think we would drop into League 1, especially after the narrow escape when Nigel Pearson kept us up. I thought that that'd be a great wake-up call, but in 2008–09 we lurched from disaster to disaster, culminating in administration and a 10-point deduction by the Football League. They automatically impose that penalty on any club going into administration. If it happens before the last Thursday in March then the points are lost immediately; if the club goes into administration after that date then the points are deducted at the end of the season if they avoid relegation. If they go down anyway then the penalty takes effect at the start of the following campaign. It's a strange rule, a case of having your cake and eating it. But then the Football League are a law unto themselves.

Like most Saints fans I breathed a sigh of relief when this year's deadline passed. All season there had been talk of financial troubles so I kept an anxious eye on Sky's *Sports News* on Thursday March 26 waiting to see if there was any announcement. I thought maybe things were not as bad as everyone said as the deadline came and went. But within a week it all kicked off. The club didn't go into administration but its holding company did. Technically that shouldn't have brought a 10-point deduction because the Football League's own rules state that that deduction only applies to clubs and *not* their parent company. But the penalty was imposed, condemning us to certain relegation and the possibility of starting the 2009 season with a 10-point handicap. Even now I can't understand why Rupert waited until a few days *after* the deadline to place the company In administration. He must have known the finances were shocking. It would have been better to take the hit and start the next

RUPERT SEEMS TO HAVE ABSOLVED HIMSELF OF THE BLAME BUT, AS THE PERSON AT THE TOP, HE HAS TO TAKE MOST OF THE BLAME.

season with a clean slate. I can see that he thought we might stay up but that was a hell of a gamble. He was risking the future of the club. I know he was trying to secure more funding and seemed confident he could get it, but it was never going to be easy in the Credit Crunch. I couldn't see any reason why he didn't take the 10-point deduction a week earlier. I could see then that we were going to get relegated.

And what happened? We dropped into the third tier of English football for the first time in 50 years, Rupert and the other directors resigned and the whole future of the club was plunged into uncertainty. At that point I was like any other fan. I watched from the outside, helpless and desperately worried. Then, at the end of April, I got a call from a good friend, Tony Lynam. He popped round for a cup of tea and told me he was putting together a consortium and asked if I'd be interested in a place on the board if he could find the right backer. I told him I'd do anything to help the club, and left him to do all the hard work. Only 'hard' isn't the word for it.

Tony worked *tirelessly* for the Pinnacle group, doing long, silly hours because it was such a complex deal and there were so many stumbling blocks. But time was against us and the situation became even more serious when the players and staff weren't paid in May. Leon Crouch again put his hand in his pocket to pay them for a second successive month, which bought us more time. Meanwhile, other groups became interested and it all got very hectic, but a £500,000 non-refundable deposit secured us a three-week exclusivity to do due diligence and complete the deal. At that point I thought we had crossed the line. I was ready to give up my job at Sky and my after-dinner speaking. Hell, I'd even have given up the occasional round of golf, that's how serious I was.

I spoke to the prospective new owner for the first time on June 8 and he seemed like a genuine bloke who'd got the bit between his teeth. He was happy to stay in the background and he wanted me to be chairman. That really took me aback. I'd always dreamed of being a footballer but I never thought I might one day be chairman. Many emotions raced through my mind but mainly panic. There was excitement at the challenge, worry about the insecurity and the pressure, confidence that I could make a difference and determination to show how the job should be done. I was flattered by the offer and by the reaction of the fans, who made it clear that they were right behind us.

I wasn't worried about them turning on me if things went badly because if I couldn't do the job properly I'd let someone else take over. I wouldn't arrogantly cling to power. And it was a big decision for me because I had such a good lifestyle. I had a steady, secure, one-day-a-week job with Sky which I really enjoyed. That was enough to finance my golf and other expenses. I even got a text from Phil Thompson saying, 'It's good for Saints but bad for us – honest!'

It seemed as though it was All Systems Go – until the Football League threw in a major obstacle. I think they realized they were on slightly dodgy ground with the 10-point deduction which, in my opinion, broke their own rules, so they tried to railroad it through. They said they would only approve the take-over and grant us a League licence if we confirmed in writing that we wouldn't appeal against the decision. But every club should have the right of appeal. The Football League exist for the interests and benefit of their members, and we were looking for help. We weren't asking for the 10 points back – just for the right to query the decision. Every other club losing points had been allowed to appeal, so why should we be treated any differently? The reason is they were scared of losing.

Their chairman Brian Mawhiney wouldn't bend and that was incredibly frustrating. I still resent the fact that he laughed during the Sky interview when he announced the 10-point penalty. I have never disliked a man I have never met as much as then. It was almost as though the Football League had their own little world of rules, exempt from the laws of the land. It was a case of 'These are our rules and this is how it is going to be.' That sort of arrogance drives me crackers, and it actually put me off wanting to be a chairman if it meant regularly dealing with people like that.

But I was so desperate to do the job that, in the end, I said to the rest of the Pinnacle group that we just had to bite the bullet and accept the points deduction. Eventually I talked them round, but the document presented by the Football League was something we just couldn't sign. It also revealed the possibility of future sanctions, including further points deductions. We couldn't be party to that. We had to pull out. And then the Football League promised there would be no further sanctions. Suddenly Pinnacle were back in the running but, by then, a Swiss consortium and another English group had made up ground and were rivalling us. In the end the Swiss group gained control. By all accounts, Markus Liebherr, the new owner, is pretty minted. The good thing is that the club was saved from going out of existence and hopefully Saints will at last find the stability that has eluded them for so long.

23

THEY THINK IT'S ALL OVER

'I SEEM TO HAVE WORKED HARDER IN RETIREMENT
THAN I EVER DID WHEN I WAS PLAYING.
THAT CAN'T BE RIGHT ...'

In the end I was actually quite looking forward to retirement. I knew I was going to miss playing and the day-to-day banter but the previous two or three years had been riddled with injury. Repeatedly trying to get back from one muscle strain, only for another to flare up in its place, really drained my enthusiasm. The medical room and the gym were never my favourite places, and they sucked the energy out of me. I could no longer reach the heights I had previously done on the field, and I didn't want to take money under false pretences or to drop down the leagues with people turning out to see the name and not the player. A lot of my former teammates finished up with a couple of low-key seasons at nearby Bournemouth, but that wasn't for me. I only ever wanted to play in the top division and I am proud of that record. I didn't mind people teasing me about my weight and being lazy, but I didn't want to become a figure of fun on the pitch.

I did do the *Match* on Sky1 where a team of ex-pros play against celebrities. It was good fun to have a kick-around in front of 50,000 but I was very disappointed I was only on the bench in the first series, especially as I had trained for a whole day beforehand. But £2,500 for two days work wasn't bad.

The following year was tougher; they wanted us for four days but they did increase the payment to £10,000 so I was well up for that. I even ran about in training and was rewarded with a starting place. But it all went wrong just after half-time when I again made the mistake of venturing into my own penalty area. I'm not sure why, although a friend had pointed out beforehand that you'd get good odds on the celebrities scoring a penalty in the match. He suggested my tackling was so poor that no one would suspect anything if I mistimed a challenge in my own box. But after the spectacular failure of my betting scam against Wimbledon, I wasn't up for that and actually thought I might be able to help defend a corner. The ball was whipped in and smashed me straight in the face, exploded the end of my nose and blood burst everywhere. I needed treatment on the touchline but there was no way I was going off with a bloody nose, I'd never hear the end of it. The physio managed to stop the bleeding but, as I ran back on, I pulled a calf muscle and had to go off.

The after-match party was pretty good. I wasn't a great one for getting involved in drinking binges so I went and found a quiet seat on my own. I was soon joined by Robbie Williams, who came and sat on the floor next to me. I have a lot of time for him. I like his music and his attitude. He was a top man and we chatted for half an hour about football and music, although I'm not sure he shared my taste for Shakin' Stevens. I did go and see Take That in concert with two of my aunties and I must have been the only straight male there.

I enjoyed playing Masters football, the annual tournament on Sky for ex-pros aged 35 and over. We never did very well but I did have the distinction of being the first player ever to be sent off. We were playing Chelsea and, for some reason, our former defender Ken Monkou decided to turn out for them rather than us. I flicked the ball over his head and, as I went round him, he stuck out an arm and 'clothes-lined' me. My chin collided with his arm. It was the most blatant foul you could get but referee Kevin Lynch decided to wave play on. Given that it was a family event with lots of children in the crowd, I'm not proud to admit I forgot about the game and followed him all over the pitch questioning whether he had a father and making reference to his receding hairline. He didn't even send me to the sin bin. Straight red.

I also agreed to play for Eastleigh at non-league level, but that was more as a publicity stunt to help the club. I had a lot of friends there including several former teammates, so I signed on to help their profile. It came about after I agreed to play a one-off match at Andover. Eastleigh had already cruised the league title without me so it isn't as though they needed me, but their manager Paul Doswell explained that Andover were struggling and asked if I'd play to help them get a decent crowd. I agreed and sure enough they trebled their normal gate. I was expecting a low-key, easy night but after 10 minutes we had my former Southampton teammate Phil Warner sent off. That meant we were down to 10 men, one of whom was 16 stone and very out of condition. We lost 6–1.

Eastleigh's assistant manager was David Hughes, who had been a very promising, talented midfielder at The Dell. He could have been a first-team regular for many years but for a succession of injuries at a cruelly young age. Unlike some players he really battled to try and get fit enough for the Premier League but his body couldn't take it.

Honestly, if he was a horse, he'd have been shot. He persuaded me to sign on the following season to try and help kick the club forward, and I was just doing a mate a favour. It felt a bit weird but I didn't take it too seriously though I scored three goals in six games.

All the teams I played against were very respectful. Paul Doswell made sure he only picked me for matches against teams where most of their players were Saints fans so that no one would try to make a name by 'doing' me. That was the one thing I was wary of. There weren't many occasions as a pro when an opponent ever tried to injure me, but there were a couple of tackles that made me wonder. The former Pompey midfield hard-man Mick Kennedy trod on my ankle in a Simod Cup tie at Bradford, and Roy Keane caught me in a match at Old Trafford when I felt he wasn't going for the ball. It was quite early in his United career and I was in my own penalty area – God knows why. I cleared the ball and he came in late but it was right in front of the Stretford End so there was no chance of him getting booked. His studs connected with my shin after the ball had gone. Fortunately the shin pad did its job otherwise it could have been a leg-breaker. It taught me a lesson though – I stayed clear of my own penalty area after that.

I then played beach football for England, but hated it. It was nothing like proper football. You couldn't dribble, it took a lot of getting used to and was very hard work. Eric Cantona was the big star for the French team so the organizers set up a press conference with the two of us promoting the event. Being the true professional I am, I turned up at 10.55 for an 11am start. He sauntered in at 11.35 without a care in the world and sat down next to me. I sarcastically held up my wrist and pointed to my watch, expecting an apology but he didn't speak a word to me. He didn't even acknowledge my presence, the arrogant so-and-so. No wonder fans used to bait him to the point where he exploded and famously jumped into the crowd to kung-fu kick one of them.

Talking about abuse, I never took it personally. I was so laid-back it was water off a duck's back. I'd had all the jibes about having a big nose when I was at school so I was used to that. I took it that the fans saw me as a threat and were trying to get at me. And the more anyone tries to get to me, the less I let them. I used to laugh it off and would even share a joke with the fans. I remember sitting on a wall at Upton Park during a break in play, and having some banter with their supporters who had been taunting me about a story that I had been seen playing bingo with my mother-in-law.

THEIR SUPPORTERS HAD BEEN TAUNTING ME ABOUT A STORY THAT I HAD BEEN SEEN PLAYING BINGO WITH MY MOTHER-IN-LAW.

Radio 5 Live had done a phone-in asking people about the strangest place they'd ever seen a footballer, and someone kindly rang in to say they had seen me in a bingo hall in Southampton. It was true – and I did take my mother-in-law. She had recently lost her husband and was trying to get her life back. She liked a game of bingo so I offered to take her. I quite enjoyed it and went a few times. I didn't realize it would end up making headlines on the radio or that the Chicken Run at Upton Park would keep shouting 'Clickety-click 66'. But I did have the perfect retort because I told them I had won £100 which was a week's wages at the time.

Inevitably I also got a lot of abuse when I played in a testimonial for former Pompey striker Steve Claridge. He was playing for Millwall when he called to ask if I'd play in his benefit game. I said that was fine and count me in, and went to hang up but thought I'd better check where it was, expecting him to say the New Den. Instead he said it was at Fratton Park. If ever there was time I wanted to re-wind a conversation, that was it. So I thought I may as well have a bit of fun. I knew they'd make me wear a Pompey kit so I had my own Saints shirt made up with '7 Scummer' on the back, which was what Portsmouth fans called anyone who had even driven through Southampton.

I hid it in my kit bag until just before kick-off when I told Steve Claridge I had a little surprise lined up if he could make sure we got a penalty at the Fratton end where their hard-core fans were gathered. Sure enough we got a spot-kick and I sent the keeper the wrong way to score. The boos rang out as I ran to the side of the goal, and the jeers became even louder when I took off my Portsmouth shirt to reveal the red and white stripes – until I turned my back to let them read what I had put on the shirt. It seemed to go down really well. It gave everyone a laugh – and it meant I got out alive. I wasn't worried about it backfiring because I reckoned very few of them can read.

The day was good fun, their fans gave plenty of good-natured stick but they appreciated that I had been good enough to turn out. I was gutted not to score with a dipping 35 yard volley which hit the underside of the bar and bounced out. It was pretty special even by my standards. Within seconds the crowd were chanting, 'What the effing hell was that?' It was quite a sharp response, not what you normally associate with Pompey fans. In fact, if I ever win the lottery I'll buy Pompey. And if I get four numbers …

A lot of ex-players find there is a big void after they retire but that wasn't the case with me. I was awarded an honorary degree by Southampton University in 2004. I remember being very nervous having to make that speech to a group of students, most of whom had seen me propping up the bar at the local nightclubs when I was single. Then I had a pub named after me – Le Tissier's Feet. A lot of people thought it was mine and I had to spend a lot of time denying it because it wasn't the classiest establishment. The owner asked my permission and, as I lived 200 yards away at the time, I thought it would be quite funny to have my local named after me.

I was also awarded the Freedom of the City, although I have yet to take advantage of the fact I'm now allowed to drive my sheep through the city centre. And I loved doing a radio show for a year or so, being the DJ for the club's ill-fated radio station 'The Saint', one of Rupert Lowe's worst business decisions. I believe he bought it for £1m and sold it for £1 – the business equivalent of signing and selling Robbie Keane. It did provide me with one stand-out moment when I got to interview the music legend Chesney Hawkes whose only real hit, fittingly, was called 'The One and Only'. I love that song so much. It was quite an iconic song for me because it was used as the soundtrack for my greatest goals video. I was thrilled to meet him. He was a lovely bloke and very down to earth.

I remember one scam on 'The Saint', not quite on a par with the recent Ofcom voting and competition phone-in scandals, but I feel it's time to own up. Each week we used to give away two tickets to the next home match. In those days they were all sold out. I had promised a mate a couple of tickets but had forgotten to get them. So I told him the question in advance and got him to ring up with the right answer. Mind you, in those days the radio station was only on Sky digital so we only ever got half a dozen people calling in.

I was a club ambassador for Saints for the first year after I hung up my boots, which was really only a nominal title to keep me involved in the club. It was money for old rope because all I had to do was be a match day host and entertain the corporate guests, that's in the days when the club used to have them. Effectively I was paid £500 a match to have a posh meal, the perfect job. Maybe Rupert Lowe felt guilty about the way he had treated me because that was almost as much as I used to earn as a player. On second thoughts, perhaps not.

I did feel the club probably took advantage of me over the years, knowing that I didn't want to leave. From a business point of view I can understand it but when you consider what I did for the club, I do feel they could have offered me more generous terms. That wasn't just on the field but putting bums on seats and boosting merchandise sales. Some recognition would have been nice. And on top of that Francis Benali, Jason Dodd and I put a huge amount of time and effort into helping on the community side. If ever there was an event which needed attending at short notice, they always asked one of us. And we were happy to do it. Rupert Lowe certainly never invited me to be a special guest in the directors' box. That has only happened once since I retired when I was guest of honour for the England v Macedonia international at St Mary's. It was a huge honour to be asked by the FA to meet the teams.

It's worth adding that clubs do have a tendency to look after players who they've brought in rather better than their home-grown talent. I'm pretty sure that Mark Hughes was on a lot more than me, and he did far less for the club or the community than I ever did. Most of the time I didn't know what other players were on. It was only towards the end that I began to realize. Financially I would have been a lot better off if I had been more mercenary and a pain in the backside, but that isn't in my nature.

It made me laugh when people used to speculate about how much I was on with Saints because they were always way off the mark. I remember watching a *Sky Sports* feature on wages during the final year of my contract, and they estimated that after so long at the club

I had to be on about £25,000 a week.* I wish. I did well out of my testimonial, though, thanks to the efforts of my committee who really put in the hours. I probably netted about £650,000 which went to pay off my house in Guernsey and the legal costs of my divorce, which were over £100,000. That still rankles because it was need-less expenditure. It was money which would have been far better spent on the kids. I had to pay all my own expenses and half of my ex-wife's. At one point I was £105,000 overdrawn at the bank, which was an interesting position to be in.

Over the years I let quite a lot of money slip through my hands but the bank was brilliant. It knew I was going to get my testimonial cash. The manager understood football and my situation. He was on my committee as treasurer so he knew better than anyone what was coming in. That was in the days when banks used to give credit. I'm not sure they would be so understanding now.

---

* To give you an idea how bad I was at money, I bought my first house in the late Eight-ies for £62,000 and sold it a year later for £45,000 because I wanted more space. I bought a three-bedroom place for £105,000 and then sold it for £87,000. I must be the only property tycoon to start at the top and work his way down. There was a lot of negative equity around at the time but I had been advised to invest in bricks and mortar so I did. After that, I thought I'd play safe – so I bought a nightclub! And when I was offered a new contract in my last season, in 2001, it was worth a maximum of £3,450 a week, good money by most people's standards but not then in the Premier League. Hassan Kachloul had been on around half that, but when he was out of contract he turned down an offer from Saints of £14,000 per week, describing it as an insult. I wish someone had insulted me like that. In fact they could have been really rude and offered me just £7,000 a week. Instead Hassan agreed to sign for Ipswich for around £24,000 and then changed his mind and went to Villa for £28,000 a week. He played the first half of the next season until a change of manager meant he fell out of favour and he sat in the Reserves on a huge salary for two and a half years.

I still get offers of work, and thankfully I don't have to accept the less attractive ones, like *I'm a Celebrity Get Me Out of Here*. The money on offer was nowhere near enough for a fortnight of hell, suffering such revolting creatures. But enough about Ant and Dec. Even a million pounds wouldn't have got me in the jungle eating fat live maggots with bulging eyes and disgusting bodily parts. I didn't spend a lifetime eating burgers and chips only to go and lose it all on starvation rations.

I did speak to the producers about doing *Celebrity Big Brother*. I was quite interested in doing that, and we even had a meeting in my agent's office. I thought it would be quite nice to sit around doing nothing for a couple of weeks and getting paid for it. I'd be good at that. And I would have enjoyed winding up some of the precious little luvvies and pricking their egos. It could have been good fun.

That was the year Caprice appeared. She was going out with Tony Adams at the time and I wanted to meet her just to say, 'Tony Adams? Are you sure?' But the offer never got off the ground. They kept stalling about who was going in, and all that time I was turning down offers of work just to keep those dates free. In the end I decided I couldn't afford to keep doing that so I rang and said no.

I've continued to do *Question of Sport*, though God knows why they keep asking me back because I have a shocking record. They don't give you the answers, which is a bit mean. I've done *They Think It's All Over* where they do give you the questions well in advance to give you chance to think up some funny comments. But when you have someone like Jonathan Ross on the show it is hard to get a word in edgeways. Even on his own chat show it is hard for guests to have their say because it is all about him and he just talks over them. But if there's ever a reality golf show, count me in.

24

FAIRWAY TO HEAVEN

'IT MIGHT HAVE BEEN AN UNORTHODOX WAY OF
DOING IT BUT I MADE IT ONTO THE LEADERBOARD
AT A EUROPEAN TOUR EVENT'

After football, golf has always been my great passion. Retirement has
given me the chance to play some of the world's best courses and to
see some top players close-up through caddying for my close friend
Richard Bland, who is making a name for himself in the game.

I first caddied for him the season before I retired, in a Challenge
Tour event in France, golf's equivalent of the Championship. The problem was that pre-season training began on the Monday, the day after
it finished, and the only flight I could get back was on the Sunday
afternoon. So, I caddied on the Thursday, Friday, Saturday and half
of the final round on the Sunday. When I left Richard at the eleventh
hole he was right up among the leaders, but he fell away badly without my help and guidance and only finished tenth!

For a bloke who loves his golf as much as I do, it was a great experience. Richard was quite impressed and said if he ever made it onto

the main tour he'd let me caddy for him again. I didn't think anything of it because he didn't look like getting his European tour card at that stage, but he scraped into the final event by sinking a massive putt on the final hole. It was the equivalent of Saints staying up on the final day of the season.

He had a magnificent final round to win that tournament, which catapulted him into the top 15 earners by winning his European card. And he kept his promise. I was still under contract at Southampton so I had to pick an event at the end of the season and chose The Scottish Open at Loch Lomond, a place where I'd been lucky enough to play. It went pretty well apart from the fact it rained the whole time we were up there, something I forgot to take into consideration when picking that event. The umbrella was up and down all week, and the bags were pretty heavy so my shoulder was killing me by the end.

Richard easily made the cut and was five under par after three rounds. He had a reputation for being harsh with his caddies and had already got through a couple that season, but he went easy on me as I was doing it free of charge. I said to him, 'If I make a mistake it will be a genuine one and if you shout at me, I'm off.' On the second day we were stood at the tee of the sixth hole, a par five with the loch down the right side. I stood the bag upright and, just as he was about to tee off, I noticed out of the corner of my eye that it was about to topple over. Richard was mid-swing and I told him to 'Stop', just as the bag crashed to the floor. I was so embarrassed but, fair play to him, he remembered what I had said – and eventually smiled. I picked up the bag and he went through his routine again and I thought, 'If this shot goes in the water, I'm dead.' He must have read my mind because he over-compensated and pulled it left, missing the fairway. He then left himself with a 4 foot putt for par, and I knew he'd blame me if he dropped a shot. The ball hit the side of the cup, looped around it and, almost in slow motion, dropped in.

As he was playing the eighteenth on the final day, he looked at the scoreboard intently and said if he birdied that hole it would probably qualify him for the British Open the following week because all the other players above him were exempt. He asked what I was doing that week, and I said I thought I could make myself available if necessary. There was a lot riding on his putt and I studied it closely, trying to look as though I knew what I was doing. It was 12–15 foot and he asked what I reckoned. I said, 'You need this putt to get into the Open and you're asking *me*?' He hit a fabulous shot which missed by just 1 inch.

Richard finished twenty-first and picked up £28,000 – and didn't have to pay his caddy who would normally have got something like £600 a week plus five per cent of the prize money – making almost as much as I earned as a footballer. Richard did pay for our room at the De Vere for the week though. With all the room service I ordered, it would have been cheaper to have paid me commission.

It was a fantastic experience being part of a big tournament, but the best moment came after the third round when Richard went to the driving range and suggested I watch. Suddenly I was aware that someone else had begun hitting balls in the next bay. I turned round and saw Ernie Els, my great golfing hero. I've always loved the way he plays and how he makes the game seem so easy and effortless. I admit I was totally star-struck, and Richard got his camera to take a picture of me and Ernie together. It is still one of my most treasured possessions. I was like a big kid and said, 'Sorry to interrupt you but I think you are a fantastic golfer.' I couldn't believe it when he said, 'And I think you are a fantastic footballer.' I was so chuffed that he had even heard of me.

A year or so later, I played a celebrity tournament in Singapore with my former teammate David Hirst, cricketer Darren Gough and rugby player Jeremy Guscott. They took their partners but I was single so I took my brother Carl and, as a result, I spent the entire tournament well under the influence. We stayed on afterwards and took part in a pro-am. I played with Richard Bland, Hirsty and Darren Gough, who has remained a mate ever since. Before our round we went to watch Ernie Els. He hit a drive to within 15 yards of where I was standing and, as he walked up to the ball, he spotted me and called, 'Alright Matt? How are you doing?' The others were gobsmacked and I felt 10 foot tall.

At that time I was jetting all over the world playing golf, but I had to come back in February 2003 because I had paid £700 at a charity auction for my son Mitchell to be the Liverpool mascot. Even though I played for Southampton he was a Liverpool fan, though now I've retired he is an out and out Saints supporter. I flew back from Australia for that – and it was a rubbish 0–0 game. I blame the mascot.

I flew back to Perth to caddy for Richard and played in a pro-am with Craig Parry and two Aussie Rules footballers with handicaps of 12 and 14. I thought they were playing off dodgy handicaps because they continually smashed the ball past mine – until they came to putt and still smashed the ball. When I caddied for Richard he put his first tee shot almost exactly where I had put mine in the pro-am. There were some tall trees in front of the ball and he said he was going to punch the shot and go under the branches. I told him it would be difficult to get the ball to stop on the green, and he'd be better using a wedge and going over the trees like I'd done the previous day.

Instead he punched the ball low and saw it fly through the green costing him a bogey. I resisted the temptation to say, 'Told you so'. He struggled to make the cut and needed three birdies from the last five holes. He had the choice of going round the water or over it. I suggested he go for the flag because he needed birdies but he played safe, made par and missed the cut. It meant he was able to have a night out and, as the alcohol flowed and tongues loosened, I asked why hadn't followed my advice. He said, 'Did I ever tell you how to play football?' And that was the last time I caddied for him, not because of that but just because we have never been in the same place at the same time, especially because of my Sky commitments. But I'll always be grateful for that experience.

The best thing about retirement is that I've been able to play a lot more golf on some wonderful courses, including St Andrews and Sawgrass, which is the best course I have played. I've also been lucky enough to play at Valderama on a charity trip where I found myself having dinner with Bob Willis, David Lloyd, Ian Botham and Paul Allot. It was one of the most surreal experiences of my life because they were all cricketers I'd idolized as a kid. I barely joined in the conversation because I was so in awe of them.

An annual treat has been the footballers' golf classic at La Manga, organized by former QPR defender Terry Mancini. It isn't just a test of golf but of who can drink the most and still swing a club. In my first year I finished second – at golf, and nowhere near the top in drinking. I'm sure the two things are related. I finally won it at the sixth attempt in 2007 when I pipped Pat Jennings by a point. But I put up a very embarrassing defence of the title. Alan McInally won it and cried during his acceptance speech because he had been trying to win it even longer than me.

The best week's golf I ever had was playing alongside Richard Bland in the pro-celebrity event at the Alfred Dunhill Masters. I was so excited I was like a kid at Christmas. I still treasure the goodie bag I received. We played at Carnoustie, Kingsbarns and St Andrew's, the home of golf. I was so nervous I was shaking. I couldn't even put the ball on the first tee properly. I was desperate not to let Richard down and, in the final round at St Andrew's, he only beat me by one shot, and that was by sinking a 10ft putt at the last.

The best moment though came at Carnoustie. We started at the tenth so the final hole was the ninth and, as I walked up to the green, I looked up at the scoreboard to see 'LE TISSIER IS A LEGEND'. It turned out that one of the guys putting the names on the leaderboard

I EVEN WON THE MBN SOCCER SPEAKER OF THE YEAR AWARD IN DECEMBER 2008 ... IT WAS MY FIRST TROPHY IN 20 YEARS.

was a Saints fan. I took a picture which I still have, so I can show everyone that my name was on the leaderboard at a European Tour event. Being an ex-Premiership foot-baller certainly does open doors and it has given me opportunities I'd never otherwise have got. And that includes the occasional after-dinner speech.

If you'd said to me that one day I'd feel comfortable addressing crowds of 500 I'd have said you were mad. I started off doing a few Q&A sessions at dinners and they seemed to go OK. People laughed in all the right places and said I should take up after-dinner speaking, but I said I was too nervous. Then Peter Osgood stitched me up, in a nice way, although I was mad at the time.

He said he had a job for me at a club near Reading in November 2005. They wanted a Q&A so I got there nice and early to find it was a real spit and sawdust working man's club with no tables laid out for dinner, and just a stage with a chair. I asked what they wanted and was told that I had to go on and do 25 minutes on my own, and then there'd be a break for a raffle before the Q&A. I asked for a pen and paper and, in the next 45 minutes, I wrote what became the crux of my after-dinner speech.

At the next dinner I was asked whether I would do a Q&A or a speech and, before I realized what I was saying, I said I'd do a speech. It was all thanks to Ossie stitching me but I quite enjoy it now – I even won the MBN Soccer Speaker of the Year award in December 2008. I was up against Craig Brown, Mickey Thomas and Duncan McKenzie. We all had 15-minute slots but I went last, which gave me a bit of an advantage because I was able to rabbit on for 25 minutes. It was my first trophy in 20 years.

25

REACH FOR THE SKY

'JEFF STELLING HAS AN UNCANNY KNACK OF ASKING ME TO SPEAK ON CAMERA WHENEVER MY MOUTH IS FULL WHICH, TO BE FAIR, IS MOST OF THE TIME.'

My career on Sky's *Soccer Saturday* show almost ended before it had begun.

I hadn't set out to become a television pundit, it just happened. Towards the end of my final season as a player I did a midweek soccer special in the studio, probably because no one else fancied doing Middlesbrough v Ipswich. Boro made lots of changes and fielded a load of kids I'd never heard of. I was really nervous, mainly in case I swore, but I managed to muddle my way through. Also on the panel was George Best who was quite softly spoken, almost shy. Everyone had their own opinion of him and his drink problems, but the whole time I worked with him he was an absolute gent. I never ever saw him drunk on air. Some days he was more lucid than others, but that was more to do with his general condition. I got on well with him and it was a very sad day when he died. I only ever saw him play at the tail end of his career with Fulham, but I've seen enough footage to know he was a great legend. At the end of his own book he mentioned me as a player to look out for, which made me feel very proud.

I must have done OK that first day because I was invited back to fill in for a few more midweek shows, as and when I was needed, until eventually I made my debut on the prestigious Saturday afternoon flagship show with Jeff Stelling. Whoever came up with the idea for that show is a genius. It must have taken real nerve to approach Sky with the idea of a six-hour show featuring four people watching matches on screens which the viewer can't see, while a presenter reels off the scores from around the country. It doesn't sound like a winning formula – but it works so well.

Much of that is down to Jeff who is absolutely brilliant and I love being part of it – although I could easily have been bombed out after making a schoolboy error on my debut. I had been given the task of reporting on Manchester United v Aston Villa. It was a crap game with hardly any goalmouth action and I was getting bored. Frank McLintock was sitting to my right watching Arsenal who were playing some really good stuff. They were 2–0 up and were having wave after wave of attacks so I sat back in my chair and started watching that match instead. Thierry Henry fired just over the bar and instinctively I cried out, 'Ohhhhhh!' Jeff came to me live on air and said, 'Matt, what has happened at Old Trafford?' I looked at the screen to see the ball in the back of Man Utd's net – and I had no idea how it had got there. I was just about to own up when the replay came on and I was able to talk through the goal as though I had seen it live. The cameraman and producer have no idea how much they saved me.

I could have gone the same way as Rodney Marsh who lost his place on the show in January 2005 after he made an inappropriate joke about the tsunami. But I did OK and was asked to take over. At the end of the season I was given a contract to be a regular instead of filling in on a casual basis. And I've enjoyed every single minute. It has been a great way of staying involved in the game – with minimal effort on my part, as ever. I have loved watching the Premier League and the fantastic stars on show, particularly the likes of Steven Gerrard, Cesc Fabregas, Theo Walcott, Cristiano Ronaldo (when he stays on his feet), Ashley Young and Dimitar Berbatov, who makes me look energetic.

I love watching Wayne Rooney but I think he is a victim of his own work-rate because he gives so much for the team that his own game suffers. He has played in all sorts of different positions whereas if he just played off a striker and did not chase so much, he would probably achieve more. My advice to him would be to stop running around so much – it worked for me.

It has been a real privilege to watch these top stars week in, week out – while getting well paid, well fed and having a laugh. My only worry was that I might put my foot in it and let slip a swear word, especially when I was watching Saints games and I felt the ref wasn't being fair. That's no longer an issue now that Southampton are right out of the Premier League but it was tough when I did have to report on them, especially when they got relegated from the top flight.

Saints played at home to relegation rivals Norwich two weeks before the end of the season and got a last-minute goal to win 4–3. I so nearly yelled, 'Effing get in there!' but I just managed to stop myself. I'm much more used to not swearing now. You just go into a zone and know that for six hours you CAN'T use any expletives. I did describe a ref as 'crap' once. I didn't think it was too bad but I got a telling-off from the producer who said through the headphones, 'I think the word you are looking for is rubbish'.

I took a while to get used to hearing the producer in my earpiece. There is a set of controls under the table so I can turn down the volume whenever Jeff comes to me for an update, but it isn't easy listening to four voices simultaneously – the producer, Jeff, the match commentary and the production people. It's worse for Jeff because he has also got to listen to the statistician. I don't know how he does it. The man is a genius; the way he copes is incredible. He has so much stuff to concentrate on – and he does it for six hours. AND he has to keep the four panellists under control, join in the banter and come up with his own witty quips for the viewers. He must be mentally drained on a Saturday night.

He has a sheet of A4 paper for every division with a lot of facts and stats written down, but it is beyond me how he manages to pick out the right one at the right moment and keep an eye on all the action and the incoming scores. He is definitely getting quicker with his quips and mickey-taking against us – and we give him plenty back. The fact that he is 5ft 6in and 16 stone does give us a bit of ammunition. He is the only presenter I know who needs to sit on a booster seat.

I ONCE MEANT TO SAY THAT A PLAYER HAD BEEN TACKLED FROM BEHIND BUT ACTUALLY SAID HE HAD BEEN 'TAKEN FROM BEHIND'.

Jeff has a great way of building up the expectation before he goes to a live update at one of the grounds. He'll make people think the goal has gone one way before reeling in the viewers with the news it has gone to the opposition. But he also knows when it is funny and when it is just too painful. In the closing weeks of the season, when every point matters so much, he'll build up the suspense but he does not clown around or build up false hope. As it said on the cover of his own autobiography, *Jelleyman's Thrown A Wobbly,* he knows our joy and our pain – but mainly he knows our pain. That's so true and it comes though very clearly in his book which, fittingly, is very short! It is just as well his surname begins with the letter 'S', given that books are usually stocked alphabetically. If his name began with 'A' he would never be able to reach the top shelf to get a copy!

He is so sharp though that all the panellists are on their guard to make sure they don't say anything stupid or stumble over their words because you know he will pounce on it. I once meant to say that a player had been tackled from behind but actually said he had been 'taken from behind'. I was crucified. And I still laugh every time I remember Frank McLintock being handed a team sheet and asking Charlie Nicholas, 'What is Dennis Rommedahl's first name?'

Likewise Jeff delights in trying to catch us out. If he knows we have just taken a bite of a sandwich, he will always try and come to us – obviously that affects me more than the others. I must admit, it is lovely to be in the warmth of the studio while some of the other lads are clearly freezing their nuts off reporting from grounds up and down the country knowing we are being supplied with Coke and sandwiches and chocolate bars. I think four chocolate bars in one show is my record – on top of the sandwiches. Normally we eat during the adverts but if I sneak a mouthful during a quiet moment, Jeff will always try and come to me. And it's that kind of devilment, fun and banter which makes the show so successful.

There's a fine line between good-natured abuse and sheer cruelty, and Jeff knows exactly where it is. When Saints needed to beat Sheffield United at St Mary's on the final day of the 2008 season in order to stay in the Championship it was far too serious for any mickey-taking, and all the lads respected that. I was going through real agonies. When they went 1–0 up it was like someone had punched me in the stomach. Saints got 2–1 in front and I thought they would be OK until United equalized and I was almost sick on screen. Thankfully Stern John quickly scored the winner. After that it reverted to being fun, and the lads were able to make fun of my reactions – and I was able to share the joke because we were safe. But the last few minutes were hell. If Sheffield had scored again or if Leicester had put one in at Stoke then we'd have been down. I was more drained after that game than I ever was playing.

We try to outdo each other predicting results in the studio sweepstake, and give each other grief over our respective teams – particularly me and Phil Thompson. Quite apart from the rivalry over who has the biggest nose, we enjoy winding each other up. And I took great delight covering Liverpool's FA Cup defeat by Barnsley in 2008 just so I could give him some stick. Some Liverpool fans took that the wrong way and thought I had it in for their team, but not so. It just made for good television. And if Phil suffered, how do you think I felt when I was jokingly told that Burnley had missed a penalty when they'd actually scored in the final home match of the 2008–09 season. That game confirmed Saints' relegation to League 1, putting them on -10 points for the 2009–10 season. That was too serious and too painful to be funny.

Likewise, when we went down from the Premiership I was actually at the ground as an analyst with Alan Parry, and he didn't even speak to me for the last 20 minutes of the match because he could see by the look on my face how sad I was. It was so hard to watch the inevitable happening as the team went down without a fight. After all the battles down the years and all the effort so many of us had put it, it really hurt to see it all thrown away so tamely.

Generally, though, there is real good banter between us. And, with my nose, it was like giving Jeff an open goal when I had an airplane named after me. Flybe made me their community ambassador for Guernsey. They also decided to put my picture on the side of one of their planes which was a real honour. George Best had had a plane named after him for the Manchester to Belfast route, so I was very flattered when they did the same for me between Guernsey and Southampton. The plane itself does not do that route too often. I've probably only flown on it half a dozen times, including one memorable occasion when the stewardess checked my boarding pass and gave me a funny look and asked, 'Do I recognize you from somewhere?' She went so red with embarrassment when I pointed to the side of the plane. At the naming ceremony Lawrie McMenemy questioned the wisdom of Flybe's marketing staff for naming a plane after a player who was slow and not very good in the air!

26

LIFE BEGINS AT 40

'I WAS SO EXCITED TO SEE ANGELA AGAIN THAT WHEN
I WENT TO MEET HER FROM THE AIRPORT, I MADE A POINT
OF FILLING MY CAR WITH PETROL. UNFORTUNATELY IT
TOOK DIESEL.'

Waking up on my fortieth birthday was horrible. Not because of the actual milestone – after all reaching 40 is better than the alternative, which is not getting there at all. It's just that the big day did not get off to a good start. My beloved wife Angela planned a surprise but wouldn't tell me what it was. All she would say was that I had to be ready at eight o'clock in the morning, wearing a suit and tie.

I don't particularly like wearing a suit and I hate getting up early. I never wear a tie, I detest them. I find them uncomfortable and even on Sky's *Soccer Saturday* I'm the only panellist not wearing one. It just looks wrong on me. So you can imagine my joy when I had to get dressed up. It was my birthday so I should be doing what *I* wanted, not poncing around like a tailor's dummy. I couldn't think of any possible birthday treat which would require me to wear a suit and tie. I ate breakfast with a face like hell, getting more and more wound up while Angela took pictures of me. I did wonder briefly why she wasn't dressed up. I said, 'If I'm smart, you should be too.' She snapped, 'Don't be cheeky, I AM smart!' The day was rapidly going downhill.

Then there was a knock at the door and I was confronted by three of my best mates in golf gear wondering why I was looking like a lemon in a shirt and tie. Talk about being set up. Angela had booked a round of golf for us at Wentworth. I couldn't get changed fast enough. That was followed by a surprise dinner in town with a large group of my friends. It was a milestone and a moment to take stock of life, and I have to say I am pretty happy with where I am and who I am, with the life I have had and with the way the future is shaping up.

I have a job I enjoy which allows me to play as much golf as I like – and a wonderful wife who also allows me to play as much golf as I like. Fittingly, I proposed to her at a golf club. I had played in Ronan Keating's Charity Golf Day at the K Club, which must have raised £200,000 from the auction alone. I was so enamoured with the venue that I took Angela there for her thirtieth birthday and proposed to her – without a ring. When I'd previously been there I saw the perfect engagement ring on display in the hotel lobby, so I planned to go back with Angela, buy it and propose. I didn't realize the display was just samples from a jeweller in Dublin. So I forgot about buying the ring and just proposed – 11 years after

I STOPPED AT WINCHESTER SERVICES TO FILL UP WITH PETROL – AND IT WAS ONLY TWO MILES DOWN THE ROAD THAT I REMEMBERED MY CAR TOOK DIESEL.

we had started going out together. We had split up for about eight years in that time and Angela left the country. She worked in Dubai and then South Africa but we stayed in touch part of the time, and our feelings for each other were still as strong as ever.

Angela came back for good in March 2007 but it wasn't the best reunion because I was flying out to Mauritius the following day for a week-long golf tournament. I thought I was being considerate giving her a week on her own to sort her stuff out. We didn't even have that first night together because I was speaking at a function in Peterborough. And driving back from meeting her at Heathrow, I stopped at Winchester Services to fill up with petrol – and it was only two miles down the road that I remembered my car took diesel. I'm surprised she didn't get on the next flight out of there.

Thankfully she stuck around and we were married in Mauritius on May 19, 2008. It was purely coincidence that was the same date when I scored the last goal at The Dell, but it should ensure I don't forget my anniversary. It was very romantic. We married on the beach without shoes and with vows we had made up ourselves. We grabbed a couple of witnesses who were on their honeymoon. Nick and Lisa Yates were lovely and she fell pregnant not long after Angela. It was all very low-key but it was hardly *Hello!* magazine material. Neither of us are like that. We now have a beautiful daughter, Ava Belle Eileen, who arrived on March 20, 2009, and in her short time on this planet she has already filled our lives with such happiness. It's amazing how a small thing like her smile can fill your heart with such pride and joy and you suddenly find levels of patience you didn't realize you had when sleep deprivation kicks in. Clearly I'm talking about Angela because I do possess the ability to sleep through earthquakes.

From my first marriage, my son Mitchell and daughter Keeleigh are growing up into wonderful young adults. I try to get back to Guernsey to see them and my parents every week. I will always be incredibly grateful to my mum and dad for all they did for me, not just to make it possible for me to have such a long career at the top of the game but also for instilling me with all the values which make me the person I am.

I feel very privileged to have such a fantastic family and to have had such an enjoyable life both inside and outside of the game. But what does the future hold for Matt Le Tissier? The answer is simple ... Buy the bloody paperback and find out!

27

THE BETS ARE OFF

'WELL, THAT WAS AN INTERESTING FEW WEEKS! I WAS ON EDGE TO SEE WHAT SORT OF A REACTION THERE WOULD BE TO THIS BOOK WHEN THE HARDBACK VERSION WENT ON SALE. I DIDN'T HAVE TO WAIT LONG.'

I was hoping for a bit of press coverage but I never expected the headlines that followed. Maybe that was a bit naïve of me. I thought the press would pick up on my views on Bruce Grobbelaar or Glenn Hoddle or Rupert Lowe – I didn't expect the storm over the 'betting scam'.

After all, it had been 14 years earlier, it could not possibly have affected the outcome of the match and I messed it up so badly that not only did I not win anything, I almost lost a fortune. I honestly thought it would be taken in the spirit it was intended. Those who know me will have realised I was just having a laugh at my own expense. Instead it got blown up out of all proportion. I think it must have been a quiet day on TalkSport.

I didn't hear the debate – I was playing golf at Loch Lomond. But plenty of people told me all about it. The presenter, Mike Parry, fuelled it and kept it going, which is fine. I don't have a problem with that, it's his job. Funnily enough, I saw him at a dinner a couple of weeks later – but he didn't seem to want to talk to me. He probably thought I was going to have a go at him but I just wanted to let him know I was fine about it.

The headlines and the flak didn't bother or upset me – and I certainly didn't worry about the scare stories suggesting the police would be investigating it. They stemmed from the *Southern Daily Echo* who didn't help the situation by constantly asking the cops for a comment. I know how the media works – everyone always wants a follow-up to any halfway decent story so they can get their own angle. The strange thing is that the *Echo* could have had the story to themselves. They had the advance serialisation rights and this was not one of the stories they chose to publish. Either they just missed it or someone didn't read the book properly, but I think they probably felt they had a bit of egg on their face when all the nationals ran with it. Maybe some of the people at the top began asking why they had missed it and so they felt a need to move the story on by pestering the police to see if they would investigate. Of course, they were never going to because it was so long ago – and nothing came of it.

The initial response to the book was amazing. We had a big launch at St Mary's and there were plenty of press people there – which was just as well as I would have looked a bit silly standing on my own. I must admit I felt quite proud as the books were handed out and I saw my family, friends and even the journalists reading them and smiling at some of the stories.

That was followed by a signing session at the Saints Megastore. I thought this would only take an hour or so at most but even an hour before the doors were due to open there was a queue that stretched the length of one stand and halfway down the other. I couldn't believe so many people had turned out and waited so long in the cold.

I made a point of signing proper named greetings and taking a few minutes to chat to each of them – even though it meant I was still there four hours later. I made sure everyone went away happy. It really annoys me when celebrities literally scrawl their name without even acknowledging the person who is asking. I know it can be intrusive at times, especially if the request is rude or abrupt or if it comes when you are out having a private dinner somewhere, but it takes just a few seconds and it can make someone's day to get an autograph – perhaps even more importantly, they would never forget a refusal.

I remember a former Saints manager telling a group of a dozen or so youngsters he didn't have time to sign their scraps of paper as he drove out of Staplewood after his very first training session with us. He told the kids to come back on Monday – when they would have been back at school. Even though he was not my favourite person, I am sure there was no malice, it was just thoughtless. But they will still remember it while he will have forgotten it the moment he turned out of the gates.

Likewise, there was a Manchester United legend who was asked for his autograph in the car park at The Dell and said he was in a hurry. The youngster bravely persisted and said it would only take a couple of seconds – so the former England international said: 'How about half an autograph?'

I worked hard promoting the book – I know, it came as a surprise to me too. There were signing sessions across most of the south coast and I did plenty of interviews for the media, including Simon Mayo's show on 5 Live, which was good fun. I never got to go on *Friday Night with Jonathan Ross* though, probably because I would have wanted a 50–50 split of speaking time. I don't think he ever got back to me; maybe I should get an answer phone?

Most of the interviews were about the 'betting scam' and whether I worried fans would think less of me. I never thought they would because it was hardly going to influence the outcome of the game. It's not like I was a goalkeeper and decided to push the ball into my own net at Coventry or anything like that.

In hindsight, maybe it wasn't the wisest thing to put in the book, but hey, sales went well! There's no such thing as bad publicity and it certainly got people talking. Having said that, I would probably have omitted that story if I had become chairman of Southampton as I would have had to become the first chairman to sack himself – and even Rupert didn't manage to do that!

Now that the dust has settled, I'm quite glad our takeover bid didn't work out. I think it was probably best from the club's point of view as well as my own. I was always a bit apprehensive about having a full-time job and I did worry how I was going to fit in my golf (the sport, *not the car*). Also, I really enjoy working for Sky. I love doing *Soccer Saturday* and if I had become Saints chairman then it would have been impossible for me to continue with it.

Our group was deadly serious about the takeover, and we did come very close, but we were seeking funding from a Swiss bank that suddenly pulled out citing a conflict of interests. I never found out exactly what that was … but it left the way clear for Swiss-national billionaire Markus Liebherr to take control. It was a huge relief when he got the green light because it meant the club was saved – and thankfully in a stronger position than it had been before.

Our group would have had enough funding to finance a promotion push. We could have afforded Rickie Lambert and a couple of other players and we could probably have got the club into the Championship but then we would have needed more investment to take the club forward. We got as far as sounding out possible managers in case we took over and I spoke to a lot of people with Southampton links.

I had a good chat with Gordon Strachan but at that point he wasn't looking to get back into management – though he did leave us with quite a few names of Scottish players who would have been useful in League One. I spoke to Alan Shearer who certainly did not rule it out, and Iain Dowie was also pretty interested – not pretty AND interested, by the way. I also held talks with Kevin Keegan – everyone already knows that thanks to the contractors working on the house next door. They thought it would be a good idea to take a picture of Kevin in my driveway and send it to the *Echo*. I wasn't too happy about that!

Funnily enough, Alan Pardew wasn't on our radar – mainly because we were looking at people with Southampton links. But you can't knock the job he has done. After a slow start while it took time to rebuild, he has turned the cub around and has proved to be a pretty good choice. I have to say the takeover has been very good for the club, at least on the playing side.

Off the field, there are still some question marks about the way the staff are treated. From the outside it appears that the manner in which the club is being run on a personnel level has not changed too much from Rupert's time. Apparently, it makes him look like a woolly liberal which takes some doing! It remains to be seen if the same spirit is there. But you cannot knock what is being done on the field.

The new owner is investing in the team and it is great to see that kind of commitment from him. The level of funding is very high for a League One side and we have brought in some top quality players. Rickie Lambert has been a superb signing. He has been a revelation for us. He has a very good touch for such a big man, is a real handful in the air, knows where the goal is and has scored some fantastic free kicks. I am very happy to see him wearing my number 7 shirt; it is about time the fans had a real hero to hang their hopes on.

Having swapped the stadium for the Sky Sports studio, I still revel in one spectacular success at the beginning of the 2009–10 season: when Burnley beat Manchester United at Turf Moor – and I called it! I got slaughtered for my prediction before the match by presenter Ed Chamberlin and the rest of the panel but I had the last laugh as it was one of my finest moments on the show. Paul Merson went as far as to say I should be sectioned while Ed did a double-take. He just assumed I was going for an away win like everyone else and when the penny dropped, it momentarily stunned him into silence. It was worth doing just for that. I thought Sir Alex Ferguson had taken a few liberties with his line-up and did not pay Burnley enough respect – especially as it was their first home game in the Premier League. I remembered how we had gone to Charlton in similar circumstances and they battered us 5–0 so I knew the Burnley players and their fans would be on a real high. I was so smug when Burnley won and I was proved right. Just a shame it hasn't happened again since.

Not getting involved with Saints has given me the chance to spend more time with my wife, Angela, and baby daughter, Ava, who enjoyed her first Christmas and was thoroughly spoiled by both families. I'll have to put a stop to that. My son Mitchell has passed his driving test which is great because it saves me £30 a time on car hire when I go over to Guernsey. Mind you, it's a false economy because, mysteriously, he never seems to have any petrol when I go over! My eldest daughter Keeleigh has fantastic teeth now her braces have been removed after 22 months. She has a beautiful smile so it was well worth it. I wish I had had it done when I was her age instead of being a stubborn little git.

With Saints on the up once more and Pompey in decline, my family life settled and happy and *Sky Soccer Saturday* going from strength to strength, the future looks very rosy.

28

WHAT THEY SAY ABOUT MATT

Lawrie McMenemy
Southampton manager Dec 1973–June 1985, during which time Matt signed as a schoolboy for Saints; England assistant manager, July 1990–Nov 1993; Southampton Director of Football, Jan 1994–June 1997

'I told the players to sicken him with the ball because he is special. I told the others, "I know he is special and you know he is special" so they had to make sure they gave him the ball at every opportunity and "sicken him with it" – that was the key phrase. I said if he collapsed with exhaustion then Bally and I would walk on and carry him off. Then we worked on some set-pieces – two of which came off the next day at Newcastle. It was a great start and the beginning of a terrific run. Matt really enjoyed his football under Alan, who was his type of coach. He concentrated on ability, touch and vision far more than running which suited Matt down to the ground.

It's a bit of a myth that we had as many offers for Matt as the press made out, but that was probably because clubs knew he was happy at Southampton. I remember the Chelsea director Matthew Harding once doing an interview in a national newspaper extolling the virtues of Matt and how he would love to have him. At a charity lunch he was collecting autographs and, as I signed his book, I said, "Can I give you a tip about being a director? Don't tap up other people's players in public." I did it tongue-in-cheek but he was slightly embarrassed. I said, "If you like him so much I suggest you come to Southampton with a cheque for £7m and put it into our club then you can watch him every week." He said that if he did that he'd have to rename the club Chelsea-on-Sea. At the end of the lunch he handed me a cheque for £7m made payable to Chelsea-on-Sea. I still have it.

I signed Matt as schoolboy after we got a call from a schoolteacher one day. He had brought a group of kids over from Guernsey. They had a few hours to kill so he asked if he could bring the kids to The Dell. I said yes and afterwards he wrote to thank me for the hospitality and said if there was anything he could ever do then to let him know. I wrote back and said if he ever had any promising players then he should let *me* know. The result was he sent over Matt and Graeme Le Saux. Graeme was homesick, which tended to be a feature of youngsters coming over from the Channel Islands. Matt is a very family-orientated man, very laid-back, grounded, down-to-earth and loyal, and that had a lot to do with him staying here.

Graeme eventually signed for Chelsea while Matt joined Southampton. By the time I returned to the club as Director of Football, Matt was an established top-quality player. He should have won more caps on ability – but you have to work closely with him to realize that. Having been an international manager, I can see both sides. If you only saw Matt now and again – and England managers only really saw him when Southampton were playing away to the big clubs – then it was hard to get the full picture of what he could do. But he had supreme natural ability and great self-belief.'

Iain Dowie
Centre-forward, Sept 1991–Jan 1995

'Matt was the jewel in a side full of great spirit. A lot of us weren't the most talented and got by on work-rate, but he had the most unbelievable talent. Before training Francis Benali and I would go out early and do all the right stretches to warm up. Then, at one minute before 10am, Tiss would amble out of the dressing room looking as though he was off down the park for a kick about. Every day I would throw the ball to him out as he crossed the touchline and challenge him to hit the crossbar from there. And about eight times out of 10 he'd do it.

He really enjoyed his football. I remember one night when we'd both been dropped into the Reserves and a lot of players would not have fancied it. I remember flicking the ball for him to run clean through and, as the keeper came out, Matt flicked his head as though he was going to nod the ball at goal. The keeper bought it and dived only for Matt to chest the ball down and calmly roll it in the net. He just laughed.

He was a magnificent finisher but didn't care if he missed. It never affected him or dented his immense self-belief. He was a big character who used to love the banter and having the mickey taken out of him. We had some hard drinkers in that team but he was quite happy with his Malibu.

Matt was very much a team player, though he isn't given enough credit for that. Even when he scored a spectacular goal, he always gave credit for the assist. Everyone remembers the stunner he got against Newcastle; I gave him a crap flick-on but he made it good. The ball dropped behind him but he dug it out and scored a very special goal. He was the only player who could have a packet of crisps and a can of Coke on the way to a game and still be magnificent.

I have been fortunate to play with, and against, some top players in my time but I have never seen anyone strike a ball like him. Alan Shearer had unbelievable power but in terms of skill Matt was the most natural striker of a ball I have ever seen. He was second to none. It was almost like a golf shot off the tee because he'd hit the ball with bend and whip. He was also a good athlete. He could run well; he just chose not to.'

Ian Branfoot
Southampton manager, June 1991–Jan 1994

'A lot of fans thought I didn't appreciate Matt's ability – that couldn't be further from the truth. He is one of the most talented players I ever worked with. I just wanted him to work harder, not just for Southampton but for himself.

People would compare him with Alan Shearer. Matt had far more skill but Alan's work-rate was incredible. He was a fantastic example and would put in so much effort chasing and closing down to defend as well as leading from the front. You have to ask why didn't the top managers take Matt? Great players play for great clubs. I never had too many enquiries about him when I was manager.

I don't have any regrets about the way I handled Matt, but if I had known then what I know now I would have played him in a different position. Part of the problem with Matt was that no-one knew what was his best position, and I think that was one of the things which stopped him winning as many England caps as his talent deserved. He was being played on the wing when I arrived at the club so I kept him there, but it wasn't his strength. He was never going to provide any protection for the full back who must have hated having him in front of them. In hindsight I should have played him just off Alan

Shearer playing more of a 4–4–1–1 formation. We could have got away with it because of Alan's phenomenal work-rate which would have compensated for Matt.

I wouldn't have built the team around him but I would have given him more of a free role. As long as you have 10 other players working hard you can get away with it. I did have players like Glenn Cockerill and Terry Hurlock coming to me complaining about Matt's lack of effort and saying they were working their socks off while he wasn't putting it in. That gave me a problem because they were honest lads and that was one reason I left him out before the Newcastle game.

Contrary to what he might think, I wasn't going to sub him just before he scored that great goal and I was delighted that the kick up the backside had worked. As a character I had no problems with him at all. I just questioned his work-rate and ambition. Matt is a smashing lad and he chose to stay at Southampton where he knew he would be a regular and it was close to the Channel Islands. I think his upbringing had a huge effect on his character and, in many ways, he did well to break away and to establish himself as a top player. He had a very successful career and is still a big hero in and around Southampton. That was his choice and I can't blame him for that.

I liked Matt as a person, there are a lot worse than him around. He was an intelligent lad, a nice lad – we just had very different ideas on the way the game should be played. He is bright and articulate with a good sense of humour which you can see on *Sky Sports*. That is the perfect job for him because it doesn't require him to move. I was just frustrated that he had so much talent. I wanted him to play for England and to fulfil his potential. You don't get a second chance in football, and I wanted him to be as big in the game as he could possibly be.

I do wonder if he ever regrets not doing what Shearer did, moving away to test himself at the top? I was desperately disappointed when the board decided to sell Shearer as I would have loved to have played them both together. I had no choice in the matter although I still smile at an approach from Manchester United. We had played them towards the end of the season on a Thursday night. They won 1–0 and at full time I went to shake Sir Alex Ferguson's hand and he told me to eff off as he didn't like the way we played. A few weeks later he rang me up wanting to buy Shearer. I said, "Alex, you remember what you said to me last time we met? Now you can eff off." And we sold him to Blackburn.'

Micky Adams
Full-back, March 1989–March 1994

'I always prided myself on my fitness, which I got because of Tiss. A lot of managers wanted to play him wide, to get him out of the way. That meant he was often playing in front of me on the left. Players would give him the ball and I would go flying past him on the overlap. He used me as a decoy and would go on a run with the ball, and then I'd have to go chasing back.

He had fantastic natural ability, but he did practice as well. He worked at those skills to hone and perfect them. I remember Ian Branfoot used to make us practice set-pieces for hours on a Friday. He'd make Matt take corners in a certain way and Tiss did everything he asked, raising an arm if it was going short or placing the ball down twice if it was going long or whatever code we had developed. And then on the Saturday he'd completely ignore all those instructions and shoot from the corner flag. He always reckoned he could score from a corner and he actually did it a few times. Now I am a manager that would drive me absolutely mad. But that was Tiss. He had such confidence in his ability to put the ball exactly where he wanted. If we got a penalty he would ask which bit of the net we wanted him to hit – and he always did it. He was the best player I ever saw, that's for sure. His control and touch were unbelievable – but he did work at them.

He showed amazing loyalty by staying when he could have made a lot more money by moving. Southampton would have been relegated many years earlier if it hadn't been for him. Fans might not like me saying this but I believe he should have left. I think it suited his home life at that time because there was a nice flight from Southampton to Guernsey for him and his wife. I know he had numerous offers to leave the club but I don't think his wife wanted him to move. He enjoyed being in Southampton and it suited him, but I would like to have seen him test himself and have a real go at it at a bigger club. He would certainly have won more England caps.

I believe he was stitched up when Terry Venables picked him to play in the ill-fated game in Ireland. I think he thought it would be a physical game against a robust side, probably in the wind and rain and on long grass. And I think he thought Matt wouldn't fancy it. He was under a fair bit of pressure to play Matt so I think he picked that match deliberately, setting him up to fail. That way he could say he had given him his chance and he could then leave Matt out. As it turned out the game was abandoned early on because of crowd trouble so no one really got a chance to show what they could do – yet Matt wasn't even in the next squad.

There were times when he was a liability and I know Ian Branfoot got frustrated with him but, as players, we always forgave him because we knew he would get us a win bonus. At some point he would score a goal out of nothing and win us a match we didn't expect to because he could do things no one else could do.'

Tim Flowers
Goalkeeper, June 1986–Nov 1993

'I have won a Premiership medal, played for England and had a fairly decent career. But all anyone ever asks me about is THAT goal, the one that got Matt the 1994–95 BBC Goal of the Season at Ewood Park.

It was a complete fluke. I'm sure he was trying to chip a pass for someone else. I knew as soon as he hit it that I wasn't getting near it. My heart sank as the ball flew in. I was devastated because I knew he would never let me forget it – and sure enough I looked up from the bottom of the net to see him abusing me from the halfway line. Even now, half his after-dinner speech is about that goal. That's why I have saved my win bonus from the game just to remind him who came out on top.

But I don't feel bad because he could beat any goalkeeper from anywhere. Some forwards you know will hit the ball with pace or bend but, with Tiss, you never knew what was coming. He could do you with any type of shot from the most powerful strike to a delicate chip, as Peter Schmeichel found out to his cost. To beat someone of 6ft 4in requires phenomenal skill. And his dead-ball delivery was tremendously accurate and he really should have played for England many more times than he did.

In fact he could do anything with any kind of ball – tennis, golf, cricket or snooker. He used to take me to the 147 Club and, in the end, I bought a pair of white gloves so I could dust the balls down while he potted them. He didn't get to beat me at golf too often, simply because I never played. I have never been able to play that game so I just used to carry the bags on pre-season tours. I was persuaded to play once and as I drove off at the first tee the ball exploded. Tiss had swapped it for a trick one filled with talcum powder. I should have guessed with seven players all crowding round to watch me hit it. It frightened the life out of me while Tiss fell about laughing.

We got on really well. I enjoyed his company even though he was a bit of a weirdo. While everyone else was on the beer, he would be happy with a Coke. Some people can tell a wine by sniffing it, he could do the same with cola. He could tell by smelling it whether it was Coca-Cola or Pepsi or own brand or, God forbid, diet.

Diet wasn't something he cared about. Before training he used to have a sausage and egg McMuffin, and still used to beat me from outrageous distances. I have no idea how he ate what he did and still play at the highest level. He should leave his body to medical science, or maybe just melt it down for chip fat.

He actually eats less now than he did when he was playing. Maybe it is a trick of the television cameras but he looks slimmer on Sky's *Soccer Saturday*. And it is good to see that Just For Men is working. I am not surprised he has been such a success on that show because he has always been funny and eloquent and spoken a lot of sense – one of the few who does on that panel. He is honest and open and speaks his mind, and he has a lot to say. I'd never tell him but he is a real top man.'

Mike Osman
Comedian, long-time friend, business partner

'Matt is the greatest player I have ever seen in a Saints shirt. I have been watching the club since 1964 and I have seen some magnificent players including Kevin Keegan, Mike Channon, Alan Ball, Peter Osgood, Frank Worthington, Terry Paine and many more. They were greats but Tiss was the best. I have never seen anyone dribble or pass or shoot like he did. He was the best crowd-pleaser of his generation.

If I went to a game and he got injured, I felt like going home. I only ever used to watch him. He has given me more pleasure than anyone else on earth – in a manly way. I would pay anything to see him play again now. He consistently kept Saints in the Premier League playing in what was often an average team. And you wouldn't get his kind of loyalty now – it was unusual even then. I was with him on several occasions when he was offered big money to leave but he turned it down, time after time, to stay with Southampton.

As a business partner he was a mathematical genius. Unfortunately I always came bottom at maths which is why the nightclub went down the pan. Quite genuinely, he has said if he hadn't been a footballer then he would probably have been an accountant. Maybe he should have been keeping an eye on the books at St Mary's?'

Richard Dryden
Centre-back, Aug 1996–Feb 2001

'He calls me thick? Well, how's this? I had a big white Mitsubishi car which he nicknamed "The Ambulance" because that is what it looked like. I used to drive him from The Dell to the bookies at Bedford Place where we would place our bets. One day I had finished putting my bets on so I went to wait in the car. He came out and jumped in only to find it was the wrong one, and he was sitting alongside a very startled man with his wife and baby.

But he was an unbelievable player. Before I signed for Southampton I used to watch him on television and wonder if his goals were flukes – until I saw him do it day after day in training. He was a great player and a great character. He wasn't big-time in any way. When I signed, he was the first one to come up and introduce himself and look after me.'

Francis Benali
Full-back, Jan 1987–June 2003

'Goal-scoring was not my strong point so Heaven knows what possessed Matt to pick me out with that cross [against Leicester, in December 1997, for my only league goal]. Maybe he thought on the law of averages I had to score sooner or later. But it was really nice that he was the one to set up my one and only goal because we had come through the ranks together.

He was an inspiration to the rest of the youth team because he pretty much leapfrogged the Reserves and went straight to the first team which showed that it could be done. We had a strong youth set-up at the time and he paved the way for others to follow. You could see even then that he was a bit special. He could do things which none of us could get near, no matter how hard we practised. He was an awesome player and I felt very privileged to be his teammate over many years and to see up close his special talent. He was a massive part of the club's success in staying in the Premier League for so long. As the title of his DVD says, he was *Unbelievable*. He never used to score tap-ins – just spectacular strikes.

I cannot speak highly enough of him as a player or as a person because he had no airs and graces. He really mucked in and did his bit for the community and was always the first one to put himself forward when a presentation needed doing. He is a fantastic person and someone I have an awful lot of time for. He was a top player with wonderful ability – and a good friend.'

James Beattie
Striker, July 1998–Jan 2005

'I grew up in Blackburn and supported them as a kid so I was in the stands the day Matt beat Tim Flowers from 35 yards. The goal might have been against my team but I couldn't help applauding – along with the rest of the crowd. It was that good.

His DVD was called *Unbelievable* and rightly so because that's what he was. His skill, touch and finishing were second to none in games and in training. It was ridiculous what he could do with a ball. I was delighted when I found out I was going to be playing alongside him, even though he was just starting to dip past his prime. He had pigeon-vision because he saw things so quickly. I knew if I made a run then he'd spot it and find me because he had the ability to put the ball wherever he wanted. I would love to have had more time alongside him, and I am proud to have played a part in him scoring the last ever goal at The Dell.

Matt was different class not just as a teammate but as a friend. He has that great ability to laugh at himself and not care what anyone else thinks of him.'

Dave Jones
Southampton manager, June 1997–Jan 2000

'Matt is the most gifted player I have ever worked with. He did things in training that left you wondering how on earth he did it. If he had worked a bit harder on his fitness then he might have been an even better player.

People say he might not have been the same if he didn't have that laid-back, devil-may-care approach. That might be true – but he might also have gone on to become one of the all-time greats. We'll never know.

I remember we had a cup-tie at Brentford and it came in the middle of a very crowded fixture programme so I told him if he scored me a couple of goals, I would take him off for a rest. He promptly banged in two in the first 20 minutes – and asked to come off!

He didn't look like your typical footballer – and I did ask for the stripes on our new kit to be made narrower so they suited him better. He could never have played for a team which wore hoops – especially if they were sponsored by Dunlop.

I perhaps didn't pick him as much as some people would have liked because he was coming towards the end of his career and was starting to pick up a few knocks and, unfortunately, I was the manager who perhaps pushed him towards the end of his career.

I'd love to have managed him at his peak because he was an icon to the club. I enjoyed having him around the place because he is a great character and now a good friend.'

Stuart Gray
Full-back, Sept 1991–Nov 1993; Manager, Mar 2001–Nov 2001

'Only Matt could have scored that last goal at The Dell. I don't think any of the other players would have been capable of finishing that chance the way he did. And it was so fitting that he got it. But it wasn't sentiment that made me put him on. It was for a very specific purpose. I told him I wanted him to play as far forward as possible – and told him if he came back over the half-way line, I'd take him off. That must have been music to his ears.

When he put the ball in the net to give us a 3–2 win, I have never heard a noise like it. Dennis Rofe and I were half-way to the centre circle celebrating. It was a privilege just to be there for such a special moment. It still makes the hairs stand up on the back of the neck just thinking about it.

I had the privilege of playing alongside him and managing him, and he was an incredible talent, the most gifted player I ever worked or played with. I would stand looking in wonder at some of the things he did in training. He didn't like the physical side but he knew he had to do it because he couldn't rely solely on his amazing skill. To be fair, he was never one to miss training and often would embarrass his teammates with a finishing session. It might take them six or seven attempts to hit the target while he would do it every time. What he did for the club was fantastic, not just on the field but with his great loyalty. Even now, you can still see his passion for the club on Sky.

I felt for him when he was left out of the World Cup squad after he had got that hat-trick for the England B team. You see Fabio Capello picking David Beckham because of the quality of his set-plays and Matt is very much in the same vein. If you got a free kick anywhere near the 18 yard box, you knew it would go in or, at worst, hit the woodwork.

As a teammate, I was happy to be one of those who did his running for him because we knew if we could get the ball to him, he'd win the game for us – as he proved in that last match at The Dell.'

Paul Telfer
Full-back, Nov 2001–Aug 2005

'My goal [in Saints' last home match against Newcastle, in Matt's final season] was probably the sort Matt would have scored, only he'd have done it 10 times better and with more style. And people would have known he meant it. That probably should have been his moment because the plan was for him to come off the bench and it would have been a great way to finish his career.

I wish I had met and played with Tiss when he was in his prime because he was a fantastic player. He was in his last season when I joined Southampton but, even then, the things he did in training took the breath away. I have played a lot of golf with him and he is a top man off the field too. My only disappointment is that I didn't see him at his best.'

Jeff Stelling
Sky Sports colleague, Jan 2005–present

'Matt is a joy to work with in every respect. Being a football pundit may look easy but it is bloody difficult to find someone who has all the right qualities, but he fits the bill perfectly.

He came in as a direct replacement for Rodney Marsh who had been the kingpin of the show – spiky, opinionated and full of himself, which was just what we wanted. Matt had to fill his boots which was a tall order – but he did it just by being himself. He was still opinion-ated and still funny, but his humour was much more subtle. We had a few teething troubles in terms of his appearance. He came in looking like Worzel Gummidge dressed by a charity shop. The managing director personally went into Richmond to buy him some new shirts and ties – and after a couple of weeks Matt discarded them because he looked even worse dressed like that.

But the great thing about Tiss is that he can laugh at himself and he does not mind people poking fun at him about his work-rate as a player, his dress sense and his taste in music. He doesn't care what people think about him. He's very stubborn and refuses to change. We have a cast-iron rule that mobile phones are completely banned in the studio, even if they are on silent. But he always has his on. On one occasion there had been a lot of transfer speculation about James Beattie and Matt was fiddling under the desk as I got to him. I asked what he was doing and he said he was texting Beatts to see what he should say. I asked what the reply was and he said, "Tell them Eff all."

But Matt gets away with it because of the character he is. He slots perfectly into the panel because he does not mind setting himself up to be mocked. It was the same when he revealed that he likes Shakin' Stevens – that's the singer not a hobby, by the way! I once said that West Brom hadn't won old Trafford since 1984 when Shakin' Stevens was Number One with 'This Ol' House'. Matt said, "I think you'll find it was 1981." I checked and, of course, he was right so I asked how he knew and he admitted that it was the first record he ever bought, and that he had seen Shaky in concert several times. He knew we'd give him merciless stick for that but he was up for it because he knew it would make good television.

The chemistry of the panel is so important and the others regard him as a mate. If they don't like you then you won't be coming back too often, but they all get on well with him. They like him as a person, respect his opinions and, of course, they admired him as a player. We have tried a lot of ex-pros on the panel but not too many can slot in, and certainly not as comfortably as Matt.

It isn't as simple as just sitting there talking about the match. Yes, you've got to know the game but you need a quick wit, a good sense of humour, clarity of thought and the self-belief to stand up to three grizzled pros who jump on your every mistake. He has to be able to watch a match on a screen and talk to me and listen to the producer all at the same time, but he is as sharp on screen as he was on the field.

He was a terrific player who was admired by fans of all clubs. He wasn't at a club that a lot of people hated, and he was the sort of player most fans wanted to be. He scored brilliant goals but he felt like one of them – very ordinary, a bit lazy and overweight but tremendously loyal. That counted for a lot in the game. Fans get very resentful if they see their best players leave for the sake of a few more quid when they are already very well paid. But Matt had an old-fashioned sense of allegiance to a small club. Southampton were never a threat to the big boys so opposition fans never hated him; they just enjoyed watching him play. And they enjoy watching him just as much now because he says what he thinks. A lot of ex-pros can be loathe to criticise while others can do it just for effect. Matt gets the balance just right. He is always willing to have a dig if it is required, and he has been very outspoken on Steve McClaren, Emile Heskey and (surprise, surprise) referees. But he never overdoes it, showing the same balance, composure and entertainment factor as he did as a player.'

Phil Thompson
Sky Sports colleague Jan 2005–present

'Matt is the same in the studio as he was on the pitch – very laid-back but very sharp. People sometimes look at Matt and think he's disinterested in the game, but nothing could be further from the truth. As a player he would appear casual and lazy, then suddenly he'd pounce on a half-chance and conjure something out of nothing. He's the same as a panellist. He's a real student of the game and really watches it. That might sound obvious but not everyone does it. And he has a great way of putting his point across.

He fits right in with the rest of us because he can laugh at himself, which is absolutely essential, and he has really added to the chemistry of the panel. We have some great banter – not least because we are both well blessed in the nose department. Matt must be delighted to have me in the studio with him. All through his career he got stick from fans for the size of his nose but he is only in the Championship compared to me. I'm in the Premier League when it comes to noses!

We both started to be regulars around the same time and I enjoyed getting to know him. I likened him to Alan Hansen in many ways because they were both players I looked at and thought they weren't management material. But just like Alan, Matt has found his niche. His biggest asset is that he is not scared to give an opinion. If someone isn't pulling his weight in a game then Matt will not hesitate to say so – even though he was hardly the hardest worker himself.

I remember when Liverpool were twice behind against Havant & Waterlooville in the FA Cup and Matt absolutely slaughtered me. Then Sky gave him the next round when Liverpool lost at home to Barnsley and he was screaming at me. Some of the Liverpool fans thought he had a down on the club but that wasn't the case at all – it was just his way of having a dig at me. If it had been Arsenal losing to Barnsley he'd have made fun of Charlie Nicholas. It just made for good entertainment.

Sometimes though it is too intense for mickey-taking. I remember the last day of the 2007–08 season when Southampton were in danger of being relegated from the Championship. Matt went through hell that day. He had fought so hard for so long to keep them in the Premier League. When they came from behind to beat Sheffield United 3–2 you'd think they'd won the cup. He was absolutely DELIGHTED. Even though he had hung up his boots after a great career he still loves his club, even in the bad times.'

Charlie Nicholas
Sky Sports colleague, Jan 2005–present

'I should get danger money from Sky whenever I have to sit between Phil Thompson and Matt, with two of the biggest noses I have ever seen. They could take someone's eye out if they suddenly turn round.

When Matt first joined the panel, Sky tried to smarten him up. But he isn't that type of guy. Vic Wakeling was the Managing Director of Sky Sports, a really important guy but not too busy or important to take it upon himself to go shopping on Matt's behalf. He bought him four shirts and four jackets because he couldn't take any more of what Matt was wearing. In all my time in television, I have never seen anyone being told what to wear. But even he gave up trying to make Matt wear a tie, and rightly so because it just looks wrong on him.

A lot of footballers are very image conscious and spend a lot of time on their grooming but not Tiss. He is just very down to earth. He is very easy-going and seems embarrassed by any compliments he gets. And that is why he is so loved by the viewers. They know he was a terrific player and most of them loved to watch him even when he was scoring against their side. But despite his immense ability, he has never been flash or flamboyant.

He has dreadful taste in music, he has the worst ring-tones ever and he asks for girlie drinks whenever we go on a big night out with Sky. We will be on champagne and cocktails and he will ask for Malibu and Coke and never worries what people think.

He also scored some of the most spectacular goals I've ever seen. He was a genius with the ball and I'd admired him from afar but the first time I ever met him was at Paul Merson's testimonial. He was magnificent that night with his control of the ball and the way he nutmegged household name players for fun. I wondered why he had stuck with Southampton all those years but he can be very stubborn and never felt a need to move. I think his talents would have been even more widely appreciated if he had been at a bigger club but what he did for Southampton has to be applauded. People there must think he is a God.'

Alan Ball
– My Tribute

Even after Alan left the club in the summer of 1995, we remained great friends and often saw each other socially. The day he died was one of the saddest of my life. It was three o'clock in the morning on April 25, 2007 when I got a phone call from Big Dave, a mutual friend who used to drive Bally to all his social functions so that he could have a drink. Dave used to look after the players lounge at The Dell when Lawrie McMenemy was manager and is one of the most loyal blokes you are likely to meet. As his nickname suggests, he is a big lad with sovereign rings, no hair and not too many teeth because they had all been knocked out in fights.

I was at a Cornish golf festival and had put my phone on silent but, bizarrely, I heard it vibrate on the bedside table. It was a weird moment but I answered it and was knocked for six by the news that Bally had suffered a heart attack and had died. At first I thought I was in a nightmare but when I realized Alan had gone, it hit me hard. It was a massive shock because he was so full of life and seemed in really good health. He had bounced back strongly from the death of his beloved wife Lesley and had rebuilt his life.

The send-off at Winchester Cathedral was outstanding. It was an autograph-hunters' paradise as household names from every era of the game turned out to pay their respects, with hundreds of fans crowding outside to hear the service relayed over speakers. And the news coverage was incredible. It showed how highly he was thought of – and the sad thing is that I don't think he ever realized that while he was alive. He was a fantastic player, great company and the best manager I ever had. He had as much belief in my ability as I had. He wasn't interested in the many things I couldn't do, he just focused on what I could do well and how he could fit that into the team. It wasn't often in my career that a manager had that faith in me and it meant a lot.

I loved spending time in his company. Very often I wouldn't even join in the conversation but just listen. He had such enthusiasm for life. He was inspiring. And he was a brilliant after-dinner speaker. Not everyone in the squad liked his methods, but you get that at every club under every manager. But he was brilliant for me.

Matt Stats

Born: Guernsey, October 14, 1968
Height: 6ft 1in
Weight: 13.5st (though for some reason the club scales kept saying 14st)
Nickname: Tiss, Le God.
Family: father Marcus, mother Ruth, brothers Mark, Kevin, Carl, wife Angela, children Mitchell, Keeleigh and Ava, dog Bella
Appearances: 540
Goals: 209

Honours

Eight England caps (see page 282)
Barclays Young Eagle of the Year 1990
PFA Young Player of the Year 1990
Saints Player of the Year 1990, 1994, 1995
ZDS Cup runners-up medal 1992
Footballers Golf Classic 2007
MBN After-dinner Speaker of the Year 2008

England caps

Denmark H 1–0 March 9, 1994 (on as sub, 67 mins)

Greece H 5–0 May 17, 1994 (on as sub, 62 mins)

Norway H 0–0 May 22, 1994 (on as sub, 77 mins)

Romania H 1–1 Oct 12, 1994 (played 90 mins, all of the subs must
have been used)

Nigeria H 1–0 Nov 16, 1994 (on as sub, 78 mins)

Republic of Ireland A 0–1 Feb 15, 1995 (started, match
abandoned, 27 mins)

Moldova A 3–0 Sept 1, 1996 (on as sub, 81 mins)

Italy H Feb 12, 1997 (withdrawn, 61 mins)

Hat tricks

Leicester H 4–0 March 7, 1987

Norwich H 4–1 Feb 27, 1990

Wimbledon A 3–3 March 17, 1990

Chelsea A (ZDS Cup) 3–1 Jan 29, 1992

Oldham A 3–4 May 8, 1993

Liverpool H 4–2 Feb 14, 1994

Norwich A 5–4 April 9, 1994

Huddersfield H (League Cup) 4–0 Oct 5, 1994 (scored all four
goals)

Nottingham Forest H 3–4 Aug 18, 1995

Russia B (Loftus Road) 4–1 April 21, 1998

Penalties
1989–90
Wimbledon H 2–2 Sept 30

QPR A 4–1 Oct 14

Chelsea A 2–2 Nov 18

Millwall A 2–2 Dec 2

Sheffield Wednesday H 2–2 Dec 30

Oldham H 2–2 (League Cup) Jan 24

Wimbledon A 3–3 March 17

Coventry H 3–0 April 28

1990–91
Wimbledon A 1–1 Nov 3

QPR A 1–2 Feb 23

Chelsea A 2–0 March 23

Sunderland H 3–1 April 13

Derby A 2–6 May 4

1991–92
Luton A 1–2 Sept 4

Nottingham Forest A 3–1 Oct 26

West Ham H 2–1 (ZDS Cup) Jan 7

Chelsea A 3–1 (ZDS Cup) Jan 29

1992–93
Middlesbrough H 2–1 Aug 29

Gillingham H 3–0 (League Cup) Oct 7

Ipswich H 4–3 March 13

Nottingham Forest H 1–2 SAVED damn him! March 24

1993–94
Coventry H 1–0 Jan 15
Liverpool H 4–2 (two pens) Feb 14
Norwich A 5–4 April 9
Blackburn H 3–1 April 16
West Ham A 3–3 May 7

1994–95
Spurs A 2–1 Sept 12
Nottingham Forest H 1–1 Sept 17
Huddersfield H 4–0 (League Cup) Oct 5
Norwich H 1–1 Nov 2
Sheffield Wednesday A 1–1 Jan 2
Luton H 6–0 (FA Cup) Feb 8
Spurs A 1–1 (FA Cup) Feb 18
Spurs H 2–6 (FA Cup) March 1

1995–96
Nottingham Forest H 3–4 (two pens) Aug 18
Blackburn H 1–0 April 6

1996–97
Leicester A 1–2 Aug 21
Sunderland H 3–0 Oct 19
Sheffield Wednesday A 1–1 Nov 2
Sheffield Wednesday H 2–3 Feb 22

1997–98
Barnsley H 4–1 Nov 8
Coventry H 1–2 Feb 18

Everton H 2–1 March 7
Newcastle H 2–1 March 28

1998–99
Nottingham Forest H 1–2 Aug 29

1999–2000
Sunderland H 1–2 April 1

Fat stats
The M-Plan diet:
Breakfast: Sausage and egg McMuffin
Lunch: Jacket potato with tomato ketchup and as much cheese as I
could nick from the players' canteen
Afternoon: Two cans Coca-Cola (not diet), pack of crisps, bar of
chocolate
Tea: Chicken Kiev, chips, beans, pint of Coke

Dream Team
Matthew Le Tissier in free role and 10 hard workers.

Best Saints XI
Tim Flowers
Jeff Kenna   Claus Lundekvam   Michael Svensson   Francis Benali
Jimmy Case   Chris Marsden
Ronnie Ekelund   Rod Wallace
Matthew Le Tissier
Alan Shearer
Manager: Alan Ball

Saints XI I would least like to play in

Chris Woods

Ray Wallace   Peter Whiston   Tahar El Khalej   Graham Potter

Matthew Le Tissier (in midfield holding role)

Sergei Gotsmanov   Kleber Chala

Ali Dia   Paul Moody   Agustin Delgado

Manager: Ian Branfoot

Hard Men XI

John Burridge

Barry Horne   Neil Ruddock   Francis Benali   Mark Dennis

Jimmy Case   Terry Hurlock   Chris Marsden

Mark Hughes

Iain Dowie   Alan Shearer

Manager: Graeme Souness

Fittest XI

John Burridge

Paul Telfer   Ken Monkou   Francis Benali   Micky Adams

Sergei Gotsmanov   Carlton Palmer   Barry Horne   Rod Wallace

Brett Ormerod   Alan Shearer

Hospital XI

Ian Andrews

David Howells   Barry Venison   Scott Marshall   John Beresford

Perry Groves   Ronnie Ekelund   Mark Draper   David Hughes

Agustin Delgado   Marian Pahars

Pundits XI

Peter Schmeichel

Phil Thompson   Ruud Gullit   Alan Hansen

Paul Merson   Jamie Redknapp   Graeme Souness   Charlie Nicholas

Matthew Le Tissier

Andy Gray   Alan Shearer

Manager: Martin O'Neill

Worst refs

1. Roger Milford (once booked me in the tunnel for arguing after the final whistle)
2. David Axcell
3. David Elleray
4. Jeff Winter
5. Neale Barry

Best refs

1. Paul Durkin
2. Dermot Gallagher
3. Errr … That's it.

My top 10 goals
1. Blackburn A 2–3 Dec 10, 1994

My all-time favourite goal, mainly because it was against my old mate Tim Flowers. I beat a couple of men and hit the ball from 35 yards. It went exactly where I wanted it to go, in the top left corner. And it left Tim floundering helplessly. But, as he always reminds me, they won the game.

2. Arsenal H 3–2 May 19, 2001

Just beaten into second place by the Blackburn goal. I had a strong feeling I was destined to get the last goal at The Dell, and I hit it perfectly – despite Chris Marsden's attempts to get in my way.

3. Coventry A 1–1 Oct 13, 1996

Live on Sky I hit a 30 yard shot which bent away from Steve Ogrizovic and into the top left corner before he could even move.

4. Newcastle H 2–1 Oct 24, 1993

The first of my two goals that day. Iain Dowie's header dropped behind me and I stuck out my foot and managed to flick it forward, with the sole, before lobbing it over Barry Venison and steering a shot on the run into the far bottom right corner. It was a slight scuff which is why this goal isn't higher in the list. Being a perfectionist, it rankles that it wasn't a crisp shot.

5. Liverpool H 4–2 Feb 14, 1994

The sweetest half-volley I ever struck. It came after just 27 seconds and I absolutely smashed it past Bruce Grobbelaar into the bottom right corner.

6. Liverpool A 2–4 Oct 30, 1993

Even the Kop applauded as I turned Mark Wright inside out and back again in front of them, before firing a left-foot shot across goal and just inside the right-hand post.

7. Wimbledon H 1–0 Feb 26, 1994

Towards the end of a dour game, Jim Magilton rolled a free-kick back to me 25 yards out. I flicked the ball up and hit it on the volley, over the wall and just inside the right post.

8. Newcastle H 2–1 Oct 24, 1993

My second goal in the match, and my best ever double. I controlled the ball on my thigh, turned and hit a sweet dipping 20 yard volley inside the far right post.

9. Norwich H 4–1 Feb 27, 1990

The second goal in my hat-trick as I beat my old mate Andy Townsend and then got past him again, before shooting in off the base of a post.

10. Manchester United H 6–3 Oct 26, 1996

A perfect lob over Peter Schmeichel. I remembered he had been lobbed by Philippe Albert the previous week, so I gambled he'd be in the same position. After beating a couple of men, I chipped the ball without even looking and it dipped just under the bar.

What the Fans Say

Thank you, Matt, for all the wonderful memories, held even closer in these troubled times. You were a legend on the pitch and you still are off it. Love watching the laughs you have on *Soccer Saturday*.

Matt and Holly

My most recent happy memories of supporting Saints are filled with joy from watching the most skilful English player to have come through in the last 30 years. His vision and technique were ahead of his time, and I had the pleasure of watching him play for my team! What a decent, witty bloke as well, who would have a laugh with opposing supporters, especially in his latter years!

Dave Carr, Andover

Back in 1995 I was running the school football team at Mansel Juniors. We won through to the final stages of the Hampshire Soccer Challenge to be played at The Dell, before Saints' game against Sheffield Wednesday. Unfortunately, we were playing in rags and were desperately in need of a new kit for our big day. Not only did Matt provide us with a new gold and black kit, but he promised us a slap-up lunch at Celebration Plaza if we won. With an offer like that my team couldn't fail to win the final. Matt was true to his word, gave the kids a great lunch, chatted away to them for a good hour and even waited on their tables! I'll never forget the smiles he put on those kids' faces – thanks Matt.

Mark Nutting, Southampton

Quite simply, Le Tiss was an absolute legend and my hero growing up. He provided so many of my greatest memories from the Dell era and it is a real shame we never really got to see him at St Mary's. How we could do with him now! I have lost count of the amount of breathtaking goals he scored. I don't think I will ever witness another Saints player quite like him in my lifetime.

Kevin Willsher, Hedge End

Watching you play football has been one of the genuine pleasures of my life. Thank you for sticking with us – we may be unglamorous, we may have always been last to be shown on *Match of the Day*, we may not have won much … but with you in the team we didn't much care.

Sue

The first time I met Matt Le Tissier was on a cold, blustery day in Belfast. I was mascot for the team that day prior to a surprise 2–1 defeat at the hands of Linfield, albeit in a friendly. I will always have fond memories of taking a penalty against my Saints hero prior to kick off – only to have him save it with an audacious back heel! A wonderfully nice man, and the football speaks for itself.

Steven Smith, Newcastle upon Tyne

Matt Le Tissier is quite simply the best player I have ever seen at Southampton. With his laid-back attitude on the pitch, he oozed confidence and gave the fans hope when we thought there was none.

It was not just his ability to score from anywhere and in any situation that we loved, but his all round play, his creativity, his touch and his ability to find space in the most packed midfield. He is, quite simply, class.

Aaron Swain, Dunstable

Le Tiss, Le God, Le-gend! Thank you for your loyalty, dedication and the unbelievable memories you have given me and all Saints fans to cherish forever. The debt we owe you for single-handedly saving us from relegation each season can never be repaid, your hero status will never be equalled, and your loyalty and genius will never be matched. You inspired me to love football and forever support Southampton Football Club, while your legacy continues to give me faith in integrity and decency in football. A great man and simply the greatest footballer ever to grace the game.

Martin Hiley, Southampton

There is only one word to describe a talent like Matt's: unbelievable! He is a true one-off, not just because of his passing, his touches, his incredible penalty record, his set-pieces and his sensational goals, but also because of his presence and the hope he gave to both a struggling team and struggling fans. He is a warm, helpful person who would give anything to make someone's day. He also does a fantastic job on Sky where he is as witty and articulate as he is in person.

Tim Hiley, Southampton

What a privilege it has been to witness the majesty and brilliance of Matt throughout his career. I shall never forget the moments of magic that had the whole crowd gasping week in week out. The fact that he was loyal to Saints throughout his career and almost single-handedly kept us in the Premier League year after year adds another dimension to the esteem in which all Saints fans hold him. The last goal ever at The Dell is the epitome and pinnacle for me. So glad I was there. He is truly a great bloke, too. A genius.

Claire Taylor, Hertfordshire

What can you say about Matt Le God but simply a genius and a true legend.

Roger Hill

Thank you for all you did for the Saints. Thank you for your loyalty. You were the greatest player I have seen and you should have won many more caps for England, but their loss was our gain. Your hat-trick against Norwich at The Dell the best I have ever seen. I even got to play against you when you went to Eastleigh. You nutmegged me and called it, which I loved.

Coxy, Fareham

When I was 12 I saw Matt, my hero, in Sainsbury's. I stood by his jeans for five minutes patiently waiting for him to finish paying, and he almost missed me until he tripped over me! But he wasn't angry enough to refuse an autograph which I still have 12 years later! I wanted to be like him, and from that moment forward I stopped caring about my hair.

Doug Clutterbuck, Woolston

Matt used to live a few doors away from me when he first started playing for the reserves. We had a party one Saturday night and I invited him over, not really expecting him to turn up. He did arrive, albeit rather late, but with a couple of bottles of Brut champagne. Not really what my mates were used to drinking and they made an impromptu grand prix-type celebration and sprayed it all over the kitchen. I never got to taste the Brut but Matt's football really was champagne!

Gary Gibbens

Matthew Le Tissier showed loyalty to Southampton FC which you just do not see any more in the modern game. Watching him play was a breath of fresh air. He could change a game with the slightest flick or goal from nowhere. Quite possibly the laziest player I have ever seen play but at the same time the most amazingly gifted player to ever pull on the red and white shirt. He was never given a proper chance for England but I know that, if he had, he would be as much of a legend to England fans as he is to Southampton.

Scott Ingate, Woolston

Matt, it has been a real privilege to witness many of the special moments you provided in a Saints shirt, even if one of them cost me over £200 when my specs got trampled in the Archers during the cele-brations of your last-minute equaliser against Newcastle in 1997. Even my eight-year-old son always insists on having number 7 on his shirt, and he has only seen you play on DVD. Thanks for all the wonderful memories.

Andrew Parry, Massachusetts, USA

I'll never forget an injured Le Tiss (I think he had delayed having surgery until the end of the season) coming on as sub in our must-win home game against Blackburn at the end of the 1996–97 season. We were 1–0 up but struggling to hold on when Matt was brought on hopefully to provide another bit of magic. With 15 minutes to go and practically on one leg, Le Tiss cut in from the left touchline and provided the sort of finish only he could. His celebration was more of a hobble as he went over to the fans – it was obvious that he was in pain – and it clearly highlighted what set him apart from most other players, namely that it meant as much to him as it did to all of the fans. Brought tears to my eyes – what a legend!

Steve Hall

One of my favourite Le Tiss memories was his hat-trick against Liverpool on St Valentine's Day 1993, the first home game under Alan Ball at The Dell. After Ian Branfoot got sacked it seemed like a weight had been lifted off Matt's shoulders, and he took precisely 27 seconds to score a cracker from the edge of the box past the diving Grobbelaar. We were 2–0 up after six minutes when debutant Craig Maskell scored. Two Le Tiss penalties in a 4–2 win in the driving snow made it a magical night and the perfect way to celebrate Valentine's Day. There may have been more important games but this seemed like a turning point in Matt's and Southampton's history.

Simon Rea, Oxford

MLT was, and for ever will be, a god of football and a true Saint. Matt is an inspiration for any true sportsman or for anyone who loves the beautiful game. His dedication, passion and loyalty will never be matched. Today's footballers could learn a great deal from the undying loyalty and commitment that the legend demonstrated every time he put on his sacred number 7 shirt. His talent, charisma, pure goalscoring ability and infectious love for the game were a joy to watch.

Ellen Hunter, Farnham

Remembering Le Tiss weave his magic at The Dell in my mind's eye still to this day makes the hairs stand up! I remember shouting 'give it to Le Tiss' and then being crushed by the sea of fans as he creates the unbelievable and scores. 25 years on my only excitement comes once a month and it's not at the Saints' ground! God bless Le Tiss.

Mark Hines

On my 50th birthday my kids bought me a Saints shirt with 'Le Dad' and the number 50 on it ... says it all. Different class, and the best player I have ever seen 'live'.

Pete Dowling

It's been an honour and privilege to have paid to watch arguably one of the top players to have graced this country and the Premier League, as well as Southampton Football Club. I used to love watching Matt Le Tissier play. He was lazy and for periods in a game would look disinterested but he could produce special skills out of nothing and his goals were phenomenal! I think it's a tragedy that a player with the skill, vision and undoubted talent did not get the opportunity to grace the international stage he richly deserved. I know I will never see a player this good and special ever play for Southampton Football Club again.

Gary Clark, Totton

Our special memory comes from the final competitive game at The Dell on 19 May 2001. As the last minutes of the game approached, I turned to my son Andrew and said, 'Do you think we still have one special moment left to come?' Within seconds of saying this, you controlled the ball, swivelled and hit that superb left foot volley into the top corner of the Arsenal net to give us an amazing 3–2 win! It is a memory that will stay with both of us for ever and, in my 40 years as a Saints fan, is the best so far!

Dave & Andrew Waterman Horndean

A living legend, no club could have hoped for a greater player than Matt Le Tissier! My father, brother and I had the privilege to be part of the 15,000 faithful who, on 26 October 1996, bore witness to Southampton beating Manchester United 6–3. Matt's contribution was outstanding and his goal that day was still one of the best the Premier League has ever seen. Even now as a pundit on Sky Sports, his passion for the club is as strong as it was when he was playing and for that he will forever be one of a handful of players who really lived up to their nickname. 'Le God'!

Lloyd Hiscox, Bristol

Having someone like Matt in your football team, it didn't matter to me where we finished in the league and that was just as well as it was usually at the wrong end. All that mattered to me was him running through defenders and scoring great goals.

Gavin Dyer, Romsey

When I was about ten I took part in the Saints Soccer Schools during school holidays. On one of the days we went to watch Saints train at Staplewood. Throughout it all Matt was nowhere to be seen. Until, that is, after the training when he stumbled over to us all in the stand wearing … slippers and I think a robe to do autographs! I didn't think much of it at the time, but now I think, well that's our Matt: brilliant with little effort.

Mike Reed, Thornhill

Le God gave me untold memories to cherish but the one that come most to mind is the match away at Upton Park in 1994. We were in our perennial battle for survival and it had come down to the wire: the last game of the season and a win would ensure safety. Although Le

Tiss scored two goals that day, one other moment is etched in my memory when he weaved his way to the corner flag, tracked by a full-back. He looked up and saw that the rest of the team were struggling to get forward (some things don't change!). This prompted him to 'turn' the poor full-back four times. By this time Neil Maddison had arrived in the box for Le Tiss to place the ball perfectly on his head for a simple finish. I remember committing to 'have his babies' at the time. As a bloke this would have been a considerable challenge so the next best thing was to name my son, born later that year, after him. Both Matthews are legends as far as I'm concerned!

Nic Armitage

As a youngster I enjoyed Keegan, Ball, Channon, Shilton, Armstrong and Wallace, amongst others. Then a lanky teenager took my football watching to another level. Maybe I'm biased, but in the eternal pub argument 'who was the best player ever?' I'll always put Le Tiss in the frame with the Pelés and Bests of the world!

Simon Bunch, Winchester

It was a privilege to see him play. Matt was the spirit of Southampton and those of us who watched him week in, week out will never forget the thrill of seeing him score another wonder goal or showing another sublime piece of skill. We were so proud of him. We just loved him.

Sean Smith, Winchester

For me, Matthew Le Tissier was THE reason to be a Saints supporter. His charisma, skill and loyalty made me proud to wear the red and white shirt. Above all, his fantastic goals are something that I will remember many years from now.

Charles Edmonds, Sherborne

There are so many words that supporters could say about your play, loyalty and overall genius. All I want to say is thank you for the memories and it was an honour to watch you.

Steve Pitchford, Telford

One of my few regrets is that I didn't see more of Le Tiss's greatest moments in the flesh rather than on TV. He was the most exciting and naturally gifted player I have ever had the privilege to be entertained by. On occasions he kept Saints in the top division almost single-handedly. Saints will never be as lucky to have a player as good as him again.

Martin Hall

I am sure that one day when I tell my future grandchildren about watching the Saints when I was growing up, the name that will dominate is Le Tissier. Matt, you provided so much happiness and inspiration to a whole generation of Saints fans. You are a true legend. That last goal at The Dell will live with me forever!

Richard Cooper, Boston, USA

Matt Le Tissier is a true Southampton legend. His unrivalled skill, loyalty and personality mean we will probably never see anyone quite like him ever again. Matt's ability to pick out a pass and make the seemingly impossible possible gave me and countless other Saints fans many hours of enjoyment.

Richard Hayward, Coventry

'Le God' … the name says it all. A god to every Saints fan for so many years and a very special player of a calibre that we will probably never see at Southampton again. I watched Matt from the time he pulled on the Red and White until the time he took it off, witnessing some very special moments along the way. I feel privileged to have seen such a footballing genius at work and I thank you for staying a Saint.

Gary Ford, Hedge End

You have given so much to Saints fans. Since you have left football, I feel something is missing in the game – the romance of the loyalty and unbelievable performances in a player whom money cannot buy. Thanks for having let me dream.

Javier Igeño Cano, Spanish Saints

We use the word legend far too easily but Matt has all the qualities to be rightly called a Saints legend. Matt stayed loyal and true, both these qualities are rare these days, and if you add them to his football ability, legend is clearly spelt out. Matt is a true Saint and it was a pleasure and an honour to see him stay and play for the Saints.

Steve Phillips, Cornwall

As a Saints fan I count myself as privileged to have had one of the most talented, enigmatic footballers to have ever graced the game playing for my team. I would always argue with my Man United supporting friends that you were as good as Cantona and anyone that saw you playing on top of your game knows the truth ... that you were better!

Dan Skinner, Sussex

The funniest memory was the last away game of the season at Derby (fancy dress as always) and I somehow got you, Flowers and Shearer to play a tune on a trumpet that I had taken. We lost 6–2.

James Palmer, Bognor Regis

You have quite possibly given me the greatest memory of all time, that magical goal against Arsenal on that final day at The Dell. I was a nipper at the time but you stamped my heart with the Saints crest for life when you hit that half-volley. The moment of seeing the man next to me cry made me realise how much this club means to many people ... and now me! It's a shame I was never old enough to remember all the other moments, but that one goal was more than enough.

Paul Knappett, Lymington

Watching a world-class player run out in the red and white of Saints is something that rarely happens. Over the last few seasons I have realised that you spoilt us all which makes the present quality of football that much more difficult to accept.

Dave Widger, Isle of Wight

They say that one man doesn't make a team but at times Matt did – the times he got Saints out of trouble were many ... and his loyalty was something you don't see today ... and why he never played more games for England I will never know. Also, how many players could make a whole DVD of their career goals? Not many.

Mick Betts, Aldershot

There was something about the way you casually sauntered around the pitch then pounced on and controlled a ball that took my breath away. Watching a Saints game suddenly became a compulsive experience where, more than at any other time of following the club, I would arrange my life so I could maximise my opportunities to bear witness to the awesome contribution you made to the game. Football is so much better when it is exquisite and leaves an imprint on the memory.

Greta Farian, Surbiton

Matt Le Tissier was magic. Every week I would watch *Match of the Day* just to watch him play – he is the pure reason for supporting Southampton.

James Weaver

The obvious goals spring to mind but one that sticks in my memory was the 3–3 draw away to West Ham, last game of the season in 1994. We looked to be heading in at half-time a goal down with no way back ... until Matt stepped up with a trademark free-kick from the edge of the box. Suddenly there was hope amongst the fans and a Matt-inspired second half guided us to safety.

Tom Smith, Bitterne Park

Matthew Le Tissier was one of the most talented players to have played the game and it was a big waste that he only got eight caps for England. While he'll admit he probably ate too many pies he could do things no other player was capable of. He made cold, wet, miserable afternoons down The Dell memorable and while many claimed he did nothing for 89 minutes, that one moment of genius would often win us the game.

James George, Salisbury

The best footballing memories I have all include Matt Le Tissier. From being a young lad at The Dell and seeing 'Le God' come over to take a corner, curl it in and then touching his shirt as he came near was magical feeling for any Saint fan. I will always be proud to say that I saw one of the Premiership greats display his touch of magic every time he touched the ball.

Ben Davis-Kearney, Dunstable

Matt is the only player I know who would make my mates move to the edge of their seats when he got the ball – and they didn't support Saints! Off the field an absolute gent who always had a word to say to you and in my mind showed what 'loving the club' really means.

Shawn Skellon, Weston-super-Mare

This man's skill is natural and can't be taught. This man's skill was productive and entertaining to boot. This man did all you thought you could ever see with a ball, and then showed you were wrong. This man scored goals from anywhere on the park, without a second thought. This man is Matt Le Tissier, a genius with the ball and now out in the public domain still showing others he knows a thing or two!

Adrian Pascal-Murray

Matthew Le Tissier is without doubt one of the most under-rated players in the history of football. At a club steeped in tradition he managed to make his mark with spectacular goals and top-quality performances. Matthew continued to win over us fans by offering something that most other players cannot – loyalty. He stuck by the club through thick and thin, and stood up to be counted in all the relegation battles.

Nick Taylor, Swanage

Le Tiss, Le God, Le Genius! My childhood hero, and you probably still are now. The one and only true Saint. The things you could do with a football were simply amazing. Countless times you have single-handedly saved Saints from relegation, and you did it in style. There will never be a player as good as you to ever put on a Saints shirt I am quite sure. My only wish is that you'd had a longer England career. What more could you have done to prove yourself? Simply unbelievable.

Gavin Harris, Sholing, Southampton

We should all feel very honoured and privileged that Matt spent his whole career with Southampton FC. He was a delight to watch, with world-class technical ability, an excellent footballing brain and loyalty too! He really was a gem of a player, an absolute one-off – audacious, nonchalant, enigmatic and a real crowd-pleaser. Matt, you will always be in the hearts of Southampton fans.

Matt Williams, Southampton

Matt's ability with the ball never ceased to amaze me week in, week out – pure genius! During his playing career Matt's hero status in our household remained unblemished, and for his loyalty, both to the fans and the club, that sentiment will remain forever more.

Jon Missin, Northampton

I will always remember Matt as a player who could turn a match with a moment of genius. In particular I recall the Zenith Data Systems final at Wembley in 1992.

Saints were 2–0 down against Nottingham Forest and I recall looking at Matt standing on the halfway line with hands on hips, having made a limited contribution to the game. Feeling rather frustrated at his lack of effort and the team's disappointing showing I shouted out words to the effect of, 'For God's sake get Le Tissier off – he is a lazy waste of space!'

Then within the space of a few minutes Matt performed two pieces of skill which nobody expected and nobody else on the pitch could have done – Saints were level at 2–2 and the crowd were ecstatic. I was reminded by a fellow supporter that my moment of tactical genius in taking Matt off would not have been a good move and I kept quiet for the rest of the game.

Colin Watts, Plymouth

Your skill was unbelievable and you brought joy to Saints fans of all generations. My daughter has a signed, framed Saints shirt in her bedroom proudly bearing the legend 'Le God'. That is how you will be remembered for years to come as people continue to pay homage to one of the finest players ever to wear the hallowed Saints shirt.

Barry Gerrard, Bedford

We feel very lucky that we were privileged to see Matt play. It was worth the admission cost just to see his skill as a footballer, and his goals were always spectacular. His talent and goals kept us in the top division season after season. How we could do with his skill now! He was first-rate both on and off the field.

Terry and Jane Smart, Hyde

With Le Tiss in the team you could be 3–0 down away from home but still not lose hope. There was always the chance that in the second half Matt would score from 30 yards, set-up the second and hit a free-kick or a penalty in the dying minutes to save the day. Again!

Mike Blake

I will always remember watching *Unbelievable* when I was growing up and being in total awe of what you could do with a football. I have many memories of watching you play and two for me stand out. The 3–0 defeat at home to Ipswich on 2 April 2001 (I know a strange game to pick), when you were warming up before the game, you were taking shots and one missed the goal and hit me on the side of the face, damaging my glasses. You came across and apologised and gave me your raincoat, which I am just about big enough to fit in! Then, of course, there was THAT goal at The Dell against Arsenal. I have never heard The Dell so loud!

James, Southampton

Our greatest memory is knowing that when Matt had the ball anything could happen ... and when we had a penalty it was a certain goal. We will never see anyone else like him in a Saints shirt. He epitomised everything that the club was at that time – exciting and entertaining.

Roger and Sarah Mein

Matt made me cry twice. When he scored the winner in the last league game at The Dell I hugged my wife and blubbed, 'It's a fairy-tale ending!' And after his testimonial at St Mary's I welled up watching his career highlights to the sound of 'My Way'. His skill made me happy countless times and I had a real laugh once. After his hat-trick for England B against Russia. I followed him down the road at QPR as he badgered his Mum to let him have fish and chips. 'But Mum, I scored a hat trick,' pleaded Matt. 'No Matthew, it's not on your diet!' came the reply.

Mike Young, Basingstoke

Everyone has their own special memories of your career in a red and white shirt. My own memory has to be Saints against Leicester City in December 1997. You took a free-kick and planted the ball straight on the forehead of Francis Benali for him to score his only top-flight goal. You had already scored the first goal but on this occasion you chose to provide the cross for the 'other fans' favourite' to have his one moment of glory.

Graham Wilkin, Poole

In an age where so many players are lured to bigger clubs by money and trophies, the fact that Matt chose to stay at a struggling Premiership side when he could have played for any club in Europe should be recognised. He scored some truly memorable goals in his Southampton career but is often overlooked as the greatest Premier League player because he didn't play for one of the bigger clubs.

Samuel Dolton, Southampton

Picture the scene: Saints 1–0 down just before half-time in the last game of the season. Relegation beckons yet again. I am sat in the main stand with West Ham supporters because all tickets have been sold for the away end. Saints get a free-kick, 25 yards out, slightly left of goal. Matt lines up to take the set piece, the wall is in place, but I know what's coming! As he curves the ball, round the right of the wall, I can tell its going to nestle in the right of the net.

I am up on my feet turning round to the rest of the stand to celebrate!

Half a dozen shaven headed West Ham supporters tell me to sit down in the nicest possible way. I don't care, Matt has saved us yet again.

UNBELIEVABLE!

Eddie Lawrence, Romsey

The only player I have ever seen who made me laugh. Not in a humorous or mocking way, but the unbelievable skill he possessed continually amazed me. I laughed at the fact that anyone could have the audacity to do what he did with a football. It was a joy to watch the confused and shocked faces of the opposing team and fans. A true entertainer with a god-given talent (and a good bloke too!).

Mark Shiner, Southampton

It is a huge credit to Le Tissier that he stayed with Saints his entire career, although looking back it's a shame so many people outside Southampton failed to appreciate just how talented he was. Not only one of the greatest players I've ever seen but without doubt the most unique. No one since has made such sublime skill look quite so effort-less. Whatever the future holds for Saints, we are forever grateful to Matt for the many great memories he has given us.

Adrian Reynolds, Eastleigh

The finest player of a generation, my first (and last) football hero is Matt Le Tissier. Watching him play for Saints was a real highlight of my life with the goals, tricks and total commitment to Southampton Football Club. The game against Newcastle at The Dell will forever be indented in my mind because of two Le Tissier wonder goals that mere mortals would never have attempted, let alone achieved. If Matt was Brazilian he would have one hundred caps; as he was English he was limited to a handful. Quite scandalous, really.

Darren Cocking, Cornwall

Quite simply the most gifted player ever to wear a Southampton shirt. Whenever I mention to anyone I meet that I'm a Southampton supporter, I'm asked about Matt Le Tissier. It was a privilege to watch you play, from your debut in the late 1980s to your premature retire-ment. Thanks so much for the memories which will stay forever.

Steve Hayden, Basingstoke

Matt, without your spectacular goals we would probably never have had a new stadium as you kept us up on so many occasions. I still get goose bumps whenever I see my personal favourite goal of yours – THAT free-kick against Wimbledon at The Dell on 26 February 1994. Love your reactions to goals on *Soccer Saturday*, Matt! You truly are Le God!

Ashley Dacre Bangor, North Wales

I saw Matt miss that famous penalty. I was gutted, shocked and at the time thought that nothing would be the same again. Then, not only did he redeem himself, but he did it with his left foot, with both feet off the ground and from outside the box. Faith restored, the world put back to rights and yet another classic Le Tissier goal. There will never be another like him – a loyal genius, unswayed by the financial gains he could have made elsewhere. A Southampton hero.

Jimmy Hayes

I often get frustrated by some of the rave reviews that current players get from pundits and fans. Be it a 30-yard free-kick, cross-field pass or volley – the plaudits are often exaggerated. For me, no other player in the history of the Premiership has achieved such excellence, or scored such fantastic goals on a consistent basis. Matt Le Tissier was truly an inspiration, a natural talent, a match-winner. His immense ability was matched only by his admirable loyalty to Southampton Football Club.

Michael Weston, Basingstoke

Never before and never again will I see a player on the same level as you were don the red and white stripes – whether it was plucking the ball out of the air effortlessly from a 30-yard cross-field pass or stretching the net with a thunderous dipping volley. The thing that I remember most though was the way you could send a player the wrong way with a mere sideways glance or a drop of the shoulders. It did not matter who the opposition were, you would carve a path in any direction with players dropping like flies around you. It is only as I am older and watching a struggling Saints team that I realise what a fine job you did almost single-handedly in keeping us up for at least four years. Thanks for the memories Matt, and although I am so glad you stayed with us it seems unfair that most of the rest of the world never got to see your undeniable talent.

Stuart O'Brien, Millbrook

Le Tissier will always be remembered by non Saints fans for his chips, flicks and an exquisite finish against Newcastle in '93. But true Saints will always remember the insane left foot wonder goal after coming in the dying minutes at the last league game at The Dell. Amazing. Pure class and a magician on the pitch. Le Tissier, Le God.

Dominic Macey Macleod, Farnborough

I watched Le Tissier from the moment he joined Saints and remember him and Rod Wallace forming one of the most formidable partnerships in the first division. You could always count on him getting us three points or salvaging a draw with a stunning goal or penalty. You were and continue to be an inspiration to many.

Damian Bryant

My greatest memory of Matt Le Tissier has to be the final league game at The Dell against Arsenal in May 2001. I remember it being a day of celebration, the Saints being clear of relegation and everyone in a party mood. Coming off the bench with five or so minutes to go, I honestly didn't think that the great man himself would score, but looking back it was probably inevitable that such a legend would have the final word. I was sitting with my dad in the Milton Road End to the left of the goal, in the front row. When the ball left his left foot, I just knew where it was going – the back of the net. An incredible moment, an incredible goal, an incredible result and the perfect way to say goodbye to The Dell.

Daniel Cook, Salisbury

I was 10 years old when my neighbour Ken took me to my first Saints game at The Dell. I queued up with all the other kids to get the players' autographs when they were warming up. Being a new fan I had little idea who any of the players were. When I retook my seat Ken told me I had got Matt Le Tissier's autograph. He told me he was a 'new lad and supposed to be a little bit special but a lazy sod too'. I'll never forget those words. Thanks, Matt, for living up to your billing. You're my sporting hero and a living legend.

Andy Weston-Green, Newbury

Matt is the greatest player I have ever seen and he is the reason the number seven is my favourite number! His goals kept us up and made the country take note.

I was lucky enough to be at his testimonial and as tears rolled down my face at the end I realised my generation will never ever see a greater, more loyal player than Matt.

Ryan Drouet, Bitterne Park, Southampton

I still take the credit for the final goal of one of the most outstanding hat-tricks I have witnessed. Trailing 1–0 to Norwich at half-time in 1989, Matt produced a second half even a ten-year-old lad in the

Junior Saints section would never forget. Having already swivelled to turn in the perfect striker's finish, Matt's second of the night was a dream of an individual goal. Having beaten one man, he then left the ball behind him, teasing two defenders in to challenge unsuccessfully, before dragging the ball inch perfectly off the far post with the sort of nonchalance we came to love so much.

The final goal of the night was the most memorable for me. Late in the game Matt broke down the left wing. Soon he was very close to my East Stand, second-row position. I could see Bryan Gunn approaching and, in my shrill voice, yelled, 'Chip him, Matt!' Matt duly obliged, delivering the most delightfully placed chip, right in the corner of the net.

I'm well aware that my input was completely unnecessary. Matt's awareness on the pitch, coupled with sublime skill to match, is something I've yet to witness since his retirement. Thank you, Matt, for the goals, the skills, the unbreakable loyalty and for being the reason I watch football.

Dr Oliver Atkinson, Manchester

For many years before you broke into the first-team my father use to continually talk about the greats he had watched in the red and white. After watching your whole playing career I now understand what he meant by GREAT. You gave both me and my father so much enjoyment over the years. I am still yet to see a more naturally gifted player and I thank you for that and the loyalty you have shown to our club.

Ian Hunt, Andover

Matt Le Tissier was my hero as a kid. Those who watched him play all share the same view. Le Tissier on his day was better than anyone. He could have played for any team in the world but he chose to stay with

Saints. That, along with his incredible ability, is what made him so special. Thanks for the memories, Matt; it's a shame you are not still playing today.

Joe Colyer, Sholing

I have three heroes ... Morrissey, Mandela and Matt Le Tissier!

Tim Muckart

Matt, thank you so much for everything you have done for my beloved Southampton. From my first season ticket in 1995–96 and seeing you lob Schmeichel, to your final goal against Arsenal and running over to us in the family centre, no other footballer has given me as many great memories. You really are a true hero.

David Rowland, Sarisbury Green

Possibly the greatest player I have ever had the privilege to support. While player loyalty is rare these days, Matt has given the fans countless fond memories and is a proud ambassador for Southampton Football Club – an achievement that medals and trophies cannot reach.

James McAlister, Chandlers Ford

I live in Portsmouth so I get my fair bit of stick. However, all I have to do is mention one name – Matt Le Tissier – and I'm untouchable. Every goal, touch and pass was always bettered by the next, and no footballer has or will come near to the things Matt achieved in the hearts of the fans. One of the most approachable and friendliest men I have ever met, you made this club.

Taylor Monk, Hayling Island

WHAT THE FANS SAY

I was one of many football kids who would shout 'Le Tissier' every time they shot. And your name is an ice-breaker whenever I am abroad or on holiday. As soon as I mention Southampton people reply, 'Matt Le Tissier!' Thank you, Matt, for everything. And for almost making me cry on my first date with my girlfriend at your testimonial when Frank Sinatra's 'My Way' came on.

David Fielder, Southampton

Quite simply, Le Tiss is the reason I am a Saints fan! A truly great footballer!

Peter Jacobs, Kent

I have three boys and sometimes we would go and see the team training. Graeme Souness was manager at the time and the first-team were playing a game of two-touch across the pitch. Every free-kick would involve a 'penalty' from the middle of the pitch to a five-a-side goal about 25 metres away. But you could only score if the ball hit the net before hitting the ground. Several players tried that day but only Matt managed it, with both feet! I remember Souness getting quite frustrated too.

Kevin Switzer

Every picture from my youth has me wearing a Saints shirt, home or away, with '7 Le Tissier' across the back. Endless repeats of great Premier League goals on obscure television channels make me very proud to say I was there. As mascot in 1995, captain Matt was particularly kind, including handing me a Mars bar – incredible, he doesn't look the kind of chap who would be easily parted! Matt is my hero, the most skilful of his generation and an inspiration.

Simon Law, Chester

I was given the opportunity to caddy for Matt at a Pro-Am competition at Dibden as one of my managers was Matt's friend and golf pro Richard Bland's brother-in-law. I had a great day talking non-stop for four hours around the course, and Matt was very honest. It made me chuckle when he said that, on the topic of Hoddle, you should never meet your hero. I didn't agree with him and at the end of the day after shooting a 71 he signed my son's Saints shirt and numerous other items. He was just a top bloke and I will remember that day for the rest of my life. It's okay to meet your hero if your hero is Matthew Le Tissier!

Dave Johnson

Matt is my all-time hero and I was a wide-eyed eight-year-old low down in the East Stand when he struck his two incredible goals against Newcastle. In today's greedy, money-driven game there will never be another Matthew Paul Le Tissier. A true legend of Southampton.

David Corlett, Bristol

I was there at your debut and I was there when we were all singing 'My Way' with tears in your and our eyes. Thank you for being such a loyal and fantastic servant to the club that we love. You were the best and it was my privilege to watch you over the years. Passion, skill and loyalty are rare commodities! Thank you.

Alasdair Duncan

What a player – what a man. I grew up watching the Le Tissier era and he is the sole reason I have such a passion for football and Southampton FC right now. It's a travesty for English football that he wasn't capped more than the measly eight times – had he been

French or Italian he probably would have hit the 50 mark. Matt was a game-turner, a rare individual who could score out of absolutely nothing.

Matthew Le Tissier is a God and an inspiration – there is no footballer I will ever speak more highly of.

Alex Stimpson

Not only was Matt a great footballer but what made him adored by all Saints fans was that he was one of us. My favourite memory of Matt, save for the great goals, was sending a poster to The Dell in the hope he would sign it. I even included a SAE and pen in hope. I had done this for other players but got nothing back. I needn't have worried: a week later the poster came back signed by the great man, who realised what these things mean to young fans.

Richard Corben

Ever since I can remember Matt Le Tissier has been, for me, the greatest player I have seen. I always get his name printed on my Saints shirts because I know he will never leave and will always be my favourite player. That last goal at The Dell ... it gets me every time! Legend.

Ed Goodall, Isle of Wight

The happiest times for me as a Saints fan were watching him entertain and embarrass the other players week in, week out. I will never forget the Newcastle home game, 24 October 1993, when he scored two of the world's greatest ever goals to keep Paul Moody on the bench and prove a point to Ian Branfoot.

Luke Prangle, Southampton

I played against Matt when my team toured Guernsey. I was in goal and he scored a hat-trick past me. We still beat them that day but a year later we invited them to Hampshire. We got completely stuffed but the highlight was taking the visitors to The Dell to watch Saints beat Spurs. Before the game the PA announcer welcomed the lads from Guernsey. If only they knew who they were saying hello to!

Wayne Palmer

My one abiding memory of Matt was my fourteenth birthday. It was 1994 and my late father took me to my first Saints game, saying to me, 'You are going to see the best player you will ever see put on a Saints shirt.' I have to admit that I hadn't taken much interest in the game until that age but after less than a minute he cracked home a half-volley and I was hooked. The next day, and for several years, I wanted to be this man. He made football seem so … simple.

Terry Couzens

Matt is the reason why I'm so passionate about football, the Saints and club loyalty. The skill and talent drift into insignificance behind the grace and poise which matched his loyalty to Southampton Football Club. Thanks for the memories; you'll always be our Number 7!

Michael O'Dea, Adelaide, South Australia

This is the man that England were deprived of. He scored many marvellous and breathtaking goals over a career that he dedicated to Southampton Football Club. Pure genius!

Phil Knowles, Exeter

I was lucky to have a fortieth birthday surprise round of golf with the man that has always been a childhood and adult hero. I was pleased to find that my opinions and perceptions of the man were not shattered in real life because he remembers to make time for the people he knows are less fortunate. He is justifiably described as down-to-earth, a gentleman, joker, legend, hero, good pundit and forever in a Saints fan's heart.

David Donworth

We will never see the likes of 'Le God' at Southampton in our days again. A one-club player, who was worth the entrance money alone, he was one of the best controllers of a football. He didn't smash it in – he caressed it into the back of the net. Fabulous player and a model professional. He turned his back on the big-money clubs because he loved playing for Southampton. Matt is a very caring person, and does so much work for local charities. Alongside Ted Bates, Matt is Mr Southampton.

Geoff Smith

Matt Le Tissier, an all-round hero of mine – great skills, great goals and, to my surprise, a great goalkeeper. I remember watching the Benali testimonial when Dave Beasant came out of goal to be replaced by the Tiss-meister, who was fantastic and pulled off many saves. So, to many he will be remembered as a scorer of great goals, but to me he was a saver of great shots and a saviour of the team at the time.

L Lowe

Matthew Le Tissier: simply the best role-model an eight-year old lad could have wished for. To be able to watch someone with your amount of loyalty, skill and personality was incredible. Thanks for all the memories of games, goals, signing sessions and primarily for making me a Saints fan for life.

Alex Cooper, Shirley

I have, and will always have, the greatest respect for Matthew Le Tissier as he has shown that football is not all about physical strength and big contracts, but that it is down to playing football for the fun and desire of it, and to stay loyal for what you believe in. I live in Denmark, but I have been a fan of Le Tissier and Saints for nearly 22 years – and I would not change this for anything.

Allan 'Dysse' Carlsen, Denmark

Matthew Le Tissier was simply a genius when he was on the football field. As someone who had the pleasure of watching his whole career, I can say he did things with a football that I had never seen any other player do. He was a one-off. Matthew's loyalty to Southampton Football Club is something that you don't see very often in the modern game. He is one of life's Mr Nice Guys, and through the pleasure he gave to the city of Southampton he has become our city's favourite son.

Steve Kill, Bognor Regis

I think the greatest tribute that can be paid to Matt is not from ourselves – we knew and saw his genius. The greatest tribute is paid by fans of opposing teams. Mention that you support Saints and they start to wax lyrical about Le Tiss – club rivalry disappears as everyone appreciates a footballer of such immense talent.

Paul Bryant, Telford

It was a joy and a privilege to have seen Matt play. His loyalty to Saints puts him on a pedestal that a mere player could never hope to reach.

Ian Strong, Whiteley

WHAT THE FANS SAY

Mr Southampton ... Mr Red and White ... Le God ... scored some amazing goals down The Dell ... kept us in the Premiership ... says it all ... pure legend!

Dean Austin, Andover

Pace and athleticism may have been missing from Matt's long list of attributes, but skill, vision, talent and great first-touch more than made up. A genuinely great guy who became a football genius, Matt not only almost single-handedly kept the Saints in the top division for so many seasons but he always had time for the fans. It was as if he was a fan himself who loved the club as much as us! Matt played every game for Southampton with his heart and for the shirt ... a rare quality

Eamonn, Australia

Matt Le Tissier, the most skilful player I have ever seen. I count myself lucky to have witnessed him keep us in the top tier of English football single-handedly on numerous occasions – and make it look like a walk in the park. Reaching 25 goals in a season is an excellent achieve-ment for any striker, but he wasn't even a striker. Season in, season out, Tiss scored 25 goals from midfield in a team that, the majority of the time, was fighting for survival. What a player he was ... football genius.

Mark Risbridger, Southampton

The one defining aspect which places Le Tissier into super status above all others is that in choosing his best 50 goals he did not include the following. In the last home league game of the 1993–94 season against Aston Villa, the ball was launched from the centre circle high up in the air by Francis Benali, it came over Matt's right shoulder, he nonchalantly one-touch controlled with his left, feinted past the goalkeeper and tucked it into the net, totally fooling the entire defence, including the keeper, in an effortless series of deft movements and caresses of the ball. It was an incredible piece of skill. That is why Le Tiss is The Biz, because that goal would feature in most strikers' top three goals; it didn't even make Matt's top 50.

Kevin Foster, Stubbington

Growing up in Southampton and having a player of your unrivalled talent and natural ability to support gave me a great sense of pride and passion, not only as a fan of Matthew Le Tissier, and Southampton Football Club, but as a fan of football in general. I'm sure I'm not alone in thinking of you as an absolute hero.

Joe Macey

During my 30 years as a Saints fan no one has given me more memories than Matt Le Tiss. I feel privileged to have watched him, thanks to moments of sheer genius and wonderful goals – especially against Man Utd and Newcastle. Who can forget the last competitive goal at The Dell, which brought tears to my eyes. One of my other favourites was scored in a last day relegation escape at West Ham, when an exquisite Le God free-kick answered the home fans' taunts about his facial features. Since retirement his appearances in exhibition games have shown a younger generation that the greats never lose their skill, while off the pitch he has been a great ambassador for Southampton.

Andy Kershaw, Chandlers Ford

Having begun watching Saints in 1973, seeing the Cup win and the brilliance of the side in the early '80s, I was used to being entertained. I was a regular, home and away, but Le Tiss brought more than I had ever seen before. Perhaps it was because there were times when he alone made games worthwhile – you knew that he would do something each match that other players could not do. He was a shining light amongst good committed Saints players, and yes, at times, he was 'unbelievable'.

Craig Foster, Ilford

I have been watching Saints for 20 seasons now and for probably only a quarter of those have we been anywhere near successful! But I kept coming because of one thing – Matty. The best player I have ever seen, and will ever see, without a doubt.

Mark Wood, Newbury

Whenever Matt was in our team, or even on the bench, I knew Saints had a chance. For his dedication to Saints, his passion to play the game his way, his enthusiasm for Southampton, his brilliant skills, goals and special ability on the ball, and, most of all, the entertainment he provided, Saints supporters will always remember him and forever be grateful. I will never forget watching the last game at The Dell, praying that Matt would get on one last time, and the feeling of the lump in my throat, tears welling up in my eyes and the heart-thumping excitement when Matt swivelled on his right foot and thumped the winner into the top corner with his left. Unbelievable!

Kevin Bound, Hedge End, Southampton

Matt would often drift in and out of games but had a major influence on the outcome due to his inspired goal-scoring and assists. I feel privileged to have had the chance to watch so many of his games. Matt was crucial to the retention of our Premiership status throughout the '90s and should be applauded for his loyalty to Southampton

Football Club rather than moving elsewhere in search of the big money available to players of his ability. However, my best memories of Matt were his obvious enjoyment of the game. Matt, you were an awesome talent, and I am very grateful for your loyalty to my club, Southampton.

Andrew Moncrieff

What a genius! Forget all these rich players nowadays, you're a legend. You could have played for anyone you wanted but stayed loyal to one club.

Mark Rice

Question 1: How did you feel after you scored a hat-trick and hit the post and bar for the England B team – and then did not get called up? It was an absolute travesty.

Question 2: Why didn't you ever run more?

Jon Ellerbeck

Matt Le Tissier is by far the greatest player I ever had the pleasure of watching; his skill was outstanding and the goals he scored were beautiful.

Dan Woodnutt, Redbridge

When I was seven I remember asking my dad, a lifelong Saints fan, which football team I should support. 'Well, son, it's up to you but have you thought about Southampton?' 'Yes,' I replied, 'but all my friends support Liverpool or Everton.' 'Yes, son, but they don't have Matt Le Tissier.' That night I watched Matt on *Match of the Day* as he scored a hat-trick against Leicester in his league debut season. My mind was made up, Southampton was my team and Le Tissier was my idol. From that moment on I watched as he weaved, tricked, volleyed and smashed his way through many arguably better teams.

Dominic Strange, Liverpool

At ten years old, I came on for the last ten minutes of a charity game – Lee's 11 against the Ex Saints 2006. Le Tiss switched sides and set me up to score our last goal. He assisted the likes of Shearer, Wallace, Pahars, Beattie and … me. I've got the photos and one day my children and grandchildren can relive my dream. Now I'm 13 I've seen Le Tiss' passion for Saints on Sky and it's in me too, so when Dad asks if we want to renew season tickets it's blatant: we're Saints through and through … because of heroes like you.

Michael Morrison

Genius, legend, stalwart, Le God. I'm not sure words adequately describe Matt's place in Saints history. He was the best player in the world under Alan Ball and it was a crime he did not make the World Cup squad. 'Unbelievable' says the video, except it wasn't; I was there to see it all. What a player, what a man. Thank you.

Steve Morrison

Matt Le Tissier was a superb player but also a very kind gentleman off the pitch as well. He always had – and still has – time for the fans to sign an autograph or have a chat – far more than many other top players.

Paul Chalk

To be blessed with such natural technical ability is one thing. Couple that with his wonderful vision and his acute eye for goal and you have simply the most gifted player of his generation – a producer of poetry in motion. To this day I am genuinely privileged to have witnessed the genius of a man aptly named 'Le God'. Truly an idol, an artist and a gentleman.

Yiannaki Loizou

When anyone asks me who is the best player I have ever seen, my answer is (and probably will always be) 'Matthew Le Tissier'!

Kelly Callaway, Southampton

Watching Matt Le Tissier play football was like watching Mohammad Ali box; they make the impossible look effortless and graceful. Genius like that doesn't come round very often; as Saints fans we are just lucky that he chose us to play for. I am glad that I got the chance to watch him so often.

Phil Cook, Bucks

Back in 1987, watching Matty tear Leicester apart on a miserable day, my dad Roy turned to me and said, 'He'll win the World Cup for England one day son.' Well, he got that wrong but he should have been right. Skill, vision, the goals ... Matty had the lot, and I – and countless other Saints fans – feel privileged to say we saw him play. Thanks for the memories, Matty, and especially the last glorious goal at The Dell, where I've never seen so many grown men, including myself, with tears running down their faces.

Dave Hunt, Southampton

Matthew Le Tissier is the single biggest reason I spent my student grant to watch the Saints all over the country during the early- to mid-90s. A few glimpses of brilliance amidst the often bland fare were priceless. I spent hours championing his cause and challeng-

ing the opinions of others who maintained that his languid, unhur
ried style wouldn't suit England. Sadly, the game is about opinions
and the day that England's World Cup squad for France 98 was
announced was the day that a large part of me fell out of love with
football.

Paul Dicker, Jersey

Some people measure sporting greatness by the trophies won or
money earned by a player. But to be great is, in my opinion, much
more than that. If we were to measure greatness by loyalty,
integrity and sheer provision of enjoyment, not to mention the
affection reserved for that player by the public, I am in no doubt
that Matt Le Tissier would be regarded as the greatest footballer of
all time.

Jack Mitchell, Reading

When my brother moved from South Wales to a flat down the road
from The Dell, it wasn't long before he invited me down to see the
Saints. Some of the goals and skills I witnessed immediately turned
me into a Saints fan. My journeys home only seemed to take five
minutes thinking of what I'd just seen and I couldn't wait for Monday
morning to tell my work colleagues all about it. The man was a god
with a football.

Nick Horton, Newport, South Wales

Le God is the most naturally talented sportsman I have ever seen and,
unbelievably, he spent his whole career at my club. He was the player
that money couldn't buy.

Robert Instrall, Havant

A truly unique footballer and rightfully regarded as the most talented player of his generation. His ability with the ball at his feet was simply breathtaking.

Ian Gibson, Christchurch, Dorset

When there was speculation he was leaving Saints, a friend took a copy of Elvis Costello's 'I Don't Want to go to Chelsea' to a Matty appearance somewhere and asked him to sign it. He did, with a smile. I now have that record sleeve, and it sums up Matty for me: a player who actually had a sense of humour, who seemed to care as much as us about Saints and a player who, more than once, had me shouting out loud, 'How the bloody hell did he do that?'

Tony Whatley, Southampton

Legend! What else can you say? He kept us up, season after season, and showed us loyalty that has not so far been matched by any other player.

Mark Pearce, Salisbury

I feel privileged to have witnessed first-hand some of Matt's greatest moments over the years. Perhaps the biggest testament to his greatness is the way he is revered by so many opposing fans – even to some who know so little of the club at all, he is still a household name. For your loyalty, for those sublime moments of skill that made me gasp in awe and for those truly magical goals that I will not tire of watching, I thank you.

Barry Clements, Cowdenbeath

WHAT THE FANS SAY

By far the greatest ever player I have seen wearing the red-and-white stripes, I feel so lucky to have been there to witness so many unbelievable moments, from his debut to his final game. We have surely missed him. So many great goals, so many great memories. Thanks Matt – You were simply 'Le God'.

Paul Gilliam, Gran Canaria

Le Tiss – truly a man ahead of his time. Quite simply, English football was not ready for you, Matt.

Duncan Goodwin, Suffolk